The New Class Conflict

Also by Joel Kotkin

California Inc. (with Paul Grabowicz)

The Valley

*The Third Century: America's Resurgence
in the Asian Era* (with Yoriko Kishimoto)

*Tribes: How Race, Religion, and Identity
Determine Success in the New Global Economy*

*The New Geography: How the Digital Revolution
Is Reshaping the American Landscape*

The City: A Global History

The Next Hundred Million: America in 2050

The New Class Conflict

Joel Kotkin

With a Foreword by Fred Siegel

Telos Press Publishing
Candor, NY

Printed in the United States of America
18   17   16   15   14   1   2   3   4

ISBN: 978-0-914386-28-5

Library of Congress Cataloging-in-Publication Data

Kotkin, Joel.
  The new class conflict / Joel Kotkin ; with a Foreword by Fred Siegel.
    pages cm
  Includes bibliographical references.
  ISBN 978-0-914386-28-5 (alk. paper)
  1. Social conflict—United States. 2. Elite (Social sciences)—United States.
  3. High technology industries—United States. 4. Middle class—United
  States. I. Title.
  HM1121.K68 2014
  303.60973—dc23

                                                              2014023194

Telos Press Publishing
PO Box 811
Candor, NY 13743

www.telospress.com

To Mandy, my partner in life and greatest source of advice and inspiration. More than anything, her love keeps me going.

Contents

Fixing the Broken Compass

From roughly 1916 to 1932 the journalist-intellectual H. L. Mencken set the tone for much of American reporting by way of his thumb-sucking pieces on the American scene, collected in six volumes of his *Prejudices*. Most of the pieces were written from Mencken's hometown of Baltimore, and on the unusual occasion when he traveled to observe the scene, as in his "coverage" of the famous Scopes trial, what he wrote was more a reflection of his prejudices than the events observed. Joel Kotkin is the anti-Mencken; for the past quarter century his richly grounded writings have been essential reading for anyone trying to make sense of American society and politics. Kotkin has toured the globe, and, more importantly for this volume, he has traveled across America to report on developments overlooked or more often misunderstood by the press. But where Mencken overwrote so that his prose often became the story, Kotkin writes in a fluid, transparent style in which the scene he is describing comes to life on the page unobscured by rhetorical pyrotechnics.

Time and again, Kotkin, informed not only by on-the-ground observation but also by a firm grounding in the nation's demographic changes, has challenged conventional accounts of American society. For example while a flood of articles from the *New York Times* and major magazines such as the *Atlantic*, the *New Republic*, and *Harper's* evoked the supposed decline of suburbia and the repopulation of America's downtowns over the past two decades, Kotkin has deflated these self-serving pretensions. The numbers he has patiently explained, time and again, do not demonstrate such a transformation. The stories being written reflect, he shows, the lifestyles and sense of self-importance of the people writing such articles and the interests of their friends and allies in "hip" architectural claques. A former New Yorker who has lived in Los Angeles for the past forty years, he has described both the city's ascent in the 1980s and 1990s and its decline over the past twenty years. His personal attachments to his adopted home notwithstanding, the evidence and not emotion has imposed itself on the argument.

In *The New Class Conflict* Kotkin picks up on a variety of themes he was the first to explore, from the hyping of the so-called "creative class," to the oligarchy that tarnishes the shine of Silicon Valley, to the growth of gentry liberalism, which he then weaves together to make it clear that our contemporary political compass is broken. The standard assumptions that fill our "quality dailies" and their aural offshoots are guided by presuppositions about what constitutes left and right that have been eclipsed by the changes of the past quarter century. To be guided by their compass is to wander aimlessly in a welter of rhetorical posturing in which billionaires who have made their fortunes in coal become the leaders of the left-wing campaign against the Keystone pipeline.

Kotkin guides the attentive reader down the byways of an unprecedented political structure in which the competing elites of the Obama era have attached themselves to dramatically different segments of society. In the new compass the true north of powerful elites points to both a new ruling class defined by the production of abstractions, digital and financial, and another rooted in the manufacture and manipulation of material objects. Similarly, when the arrow points east or west toward the middle class, it designates two dramatically different populations: one rooted in the public, the other in the private sector.

As the country shambles into the post-Obama era, Kotkin's writing serves as an essential guide to a new political landscape, one that no longer makes sense in conventional terms.

Fred Siegel
Scholar in Residence
Saint Francis College
Brooklyn, New York

Acknowledgments

More than most books, this one has had a difficult birth. It started as an idea that developed over the past decade, and which I expressed in numerous articles in such places as *Forbes*, *Newsweek*, the *Wall Street Journal*, *The Daily Beast*, and the *Orange County Register*, among others. As the ideas in the book did not fit neatly into either right or left perspectives, it proved a more difficult sale than usual.

I owe a great deal of thanks to Fred Siegel, who was originally my coauthor but who remained a strong advisor throughout the process. He also arranged for Telos Press Publishing and Mary Piccone to take on the book. I want to thank Mary, Robert Richardson, Tim Luke, and others at Telos for their advice and support in this process.

The book benefited from strong advice from a remarkable group of colleagues, including attorney David Friedman, a noted expert on land use and PhD in political science at MIT, author Aaron Renn, publisher of the *Urbanophile* blog, and demographer Wendell Cox. My brother Mark Kotkin, former head of survey research at *Consumer Reports*, provided much incisive and dispassionate analysis. Tim Luke at Telos was particularly helpful in sketching out the historical background.

I am also in debt to my many editors from the magazine world, who helped hone this message. I would like to thank, in particular, Jeremy Bogaisky, Tunku Varadajan, and Dan Bigman at *Forbes*; Mike Tipping, Brian Calle, and Rory Cohen from the *Orange County Register*; Brian Anderson at *City Journal*; and *The Daily Beast*'s Malcolm Jones, Harry Siegel, and Jake Siegel.

In terms of putting the book together, I want to thank Gary Girod, a graduate of Chapman University, without whose first-class research this effort would have been impossible. I also owe a debt to my assistant, Barbara Moroncini, who kept the files in order and did some significant research work on her own. My wife, Mandy, contributed many hours to copyediting the book, but this is hardly the extent of her contribution. Without her support and encouragement, *The New Class Conflict* would never have been finished.

I also want to express my appreciation to my mother, Loretta Kotkin, and mother-in-law, Charlotte Shamis. Both grew up in very hard circumstances, one in Brownsville, Brooklyn, and the other in Paris and later Montreal, ultimately finding her American dream in my adopted hometown of Los Angeles. Their personal stories—built on hard work, perseverance, and a sense of fair play—are the core values expressed in this book.

This effort also benefited from my relationship with Chapman University, where I serve as a fellow in urban futures. I have discussed these ideas with my fellow faculty members Chancellor Daniele Struppa and Professor Ann Gordon as well as my students.

Young people are those who will most have to live under this new class system. I am hoping that they are able to find ways to reform the current oligarchy and provide a better future than many imagine for future generations. As the father of two wonderful girls, Ariel and Hannah, I am not remotely objective about this. More than our present, it's their future we should fight for.

CHAPTER ONE

The New Class Order

I n the coming decades, the greatest existential threat facing America lies with the rise of a new class order that leaves diminished prospects for the vast majority. In this emergent society, wealth and power are concentrated in ever fewer hands and threaten to erode much of the traditional appeal of America, its institutions, and sense of promise.

Historically, the basic ethos of our modern capitalist society has rested on the premise that, with hard work and perseverance, people could reasonably hope to achieve a better future and greater material success. This was the great triumph of the second half of the twentieth century.

And indeed, until the past twenty years, Americans remained more economically mobile, except at the lower ends, than the citizens of most other advanced nations. To be sure, as Charles and Mary Beard noted in 1930, poverty in America still remains "stark and galling enough to blast human nature." But the idea that a better tomorrow beckoned was widely shared. "All save the most wretched had aspirations," they noted. There was, as they put it, "a baton in every toolkit" that could inspire aspirants up the social ladder.[1]

This legacy has allowed conservatives, such as Irving Kristol, as late as in 1997 to proclaim, with some justification, that American capitalism had created "an affluent society [that] squelches the class conflicts it was supposed to generate." Inequality may grow, he suggested, but "without class conflict," since most Americans still possessed a "set of attitudes and an intuitive understanding" that upward mobility was not only possible but normative.[2]

1

This condition, which arguably most distinguished America from other countries, increasingly no longer defines our society. Once a beacon to the world, America, according to recent research, now suffers levels of income mobility worse than those in Europe.[3] More than anything, it is a loss of confidence in upward mobility, not (as some suggest) inequality per se, that defines our current dilemma.

In contrast to the norms of the past, most Americans do not feel that their children will do better than themselves.[4] By 2013 a majority of Americans expected life to get worse by 2050, almost three times as many as those who thought things would improve.[5]

This is a reasonable response to economic trends since the 1980s.[6] Since 1973, the rate of growth of the "typical family's income" in the United States has slowed dramatically, when adjusted for inflation. In contrast, in 2012 the top one percent of the population accounted for one quarter of all American income, the highest percentage in the past century.[7]

The Emerging American Class Structure

This trend toward greater concentration of wealth and diminished opportunity is not unique to America and is more common around the world. It portends an ever more deeply stratified America, with increasingly well-defined classes.[8]

This new reality is being driven by many things, such as globalization, the growth in the return to capital as opposed to labor and immigration, and the rising role of technology. Together they threaten to create a new social order that in some ways more closely resembles feudal structures—with its often unassailable barriers to mobility—than the chaotic emergence of industrial capitalism.

Rather than birth, connections, or military prowess, as was the case in feudal society, our current class structure reflects what one economist has defined as the "strong comeback of capital" relative to labor. This can be seen as well by the increased capture of income by financial firms and those running large public firms. In 2013 alone, nine private equity investors took home over $2.6 billion in compensation just by themselves, an amount unprecedented for such a small group. In addition, there has been a rapid increase in compensation to corporate management; since 1978, pay for CEOs rose a remarkable 725 percent, more than one hundred times the increase in worker compensation.[9]

In this sense, the new class order represents the apotheosis of economic centralization, as well as a growing alliance between the ultra-wealthy and the instruments of state power. This is reflected, and glaringly so, in finance. In 1995, the assets of the six largest bank holding companies accounted for 15 percent of gross domestic product; by 2011, aided by the massive bailout of "too big to fail" banks, this percentage had soared to 64 percent. For such state-dependent banks, preserving and inflating assets, and winning friends in Washington, constitute the key business priorities; overall economic growth that creates jobs and greater wealth among the populace often seems secondary at best.[10]

This shift has been exacerbated by a Fed monetary policy that, purposely or not, has favored the interests of the wealthy over those of the middle class. "Qualitative easing," notes one former high-level official, essentially constituted a "too big to fail" windfall to the largest Wall Street firms. Before leaving office, Ben Bernanke, the architect of the policy, admitted that "there are...many people after the crisis who still feel that it was unfair that some companies got helped and small banks and small business and average families didn't get direct help." This perception has been strengthened by the fact that pay for executives at the largest banking firms hit new records by 2011, just three years after the financial "wizards" left the world economy on the brink of economic catastrophe.[11]

Politicians in both parties often denounce such profiteering by what Theodore Roosevelt would have labeled "malefactors of great wealth."[12] But in reality both parties share much of the blame for the widening social divide since both cater to the interests of the super-wealthy, albeit often different groups. Tax policy has served to increase this gap, in part by allowing the investor class to pay lower rates through capital gains even as the middle class and small business owners have been hit with rising tax rates.[13]

For the most part, it's not surprising that Republicans, with their long, historic ties to Wall Street and laissez-faire ideology, would accept such inequity. But there's something mildly risible about this discordant message of populism among a progressive administration that has targeted corporate and individual greed among the "one percent," hurting the feelings of some oligarchs, even in Silicon Valley, while pursuing an agenda that has greatly expanded their share of the national economy.[14]

Indeed, rather than a shift to a broader distribution of income, some 95 percent of the income gains during President Obama's first term have gone to barely one percent of the population while incomes have declined for the lower 93 percent.[15] As one writer at the left-leaning *Huffington Post* put it, "the rising tide has lifted fewer boats during the Obama years—and the ones it's lifted have been mostly yachts."[16]

This discrepancy between rhetoric and reality clearly exposes many progressives to charges of outrageous hypocrisy. But there is also not much here that the right should be giddy about. The inability of market capitalism, even under conservative rule, to provide a higher standard of living and increased opportunity undermines the fundamental promise of free markets. In the period between 1950 and 2000, conservative, even libertarian, perspectives were bolstered by the expansion of middle-class prosperity and property ownership. But now, with home ownership in decline and middle-class incomes stagnating, the case for "democratic capitalism," long advocated by the right, has been somewhat diminished.

The New Oligarchs

A potentially greater source of class stratification, particularly in the future, could be the melding of technology with powerful sources of capital. The current digitization of the economy, manifested in the shift of physical products and services into cyberspace, has engendered the emergence of what I will describe as a new, and potentially potent, *Oligarchy*, with influence that extends to the media and the political world.

Despite the many crimes committed in his name, Karl Marx possessed a unique foresight about how technological change, conjoined to new economic institutions such as joint stock corporations, can undermine an existing social order. The change he chronicled most closely spanned the time from the end of the Middle Ages to the beginnings of modern industrial capitalism.

At first, change came from the rise of a new group of artisans and mechanics, who increasingly led the initial transition to an industrial economy. By the early 1800s, as Marx noted, these creators of smaller scale capitalism, particularly in Britain, began to lose ground, as further mechanization associated with the industrial revolution—and the impact of the European global conquest—reordered the class system. The industrial era that drove the preponderance of wealth and power from the landowning aristocracy and the old merchant class to manufacturers and financiers also weakened the status of weavers, artisans, and small farmers.[17]

Today, our existing class order is being similarly jostled by the shift to the information-based economy. At the turn of the century, H. G. Wells identified the ascendency of a "primary and initiating nucleus of engineers and skilled mechanics" as a new force in history.[18] Over seven decades later, Daniel Bell noted that with the "rise of intellectual technology," we were witnessing "the pre-eminence of the professional and technical class" over the rest of society.[19] The emerging "post-industrial society," Bell predicted in *The Coming of Post-Industrial Society* (1973), would mean a decreased reliance on the "mass mobilization of labor," both unskilled and skilled. These inputs, he reasoned, would be supplanted by mechanization, for the benefit of those who designed and owned the machines.[20]

In our era, as in the industrial age, we are witnessing the growth of vast new fortunes among a relative handful of companies and individuals. As early as 2004, technology firm founders, largely in computer-related fields, emerged among the top ranks of the richest people on the planet. This trend has continued into recent years, with tech entrepreneurs dominating the list of moguls who are not merely inheritors. Over the coming decades, the new Oligarchs' impact will be enhanced by the fact that so many have achieved their fortunes at an early age; tech Oligarchs, mostly from Silicon Valley, represent the lion's share of billionaires under forty who are not inheritors of family fortunes. In 2014 alone at least ten new billionaires emerged from this sector.[21]

In the future, the domination of cyberspace by this rising class threatens to accelerate the consolidation of wealth, power, and influence in ways unprecedented since the height of the industrial revolution.[22] Some of the companies may fade in time, and others may rise to take their place, but the shift in wealth and power to the tech moguls will continue to shape the country, and its class structure, for decades to come.

At the same time we are now witnessing a growing sense among the tech Oligarchs—like those of the industrial era a century earlier—that they should try to shape the country's future direction. "It's becoming excruciatingly, obviously clear to everyone else that where value is created is no longer in New York, it's no longer in Washington, it's no longer in LA. It's in San Francisco and the Bay Area," suggests one venture capitalist.[23]

In the future this confluence of accumulated wealth will also express itself most effectively through the growing and increasingly politicized nonprofit sector. Yet today's "philanthrocapitalism" differs markedly from the philanthropy of the past. Instead of helping hospitals, building libraries, or supporting soup kitchens, the new Oligarchs have risen to what author David Callahan calls "affluent super-citizens," able to use their money to craft their own solutions to social problems.[24]

What Makes the New Oligarchy Different from the Old?

The characteristics of this emerging Oligarchy are critical to understanding their peculiar class nature. Rather than concentrate simplistically on the rise of the "one percent," it is more useful to focus on the differences, sometimes subtle, between this Oligarchy and those that preceded them. This takes our discussion beyond the conventional, often hackneyed analysis of the distribution of wealth and instead focuses on significant changes within the upper classes.

For one thing, the tech Oligarchs' relationship to the general population, as both consumers and workers, diverges from that of traditional plutocrats. In the last century, many old-line industries, particularly larger firms, were forced to deal with their employees and their demands, often in the form of union agreements.

As a result, whether unionized or not, large American firms that developed in the early and mid-twentieth century tended to be "very broad at the base and uncomfortably pointed at the top," as one commentator observed. The old plutocracy—the oil barons, the heads of major manufacturing firms, the owners of major utilities—may have been reactionary in many of their views, but their operations depended heavily on middle- and working-class people, both as employees and as consumers.[25]

The new Oligarchs, although they also depend on mass consumerism, base their fortunes primarily on the sale of essentially ephemeral goods: media, advertising, and entertainment. These products and services consume time and leisure more than physical space; they are less reliant on low-cost domestic energy sources, as their products are either software or built elsewhere. Indeed, many of the new Oligarchs have profited through investment in very expensive renewable energy sources that have enjoyed often lavish public subsidies.[26]

Nor do the new Oligarchs actually require a large and thriving middle class. The mass market may still be important for some products, but for the new Oligarchs mass affluence is no longer a prerequisite. There is no need for the kind of disposable income required to buy a home, or a car, or a washing machine. Even a young person working part-time as a barista or car park attendant can afford the latest smartphone, the newest video game, or, in the future, a device to lose themselves in virtual reality.[27]

The role of labor for the tech Oligarchs is also demonstrably different than for more traditional industries. For the most part, these industries employ relatively few Americans, and those that are critical to their operations are largely drawn from the ranks of the very well-educated. Overall, as of 2013, the leading social media firms directly employ less than 60,000 people total in the United States; in comparison, even a shrunken GM employs 200,000, Ford 164,000, and Exxon over 100,000. Put another way, Google at the end of 2013 had a market cap six times that of General Motors while having one-fifth as many American workers.[28]

The tech firms also have very different requirements for the workers they do employ. The bulk of the old industrial age companies have depended on highly trained workers, truck drivers, and other more blue-collar employees to make their companies work. Such employees are largely marginal in the new technocracy. As we will see later, in Silicon Valley many of these basic tasks are performed by service firms or by industrial contractors in Asia that often pay pitifully poor wages.

The Rise of the Clerisy and the Emergence of Gentry Liberalism

In the current era, the other ascendant group is what I call the *Clerisy*, based largely in the worlds of academia, media, government, and the nonprofit sector. The Clerisy's rise, as I will demonstrate later, reflects the increased influence—and employment—in such key sectors as education, government, and media. These groups, for the most part, have expanded as much of the middle class has declined.

The power of the Clerisy stems primarily not from money or the control of technology, but from persuading, instructing, and regulating the rest of society. This has particular impact given that the vast majority of the Clerisy are increasingly uniform in their worldview, especially in political matters, their approach to environmental issues, and their social values. In practical terms, such as in their support of President Obama and the Democratic Party, they are both broadly allied with the tech Oligarchs and are themselves becoming a huge center of power and influence, much as the clergy was in medieval and early modern times.

The Clerisy's power has been particularly critical in the evolution of what can best be described as gentry liberalism, a branch of progressive politics sponsored and largely shaped by the rising class of Oligarchs and their Clerical allies.

There have always, of course, been affluent individuals who backed liberal or Democratic causes out of a mixture of philosophy and self-interest. These have included those who needed government subsidies (such as urban developers) and those who sought tax breaks (such as energy companies), as well as the parts of Wall Street involved in government finance. They constituted, in the words of one leftist scholar, an odd alliance of "Jews and Cowboys," which financed the Democratic Party from the New Deal era to the presidency of Bill Clinton.[29]

These "new rich" emerged after World War II and predominantly appeared in the "tangible" sectors of the economy: oil, engineering and construction, agribusiness, and suburban real estate. Today their ties to the Democratic Party have faded, as have those of the many blue- and white-collar workers that they employ. Instead these tangible industries have now become the bulwark of mainstream Republican conservatism, including, most notably, the energy mogul Harold Simmons, the Koch brothers, and Texas homebuilder Bob Perry.[30]

As the old industries have consolidated on the right, the left or pro-gressive tendency now relies on an alliance between the new Oligarchs, increasingly concentrated in places like Silicon Valley and Wall Street, and their Clerical allies. This represents a forceful new power grouping with the potential to reshape society and politics. They may clash on specific issues and other privileges, such as the regulation of financial institutions. Yet, ultimately, the things holding them together—largely the ambition to shape the future of society—are more important than their occasional differences.

Gentry liberalism effectively amounts to a sea change in what is now widely referred to as progressive politics. In the new formulation, the great *raison d'être* for left-wing politics—advocating for the middle and working classes—has been refocused to attend more closely to the pol-icy imperatives and interests of small, highly affluent classes as well as the powerful public sector.[31] These interests, once closely linked, now seem to be diverging.

The discrepancies between the new progressive policies and social realities have been among the most unfortunate manifestations of the Obama era. In his first term, household incomes dropped by $2,600, poverty soared by six million, and food stamp rolls continued to swell.[32] Meanwhile the wealthy prospered as the stock market soared.[33]

If this had occurred during a Republican administration, many pro-gressives would have been horrified, as indeed they should. Yet despite his occasional populist rhetoric, both before and after taking office, the president has drawn much of his political support from the ultra-rich. Indeed at his first inaugural, notes one sympathetic chronicler, the big-gest problem for donors was to find sufficient parking space for their private jets.[34]

This has created a new political reality that differs from the struggle that divided Democrats in the past, which focused on issues of foreign policy, the role of labor, and the conflict between rights and obligations. In the past, Democrats and progressives still aimed their appeal largely to the middle-class yeomanry; now, progressivism depends increasingly on the largesse and support of the wealthy, notably from the media and tech sectors, as well as largely lock-step backing from the Clerisy.

Rather than an expression of working- or middle-class concerns, gentry liberalism essentially reflects the perspective of rising classes:

socially liberal, "green," but also protective of their privileges. By examining campaign contributions, the vast majority of America's wealthiest households tilt in this direction. Among the "one percent of the one percent," who increasingly dominate political giving, the leading donation recipients, aside from the conservative Club for Growth, were liberal groups such as Emily's List, Act Blue, and Moveon.org. Indeed, liberal groups accounted for eight of the top ten ideological causes of the ultrarich, and seven of the ten congressional candidates most dependent on money from such people were Democrats.[35]

In our present "age of elites," as author Chrystia Freeland has dubbed it, this ideological shift among the rich, particularly the new rich, is critical to understanding the new class order. Some of the nation's wealthiest regions, many of which were once Republican strongholds, are now among the most reliably Democratic. In 2012, for example, President Obama won eight of the country's ten wealthiest counties, sometimes by margins of two-to-one or better. He also triumphed easily in virtually all of the top counties with the highest concentrations of millionaires, as well as among managers of hedge funds.[36]

Every society needs its oligarchs, those who are able to take leadership and invest in the future; they are also necessary as creators and investors in new economic potential. It likewise needs a clerical class to serve as enforcers of social norms and spreaders of philanthropy. The great nineteenth-century robber barons, although often exceedingly unpleasant as individuals, left an enormous legacy in the form of industries, such as steel, utilities, and the railroads, that underpinned the industrial era. Only later, due to reforms and the further expansion of the economy, did that legacy translate into mass affluence.

Whether we are discussing then or now, it is critical to understand that the wealthy are not disinterested observers. They tend to push politics in a direction amenable to both their interests and their personal tastes. The railroad tycoons, who famously controlled most legislatures and much of the Senate during the post–Civil War expansion, believed they should control the direction of the country, adhering to what one lobbyist called "the politics of business." As one plutocrat said with amazing candor: "We are the rich; we own America; we got it, God knows how, but we intend to keep it."[37]

The new Oligarchy, and their allies in the Clerisy, are more subtle in their pronouncements. Nor should their efforts be dismissed as largely conspiratorial, or even malicious in intent. But throughout history, classes maintain a common interest in protecting and expanding their superior status, often at the expense, albeit unwittingly, of the lower orders. The new ruling class may not see themselves as defending their own peculiar interests, but instead they may perceive their agenda as reflecting science and the global public interest.

The Changing Attitude to Growth

Perhaps the biggest difference between the ruling classes of the nineteenth century and those emerging in the twenty-first can be seen in attitudes toward economic progress. The old plutocracy—notably energy, manufacturing, mass agriculture, and construction—generally supported and even encouraged economic progress among those below them, who also served as their customers. This fixation on growth was also shared by many on the left, including labor leaders such as Walter Reuther. Agreement that broad-based expansion was a good thing remained largely universal, at least until the late 1960s.[38]

Such industries should not be considered backwards. Indeed they are often leaders in the application of technology to their businesses. Houston, the energy capital, boasts a per capita population of engineers second only to that of San Jose. But these industries find themselves in conflict with the agenda on environmental issues, for example, embraced by much of the information technology industry, the media, and those segments of financial world, notably venture capital, that fund them.[39]

This approach has implications for the nature of growth, according to economist Benjamin Friedman. Growth, Friedman notes, is critical to maintaining a socially just order, increasing opportunity both for individuals and regions, particularly those historically left behind. For all its many environmental and social shortcomings, the old economic regime emphasized growth and upward mobility. In contrast the new economic order focuses more on the notion of "sustainability"—so reflective of the feudal worldview—over rapid economic expansion.[40]

This shift in emphasis can be seen in many of the often palpably good causes touted by Oligarchs—notably, contemporary environmentalism.

Yet while progressive in their intent, these policies in practice turn out to be socially regressive in their application. Take up less space, make a smaller impact, consume less: this has replaced the notion of accelerating economic mobility. This behavior often hurts most those "tangible" industries, such as energy, manufacturing, logistics, and housing, that heavily employ blue-collar workers. Ironically, the mandate to "live small" frequently comes from individuals who are ensconced on huge estates or in incredibly expensive trophy apartments and who travel by private jet.[41] For all the trappings of progressivism, the current ideology is remarkably degenerative.

The Embattled Yeomanry

This alliance between the Clerisy and the tech Oligarchs threatens most of all the position of America's once ascendant and still extensive *Yeoman* class. This class consists largely of small business owners, sole proprietors, and those with small property holdings. They have gone through periods of decline in the past—notably in the Gilded Age—but this class, defined largely by ownership of hard assets, has always been the critical bastion of American and other democracies. But their economic and political power has faded in the past few decades.[42]

From the origins of capitalism, the Yeomanry, often peasants or immigrants, played a critical role. At the dawn of the modern era, many of these lower- or middle-class people started businesses, in the words of one historian, "like fitful flies." They were the driving force of the market, the creators of modern cities, and among the primary beneficiaries of economic progress. The most enterprising, or connected, of these "new men" gradually overthrew the old "artisan-like" traders, and they eventually even supplanted the aristocracy, including in many countries the royal families as well. In most cases, their ascendency, although at times exploitative, generally promoted the expansion of both freedom and individual choice.[43]

But after a long, albeit sometimes bumpy, ascent, lasting well into the early 1970s, conditions for the Yeomanry clearly have worsened. Although exacerbated in recent years, this problem has remained vexing for at least the past several decades. Even at the height of the latest economic expansion, the typical middle-class American saw only one percent income growth, adjusted for inflation, compared to six percent in the period from 1995 to 2000.[44] Throughout at least the last two decades, economic change has benefited top workers at financial services companies, technology firms, and the highest-end businesses, while incomes for the middle and working classes have suffered as low-wage jobs have proliferated.[45]

At the same time the Yeomanry has endured huge increases in fixed costs (healthcare, housing, and education), as well as the demise of real pensions, the decline in unionization, mergers, and the offshoring of work to other countries. In fact, the leading causes of bankruptcy were not profligate spending habits but rather necessary spending on basic needs such as healthcare and housing.[46]

These costs have surged as overall median incomes for Americans fell seven percent for the decade since 2000, and they are not expected to recover, according to some economic models, until 2021.[47]

The Expanding Lower Classes

This fading of the Yeomanry threatens to create a more bifurcated society, with an increasing number of formerly middle-class people becoming, in a sense, proletarianized. Already a large portion—almost one-third of the public, according to Pew—considers themselves "lower" class as opposed to middle class, up from barely one-quarter in 2008.[48]

Indeed as the Yeomanry have struggled, the lower parts of the economic spectrum have expanded. In the five years following the Great Recession, the percentage of people living in poverty rose to 15 percent, the highest level in 20 years, although it was significantly higher in 1960. Equally troubling, the ability of less-skilled workers to break into high-wage work has slowed, trapping many in a kind of permanent status as working poor. Increasingly these workers are older and better educated than low-wage workers in the past. Some 43 percent of non-college-educated whites now complain they are downwardly mobile.[49]

Particularly hard hit are many minorities, notably African Americans and Latinos, whose income has also dropped more than most and whose unemployment has remained stubbornly higher. Despite the election of the nation's first African American president, in itself a considerable achievement, the gap between Anglo incomes on the one side and those of blacks and Hispanics has doubled since the recession. The black unemployment rate remains more than double the white jobless rate and reaches 40 percent among youths.

Rule from Our Betters?

The hardening of class lines, and the growing concentration of disposable income, sends signals through everything from the political economy to consumer culture. Many theorists, both on the right and the left, suggest the time has come to accept a more stratified, less permeable social order. Conservatives and libertarians, such as economist Tyler Cowen, argue that "average" intelligence and skills are no longer sufficient for social advance. Some 15 percent of the population may do very well, he argues, but the vast majority will have to accept limited prospects for themselves and their offspring.

The prospect he lays out essentially recalls the hierarchies of the Middle Ages, or at best the Victorian era. The most suitable niche for the lower orders, he notes, lies in servicing the needs of high earners, "for example as trainers, nannies, and cleaners." Rather than look to themselves for a future, "everyone who isn't at the very top will be scrambling for the attention of those who are."[50]

In Cowen's projected future, Americans should expect what they have historically resisted: deference and hierarchy. As he puts it: "There is no high morality without exclusion, no integrity without exclusion, and no corporate culture without exclusion." This defense of hierarchy would not have been out of place in America's Gilded Age, nor among many traditional conservatives as well.[51]

Ironically, a somewhat similar embrace of a culture of deference is also widely supported on the progressive left, particularly in places like Silicon Valley and among their allies in the well-funded green movement.[52] In a way reminiscent of the industrial barons of the late nineteenth and early twentieth century, who embraced the traditional Calvinist approach of the "elect," or like the early progressives, some of whom embraced the more modern Darwinian notion of natural selection, the current tech community increasingly sees itself as a natural-born elite, whose model represents the template for the economic and social future.[53]

Sadly, the vast majority of progressives generally offer little that would allow for greater upward mobility, relying instead largely on redistribution as the answer to social ills. Progressive theorists often write off the industries that have long driven private-sector middle-class incomes, in part for environmental reasons. They also, sometimes for the same reasons, denigrate any potential rise in typically better paying blue-collar jobs in such fields as energy, manufacturing, construction, or logistics. Since the 1970s, concerns about environmental constraints, noted Christopher Lasch, undermined the notion for the rising "new class" that their definition of the "good life" could be "made universally available."[54]

Thus ends the romance between upward mobility and the progressive idea. Rather than be helped in the new economic order, the once independent Yeoman class is expected to accept its new role as home care providers, hairdressers, dog walkers, and toenail painters for the "innovative class." Walter Russell Mead aptly describes this perspective as a "*Downton Abbey* vision of the American future."[55]

If left unchecked, this trend will change not only our politics but also our consumer culture. In an environment where wealth is concentrated, companies focus on the affluent minority, as opposed to the middle-class mass, which has increasingly limited purchasing power. Demographer Peter Francese points out that the "mass affluent," which comprises roughly ten percent of households, boosted spending annually last decade at a seven percent rate while overall household growth remained at a mere one percent. Even in the midst of the worst of the recession, it was luxury brands that did best, while those selling to the middle class did poorly.[56] In the years between 1992 and 2012, the share of consumption accounted for by the top five percent of earners grew from 27 to 38 percent.[57]

Ultimately, we are moving to a society where the very few dominate not only spending but also the entire political economy. Two Citigroup economists have defined this as the rise of a "plutonomy," an economy built around the spending of a relatively few affluent people, a phenomenon particularly evident in global cities such as New York or London.[58] This approach has led some, such as former New York Mayor Michael Bloomberg, to suggest that the best way to take care of the poor is not to help them find the means to enter the middle class but instead to have more wealthy people settle in your city. "If we can find a bunch of billionaires around the world to move here, that would be a godsend,"

Bloomberg, himself a multi-billionaire, suggests. "Because that's where the revenue comes to take care of everybody else."

Will the Middle Orders Revolt?

For good reason the middle orders increasingly feel alienated by people in power, in both parties, whom they perceive to have abandoned them. Almost every institution of power, from government and large corporations to banks and Wall Street, suffers the lowest public esteem ever recorded.[59] Only 17 percent, according to one recent poll, even believe the government acts with their "consent."[60] Similar levels of distrust can be seen in the European Union, Japan, India, and China.[61]

These concerns have helped shape the Tea Party on the right and the Occupy Wall Street movement on the left. It is at the core of the appeal of such disparate figures as Sarah Palin and Elizabeth Warren, even though their supporters remain divided on key social issues. Growth, and the prospect of upward mobility, notes Benjamin Friedman, has bolstered "the moral character" of the country and promoted tolerance and democracy.[62] The collapse of this widespread prosperity, along with a growing chasm between the classes, augurs a potential shift to a far less attractive social order.

The challenges of this new political epoch also undermine traditional descriptions of "left" and "right," progressive and conservative. Self-described progressives, for example, frequently side with policies that restrain middle-class upward mobility. At the same time, some conservatives embrace policies that blatantly favor the dominant corporations who use their political and financial power to limit market entries, for example for unconventional autos, and to obstruct innovative companies. They can be counted on to defend privilege, such as allowing generous tax deductions even for mansions and second homes.[63]

But the situation is not hopeless if the Yeomanry begins to understand what exactly is happening to them. Often radicals, like Marx, underestimate the ability of capitalism, through political reform, to be susceptible to significant reform and greater diffusion of economic benefits. By the end of the nineteenth century, the extreme inequality that Marx witnessed in Great Britain and other European countries was already beginning to diminish, as income gains rose for the middle and working classes.[64] This provides some hope that reform and new think-ing could produce greater income and social mobility in the current era.

The solution to the class crisis of the twenty-first century will dif-fer from that of the twentieth. In the industrial era, centralized systems and bureaucracies were critical to overcome the entrenched power of large corporations and monopoly capital. But the digital age—if it can be wrested from the control of the new Oligarchs—opens greater possibilities for decentralization. Today, centralized news sources, uni-versities, and institutes no longer possess a monopoly on information and thought. Orthodoxies may have become easier to preserve, but at the same time it is proving more difficult to halt the spread of contrary ideas.

Technology's dual character may prove critical to any attempt to undermine the new class order. Just as technology can be harnessed to concentrate wealth and power, it can also provide opportunities for an unprecedented diffusion of authority and the empowerment of individ-uals, families, and communities. Hierarchy is not an inevitable product of a science-based age.

Technology can also create the conditions for dispersed prosperity and, even more significantly, for increased physical and social mobility. Communities and families no longer have to cringe before centralized authority; they can shape their disparate futures in ways that reflect their own desires. Decentralization is the key as jobs spread. By some recent estimates, upwards of 50 percent of the workforce can operate largely at home, and some 70 percent of millennials, according to one Oracle survey, think of the traditional office as antiquated.[65]

To create this future requires a renewed focus on broad-based economic growth. Until the last decade, this would have seemed com-monsensical. Socialists, liberals, and conservatives, of course, vigorously debated how best to achieve this goal. But the goal remained the same: how to shrink slums and increase opportunity for a better quality of life for the middle or working class.

This focus on growth needs to be allied with ways to promote the dispersion of property and wealth. This may mean a greater emphasis not on particular elite geographies but on how to provide greater opportunities for ownership and autonomy in a broad section of the country and across the social classes.

Dispersed intelligence, as Alexis de Tocqueville famously observed, is the key to effective democracy.[66] In contrast, we are threatened by the concentration of intelligence and information in the hands of ever fewer companies—such as Google, Amazon, and Facebook—who then mine the collective data bounty to further their own very private ends.

In the end, the real issue lies in whether we seek to freeze class relations or re-ignite an era of upward mobility. To do the latter requires a blending of capitalist methods but in the service of fundamentally social democratic ends. It's clear from the examples of Europe and blue-state America that, by itself, a focus on welfarism and government regulation stymies mobility by discouraging risk-taking and innovation. But without preserving the prospect of progress for the working and middle classes, capitalism, in this as in earlier times, may lose both its moral compass and its base for popular support.

Is the American Dream Dead?

In his classic 1893 essay, "The Significance of the Frontier in American History," Frederick Jackson Turner spoke of "the expansive character of American life." Turner proclaimed that even as the physical frontier was shrinking, Americans would likely look elsewhere to find "a new field of opportunity."[67]

For all its limitations, the "expansive" spirit of America generated a century or more of relentless technological improvements, the gradual creation of a mass middle class, and the integration of ever more diverse immigrants into the national narrative. At times, a snapshot would reveal sometimes awful iniquities, but the overall trajectory showed a steady improvement of conditions for the middle and, later, the working classes.

Yet today, many feel this modern period of "expansiveness" is doomed, much like the prairie frontier culture whose denouement Turner portrayed. Some argue that it is better for Americans to shift from their historically "expansive" view and embrace a more modest déclassé future. This is critical not only because of the implications at home, but also for the fate of the historically radical notion—so intrinsic to the American identity—that upward mobility remains probable for those who work hard at their jobs, invest in their farms or businesses, and save diligently for the future.

It remains questionable if this ideal can make it through the new century, even in America. Rather than seek new worlds to conquer, or even hope to retain the accomplishments of prior generations, the new conventional wisdom seems to be an acceptance of ever narrowing opportunity, a kind of fatalistic acceptance of class distinction and societal stagnation.

Yet the culture of aspiration in America is not quite dead, and it may be harder to squelch than many, on both the left and the right, suggest today. As Turner contended at the end of his famous essay, it would be "a rash prophet who would assert that the expansive character of American life has now entirely ceased."[68]

The real priority is not to assert the eroded validity of the American notion of aspiration, but finding ways to overcome the economic, political, and social factors stifling its continuing health. Similar challenges—the concentration of wealth of the Gilded Age, the Great Depression, war, and environmental angst—have periodically appeared and were eventually addressed through technological innovation, as well as critical political and social changes. Rather than accept the shrinkage of the American prospect, we should seek to restore it for those who will inherit the Republic and also preserve the dream that has animated millions to come here from well outside our borders.

CHAPTER TWO

Valley of the Oligarchs

Looking back from the future, perhaps as little as a decade from now, our era may become best known for ushering in the emergence of a new American ruling class. This new force, forged largely in the marriage of technology and media, represents the most potentially dominant upper class in modern American history.

Unlike past elites in tangible industries such as energy, agribusiness, manufacturing, and construction, the emerging tech Oligarchy employ relatively few Americans, having a need largely for only highly trained workers and those who provide personal services, from accountants and gardeners to dog walkers and pedicurists. Rather than being spread out across the country, they are concentrated primarily on the peninsula between San Francisco and San Jose, with a secondary concentration in the greater Seattle area.

Indeed the top five firms of social media—Facebook, Twitter, Pinterest, Google, and LinkedIn—are located in either Silicon Valley or its urban satellite city, San Francisco.[1] As Americans disperse, seeking out affordable places and fresh opportunities, the new hegemons have tended to concentrate in what are among the most expensive, and exclusive, regions of the country.

The current tech Oligarchs differ greatly from the traditional "propeller heads" who once populated Silicon Valley. Many of those engineers were in the aeronautics, aviation, or aerospace industries that arose from the 1940s through the 1970s, and which reflected a very different, more practical attention to the real world than the new breed, whose fortunes were often made from software, social media, and Internet marketing.

Despite their technical brilliance, the old techies, whom I interviewed extensively in the 1970s and 1980s, tended to be engineering types who were relatively uninterested in politics. Even those who were more politically active, such as David Packard and Robert Noyce, were usually moderate in their politics and identified with many of the same concerns as other industrial firms. Later on, many of the earliest firms in the personal computer and Internet space were not only indifferent to governance, but even vaguely anarchistic.[2]

In contrast, the new autocrats boast far broader and more sweeping ambitions to influence politics and public policies. Like Skynet in the *Terminator* movie series, the tech Oligarchs can be said to have achieved "self-consciousness," and now recognize their ability to influence the public and the political class. "Politics for me is the most obvious area [to be disrupted by the Web]," suggests former Facebook president Sean Parker. The success with which the tech firm's technology assisted President Obama's re-election effort offers clear support to Parker's assertion.[3] Some tech entrepreneurs, following the tradition of the old British aristocracy, have even moved into districts where they could run for office, using their vast wealth to win in places with which they sometimes have little ties.[4]

This power is all the more frightening given the ability of what Rebecca MacKinnon calls "the sovereigns of cyberspace" to uncover and market our most intimate details.[5] Moving beyond the construction of more efficient platforms for communication and work, their efforts now center on breaking into the personal code of every individual who uses their technology. Historian Manuel Castells envisioned this development over fifteen years ago. "The new power," Castells wrote in 1997, "lies in the codes of information and in the images of representation around which societies organize their institutions, and people build their lives and decide their behavior."[6]

The Oligarchic Moment

Oligarchies tend to arise at critical points of economic transition. America's most significant generation of moguls—Morgan, Harriman, Rockefeller, Carnegie, and Ford—emerged as the United States transformed itself from a rather decentralized, largely agrarian economy into a mass-production-oriented industrial juggernaut.

Seizing control of a now mechanized economy, these moguls soon supplanted the old mercantile and agriculture elites that had dominated early America. By the dawn of the twentieth century, noted historians Charles and Mary Beard, masters of great urban wealth formed a "young plutocracy" with riches beyond the dreams of Midas, garnered from mines of the West, the factories of the Midwest, and the forests of the Pacific, and spent it in "the most powerful center of accumulation, New York City."[7]

In the nineteenth century, for example, vast wealth gained from cotton, silver, and other commodities helped create the foundation for such investment banking firms as Goldman Sachs, Oppenheimer, and Lehman Brothers, and for such publishing industry giants as the Hearst empire. Many of these people also went into politics, often entering the "millionaire's club" of the U.S. Senate. Their wealth, in the era before income taxes, was immense; by the 1880s the revenues of Cornelius Vanderbilt's railroad empire were greater than those of the federal government.[8]

Like John D. Rockefeller (Standard Oil), J. P. Morgan, and railway mogul Edward Harriman, the tech Oligarchs have taken advantage of the shift in the economic paradigm to garner enormous wealth and power. The information economy's emergence is allowing them to establish sway over vast sections of the economy, including such areas as advertising, media, entertainment, and, increasingly, the political system as well.

In some senses the new tech hegemons share some similarities to the oligarchs that arose to dominate the post-Soviet Russian economy. As Russia privatized its vast industrial and resource economy, certain aggressive figures, many of them quite young and some connected to the security apparatus, seized control of critical assets. In consequence, the former Communist country became dominated by ultra-rich oligarchs who controlled the country's industrial and, most importantly, enormous natural resources. Moscow, not New York or London, is now home to more of the world's billionaires than any major city.[9]

Rather than buy or steal assets from the state, as in Russia, America's tech Oligarchs benefit from access to limited pools of risk capital— nearly half of which is concentrated in Silicon Valley[10]—which for two generations has dominated the funding of major technology companies.

In this sense, notes economist Umair Haque, "Tech is something like the new Wall Street. Mostly white dudes getting rich by making stuff of limited social purpose and impact." The new boss, it turns out, looks very much like the old one.[11]

The Roots of Oligarchy

Like the Russian oligarchs, the moguls of turn-of-the-twentieth-century America have become so powerful because, unlike many firms in other industries, software giants such as Google, Facebook, Microsoft, and Oracle face still limited foreign or domestic competition. They enjoy market shares greater than the more traditional capitalists in such industries as steel, oil, gas, or automotive. Google, for example, accounts for over two-thirds of all Internet searches.[12] The fantastic wealth of Bill Gates over the past twenty years, like that of the other Oligarchs, stems in large part from these kinds of "monopoly rents."[13]

Of course, these Oligarchs, like feudal lords or rival gangs, sometimes fight among themselves—for example, the battle between Google and Apple over operating systems or, increasingly, on the hardware side of the industry. Yet this struggle between Oligarchs is far from a competitive free for all; together these two firms provide almost 90 percent of the operating systems for smartphones.[14] Similarly, over half of American and Canadian computer users use Facebook, making it easily the world's dominant social media site.[15]

By comparison, more traditional industries, such as the auto industry, appear as relative hotbeds of competition, with no firm controlling more than one-fifth of the U.S. market.[16] Major competitors, such as the Korean firm Hyundai, emerge periodically. The oil and gas business, associated with oligopoly from the days of John Rockefeller, is far more competitive; the world's top ten oil companies account for some forty percent of the world's production.[17]

More important still, the tech Oligarchs control portions of their companies that would turn most oilmen or auto executives green with envy. The largest single stockholder at Exxon, the world's largest oil company, is its CEO and chairman, Rex Tillerson, who controls .04 percent of Exxon stock. The largest automotive company, General Motors, doesn't have a single direct shareholder with over 1 percent of the stock.[18]

In contrast, Sergey Brin, Larry Page, and Eric Schmidt control roughly two-thirds of the voting stock in Google.[19] Brin and Page alone are worth over $20 billion each. Larry Ellison, the founder of Oracle, owns just under 23 percent of his company and is worth over $50 billion; in 2013 *Forbes* ranked him the country's third richest man.[20] Bill Gates, the country's richest man, is worth $78 billion and still controls 7 percent of his firm.[21] Mark Zuckerberg's 29.3 percent stake in Facebook is worth upwards of $25 billion.[22]

As a result, like their far less admired counterparts on Wall Street, America's elite tech firms—and their owners—have become fantastically cash rich. Besides GE, a classic conglomerate, the largest cash hordes now belong to Apple, Microsoft, Cisco, Oracle, and Google, all of whom sometimes have more dollars on hand than the U.S. government. Seven of the eight biggest individual winners from stock gains in 2013 were tech entrepreneurs, led by Jeff Bezos, who added $12 billion to his paper wealth; Mark Zuckerberg, who raked in an additional $11.9 billion; and Sergey Brin and Larry Page, who saw their wallets expand by roughly $9 billion.[23]

Of course, these numbers can rise and fall with market shifts, but the long-term impact of this accumulation of wealth will be profound. Perhaps most critically, the new Oligarchs have made their fortunes both quickly and at an early age. In fact, out of the 29 billionaires in the world under 40 years old, ten come from the tech sector, four of them from Facebook (whose founders are just over 30), and two from Google. The bulk of the other new rich either inherited their fortunes or are drawn from the ranks of the Russian oligarchs.[24]

The Favored .01 Percent

Great wealth and high status, particularly at a young age, often persuade people that they know best about the future and about how society should be governed. "One needs imagination to confront a revolution," observed Alvin Toffler.[25] Twitter founder Jack Dorsey, a 37-year-old resident of San Francisco, announced in 2013 that he aspires to become mayor—of New York. He hopes to follow in the footsteps of billionaire Michael Bloomberg. Like his fellow Oligarch, he maintains that his business expertise qualifies him to run the nation's biggest city, even if he hasn't quite gotten around to living there.[26]

The tech Oligarch's ascendency has made them feel somehow different—and superior. Such thinking, notes the leftist economist Thomas Piketty, has been used in the contemporary setting to "justify the extreme inequalities and to defend the privileges of the winners."[27]

This self-regard has been reinforced by public perception.[28] In 2011, over 72 percent of Americans had positive feelings about the computer industry, as opposed to a mere 30 percent for banking and 20 percent for oil and gas.[29] Even during the Occupy protests in 2012, few criticisms were hurled by the "screwed generation" at tech titans. Indeed, when Steve Jobs, a .000001 percenter worth $7 billion and a rugged capitalist of the classic type, passed away, protestors openly mourned his demise.[30]

Unlike the grandees of Wall Street or the energy industry, the tech Oligarchs have so far experienced relatively little of the criticism commonly directed at Wall Street or energy executives for their huge compensation levels. They, it appears, are different even than the other rich. Whereas the wealthy on Wall Street and elsewhere are viewed as illegitimate and greedy, the tech moguls have managed to retain an aura of earned success and enjoy almost universal admiration.[31]

"We live in a bubble, and I don't mean a tech bubble or a valuation bubble. I mean a bubble as in our own little world," Google's Schmidt boasted in 2011 to *Bloomberg Businessweek*. "And what a world it is. Companies can't hire people fast enough. Young people can work hard and make a fortune. Homes hold their value. Occupy Wall Street isn't really something that comes up in a daily discussion, because their issues are not our daily reality."[32]

One explanation lies in the relationship between consumers and the tech industry. Our society, Christopher Lasch once noted, teaches "people to want a never-ending supply of new toys."[33] People like Jobs made the kinds of toys—smartphones, iPods, iPads—that are bright spots for the new generation. These technologies, of course, have serious business uses, but those may be limited for young people unable to pay off their college debts, start companies, buy houses, or even leave their parents' basements.

But even if they cannot achieve the traditional milestones of middle-class life, the millennials can genuflect to those creating the products and services that occupy their time and keep them in touch with friends.

Indeed in a recent survey of high-performing high school seniors, Apple, Google, and Microsoft ranked among the most preferred private companies, beaten only by the traditional maker of puerile dreams, the Walt Disney Company.[34]

Technological Utopianism

The innate sense of superiority and elevated status within the information hierarchy reflects attitudes about technology as the primary driver of societal change. First nurtured in the late nineteenth and early twentieth centuries, the notion that technological change constitutes the great hope of mankind was widely shared across a broad spectrum of otherwise incompatible, even hostile, ideologies.

The development of railways, mass-production industries, the steamship, and the telegraph opened new markets as well as communications across the world. In this sense, like the Internet that followed a century later, these technologies created new business models and, for many at the time, the prospect of a more prosperous economy and an infinitely more perfect society.[35]

Electricity, according to Edison, would reduce the need for sleep, help improve the senses, and promote the equality of women. Many Americans, noted historian David Nye, believed that new technology would eliminate toil and allow Americans to settle in a pastoral utopia. Of course, much of this did not happen. Cities grew even faster and factories more oppressive as new technology allowed bosses to monitor work, and the private information of their customers, ever more closely.[36]

The Second World War, followed by the Cold War, accelerated the rise of technology-based business in the economic hierarchy. In both wars the opposing sides worked rapidly and successfully to develop technological innovations, such as radar, jet engines, and nuclear power, and to make huge advances in information processing. Out of these conflicts rose a whole new set of industries dependent on the development and exploitation of science. As a prescient Winston Churchill remarked, "The new empires are those of the mind."[37]

Despite the threat of thermonuclear war, the 1950s and 1960s were suffused with a spirit of technological optimism. In his classic study *The Technological Society* (1967), French philosopher Jacques Ellul drew a contemporary picture of the world of 2000, complete with regular shuttle service to the moon, widespread synthetic foods, and an end to both hunger and poverty.[38] These assumptions, of course, have not been fulfilled even now, but the promise of such improvements—as is the case today—captivated many observers at the time.

Both large corporations and government dominated this period of technical development. "The imperatives of technology," economist John Kenneth Galbraith suggested, would enhance centralization, fostering a "technostructure" of well-financed, highly organized firms, often closely linked to the government. "No individual genius arranged the flight to moon," Galbraith asserted. "It was the work of organization—bureaucracy."[39]

The California Model

The early days of Silicon Valley more or less followed the Galbraithian model. NASA and the Defense Department[40] were dominant among early customers, while Lockheed Missiles and Space remained easily the Valley's largest employer as late as the 1980s.[41] But as the technological revolution shifted from hardware to software, and federal spending dropped, Silicon Valley began to diverge from the Galbraithian model. These new players were animated not by conventional business thinking but by something defined by Richard Barbrook and Andy Cameron as "the California ideology," a unique amalgam of free market conservatism, social liberalism, and technological utopianism.[42]

This synthesis differed from the Galbraithian ideal in terms of corporate culture. On the individual level, the new California executives cast a very different image than the company men of earlier science-based aerospace and computer firms. Top executives no longer stayed in firms for decades or a lifetime, but shifted between companies, often starting their own. They often dressed in jeans, not suits. Even more pronounced were their differences with their rivals in Europe and Asia, who were trapped by rigid corporate structures.[43] What they relied on were not long established ties, notes analyst Anna Lee Saxenian, but "the social and technical networks" that provided funding and the critical pool of expertise.[44]

This networked system, which included a large number of specialized firms, was also markedly more supportive of younger entrepreneurs,

among them the then twenty-something Steve Jobs. This helped consolidate the Valley's supremacy over its traditional rival, the greater Boston
area. By 1990, the Valley accounted for 39 of the nation's fastest growing
electronics companies, compared to just four along Boston's Route 128.
Over the ensuing decade, Valley firms, largely through the application
of software, also overcame what had once been considered insurmountable competition from Japan.[45]

The great hope promised by this emerging, post-industrial information economy was perhaps best stated by futurist Alvin Toffler. He
distinguished between bureaucratic, top-down "Second Wave" industrial firms—which still remain powerful in their own right—and the
flatter, more dispersed, and fundamentally less hierarchical "Third
Wave" firms. The decentralization of technology, allowing people to
communicate without going through a centralized computer, Toffler
reasoned, would weaken the power of "Big Brother," promoting instead
the decentralization of power.[46] Being simply the medium of the message, software companies could not control it, it was believed, and few
considered how such companies' activities could prove harmful to the
consumer.[47]

These new Third Wave companies, noted one journalist, were seen
as "wildly productive but humane," headed by entrepreneurs who
embraced an "egalitarian" ethos that saw senior executives hobnobbing
with janitors in an almost comradely fashion. Driven by the assumption
of ever higher productivity through information technology—often
referred to as Moore's Law—these executives were widely portrayed not
as greedy capitalists but as "artists" seeking ever greater perfection. They
are here not just to make money but "change the world." Technology
enthusiast Nicholas Negroponte even suggested that "digital technology" could turn into "a natural force drawing people into greater world
harmony."[48]

From Artists to Prying Oligarchs

This sense of optimism and benevolence is increasingly hard to justify.
Rather than revolutionaries creating new paradigms of social justice
and growth, the Valley, suggests social media theorist Nathan Jurgenson, increasingly engages in a kind of "anti-capitalist capitalism" that
mints sometimes instant fortunes less on actual profits and revenues

than on the promise of being "game changers." This has worked out fine for companies that, without profits or discernible ways of becoming profitable, have made vast fortunes selling themselves to more established tech companies. He compares the Valley's pretensions with those of firms that make T-shirts with Che Guevera's picture, for sale at the local mall:

> Presumably, some people really believe Silicon Valley entrepreneurs when they say they don't care about making money. This appears to be a capitalist attempt to hide capitalism, to exploit its wealth-generating capabilities without having to assume its responsibilities and drawbacks. The post-profit Silicon Valley has, for some, been quite profitable.[49]

Yet despite its countercultural trappings and progressive ideological leanings, Silicon Valley has turned out to be every bit as cutthroat and greedy as any capitalist region—as I will demonstrate below. The technological revolution may have changed the locus of power and influence, but it did not change the fundamentally acquisitive and self-seeking realities of human nature. As Daniel Bell observed, "after one generation a meritocracy merely becomes an enclaved class."[50]

The economic fortunes of specific companies may ebb and flow, but the benefits, and the highest profits, have accrued to the same basic array of financiers, serial entrepreneurs, lawyers, and other specialists. Ultimately, any company could fail—a Facebook, a Twitter, or even a Google—but the essential tech power structure will remain in place, with built-in advantages to start newer ventures and companies, most notably due to their vast fortunes.[51]

Technology executives, however decent their initial intentions, also remain subject to the basic forces of human nature, and technology's impact is only as benign as the people implementing and controlling it. As computer industry pioneer Willis Ware warned almost four decades ago, the new communication technology, rather than simply making information more universally available, could also increase the "intensive and personal surveillance" of individuals.

Ware's proposals for greater controls for privacy were largely ignored, and they seem unlikely to be re-imposed given the economic benefits of personal data for both Oligarchs and advertisers, not to mention the requirements of the state security apparat.[52] Essentially we now have not so much a "surveillance state" as what David Lyons has termed a "surveillance society," where those who control information include not only state players but also certain well-positioned private ones.[53]

Similarly, hopeful models of entrepreneurship and competition from technology have morphed more to an oligarchic structure, with huge concentrations of both corporate market share and enormous wealth. The hopes for a more open, less intrusive reality for computer users—now the vast majority of people—have vanished, not only due to government but through the profit-seeking activities of the Oligarchal class. "The clamor for online attention only turns into money," notes technology analyst Jaron Lanier, for "a new tiny class of people who always benefit."[54]

Lanier suggests that the current Oligarchical ascendency rests increasingly on efforts to penetrate the private lives of every individual consumer. Google has already been caught bypassing Apple's privacy controls on phones and computers, and handing the data over to advertisers. The *Huffington Post* has constructed a long list of the firm's privacy violations.[55] Google, too, is renowned for mining personal information. The company's bid to use Google Plus as a platform for its other offerings represents just another attempt to create a "database for affinity" that might prove irresistible to prying advertisers.[56] As one wag tweeted in 2013: "Google motto 2004: Don't be evil. Google motto 2010: Evil is tricky to define. Google motto 2013: We make military robots." It may be time, as blogger Joshua Rivera put it, to call Google "an evil empire."[57]

But Google is hardly alone in pushing these violations of privacy. Apple has been hauled in front of the courts for its violations, while *Consumer Reports* has documented Facebook's pervasive, and often deepening, privacy breaches, including such details as health conditions (which an insurer could use against someone), travel plans (convenient for burglars), and information about a person's sexual orientation, religious affiliation, and ethnicity. Ironically, one blogger noted, even as Facebook has been loosening privacy restrictions for teenagers, company founder Zuckerberg bought several houses around his Palo Alto estate to ensure his own.[58]

It's no surprise, then, that Silicon Valley firms have worked to quell bills addressing Internet privacy both in Europe and closer to home.[59] In

VALLEY OF THE OLIGARCHS   31

Washington the Oligarchs have cultivated support in the White House, which has been eager to gain the support of tech firms and venture capitalists; and among those Republicans who rarely say no to donors with dollars.

Even faced with charges related to the release of data to the government, lobbyists for firms like Google continue to work assiduously—including with Republicans—to dampen attempts to shield consumers from prying firms' use of such data for private profits.[60] The rights of the individual computer user look increasingly like those faced by farmers or small businesspeople shipping products by rail at the turn of the twentieth century. Sitting at a home office or kitchen table, the individual user has precious little leverage.[61]

This exploitation of the Internet is central to the rise of the tech Oligarchs and their long-term strategies. Notions of control go well beyond the physical world, as was the case with past oligarchies, to the monitoring of people's personal lives in intense detail. As Google's Eric Schmidt put it: "We know where you are. We know where you've been. We can more or less know what you're thinking about."[62]

American *Keiretsu*

The fortunes that have been built in the Valley over the past few decades—even with the regular popping of bubbles—will shape our politics, culture, and relationship to technology for the foreseeable future. The new gusher of wealth also allows the Valley's investors and companies to place bets on a host of other, somewhat indirectly related industries.

In many ways today's tech Oligarchs operate in an "insider" environment that resembles nothing so much as Japan *keiretsu*—such as Mitsubishi, Sumitomo, and Toyota—which operate through what longtime journalist Karel van Wolferen calls a "combination of intertwined hierarchies." Like the tech Oligarchs, elite Japanse companies enjoyed, following the Second World War, unique access to capital and powerful links to both media and political power, and they have not been reluctant to seize their advantage.[63]

Similarly, many Valley companies maintain close, arguably incestuous ties between other tech firms and key venture firms, with many directors spread between what might even be somewhat competitive companies. This "directors club" is one way that Valley Oligarchs maintain and extend their control over the tech world.[64] Another is to develop elaborate schemes to prevent the poaching of employees so that while the top guns shift from company to company the mass of employees remain in their place. Such informal agreements between key companies such as Google or Apple are designed not only to keep technology inside companies, but also, it is alleged, to restrain wages for engineers.[65] Google and Microsoft have been accused repeatedly of using anti-competitive practices to keep out rivals, in part by refusing to license technology or through the acquisition of potential competitors.[66]

These collusive practices provide the base for the evolution of a powerful new set of dominant Oligarchic powers. As they gather huge technical and financial resources, firms such as Google have begun to utilize their dominance of critical software niches, including but not limited to Internet search, to gather enormous financial and technical resources. This has allowed them to move into a host of fields, such as robotics, energy, mapping, driverless cars, and aging, that have great potential but which are not directly related to their core business. Other tech firms, such as Apple, have made similar forays.[67]

In many ways, the shift of resources from social media and advertising to such fields as robotics and space travel has to be considered a basically positive development. The social media revolution may thrill people with games and virtual community, but it appears to have done relatively little to enhance the overall productivity of the economy. Viewed this way, investing in more significant breakthroughs, such as space travel or driverless cars, certainly represents a significant improvement in the potential returns to society of the top tech firms.[68]

This is not to say that these firms' investments will all work out well. Microsoft and Google, for example, have had their share of failures as they have sought to break out of their core businesses. But what these firms have that others don't is almost unlimited capital resources, and credibility, to enter new, often risky markets; and they frequently do so through the acquisition of companies, and talent, that lack such financial or technological resources. Google's sale in early 2014 of Motorola's mobile division, for example, at a paper loss of nearly $10 billion, would have led to bankruptcy and head-rolling at many firms. But this failure barely threatens the company, whose last quarterly revenues neared

$17 billion, whose cash on hand exceeds $56.5 billion, and whose 2014 market cap topped $400 billion.[69]

Indeed, if any of the tech powers is to become a full-fledged *keiretsu*, it's likely to be Google. In addition to their other ventures, Google's recent acquisition of Nest, a company founded by Apple alum Tony Fadell, brings Google into the "smart home" marketplace, part of the so-called "Internet of things," with its almost infinite capacity for ever greater information hauls from your once "dumb," but at least private, household appliances.[70] In splendid *keiretsu* fashion, the acquisition also helped Kleiner Perkins, one of the early investors in both Google and Amazon, gain a return of twenty times their original investment.[71]

In the process, as industry veteran Michael Mace observes, Google has stopped being a "unified product company" and is turning instead into what he calls "a post-modern conglomerate." Its goal, he notes, is no longer to dominate search, or even the Internet, but to invest in and control anything that uses information technology, from logistics and medical devices to the most mundane household appliances. In this respect, notes the *Economist*, Google recalls nothing more than an old-style industrial conglomerate such as GE.[72]

In the future, a British commentator notes, we could find ourselves literally living in a place called "Googlestan," in which the company dominates much of our daily lives:

> You will drive to work (or rather be driven to work) by your Google car. Your home and office will be automated by Google—and literally powered by Google's green energy technology. When you're not talking to your car or home, your computing will be done through a wearable Google computer. The streets will be policed, industry will be automated, and possibly even wars will be fought with Google robots. It's hard to say with any kind of certainty, but Google also has tendrils in academia and government. It's not entirely impossible that, in the future, whole countries will be powered by Google.[73]

But the Oligarch's consolidation of the economy is likely to extend well beyond the activities of one firm. Nigel Walton has dubbed "the Gang of Four" Internet companies—Microsoft, Apple, Facebook, and Google— as fitting into the conglomerate model.[74] Valley firms and investors, for example, now account for half of all venture funding invested in robotics;

they also account for a whopping 90 percent of market cap in this sector. Facebook is making a similarly bold move, spending $2 billion on a startup that makes virtual reality gear.[75]

Others are turning to fields such as automobiles, which have been dominated in the past by older industrial firms. Elon Musk, billionaire co-founder of PayPal, founded Tesla, which has emerged as a dynamic player in the electric car market, with plans to build a $5 billion electric battery plant.[76] Both Google and Apple have also made moves into the automotive market, focusing on driverless cars.[77]

In the long run, the most important drive by the Oligarchs is the one toward a field once dominated by one of the early Valley's key contractors, NASA. Although headquartered in Los Angeles, the traditional center of the aerospace industry, Space X, the largest of the space startups, was founded by Tesla's Musk, with some 1500 employees at a former Boeing plant in Hawthorne, California.[78]

Musk is not the only Oligarch with interests in space. Amazon CEO Jeff Bezos founded his own private space exploration company, Blue Origin, which has launched two vehicles into space, Charon and Goddard. It intends to build orbital space stations, and it has contracted for NASA. Critically, these two firms, as well as a third new player, Richard Branson's Virgin Galactic, are the pet projects of billionaires fascinated by space, both for travel and business purposes. If NASA continues to retreat from many areas of space exploration, it is likely that, in the future, the heavens may end up belonging to the Oligarchs as well.[79]

The New Media Empires

The Oligarchs' increasing control of the information network itself also gives them a potential influence greater than more traditional industries. A prospectus for a new lobbying group, headed up by Mark Zuckerberg's former Harvard roommate, suggests that tech will become "one of the most powerful political forces." The new group's "tactical assets" include not only popularity and great wealth but the fact that "we control massive distribution channels, both as companies and individuals."[80]

The growing media power of the new Oligarchs reflects a major transformation in the traditional structure of the information industry. In the past, more hardware-oriented companies provided the "pipelines" through which traditional media disseminated their products.

But increasingly these industries are being subsumed by the Oligarchs. On the hardware side, they seek to supplant the traditional telecommunications companies with their own series of global pipelines; at the same time, they are looking to gain control over large parts of entertainment, news, and other media.[81]

The transformation of media to online platforms has also occasioned an enormous shift from traditional advertising—largely through television and print media—to Valley-based companies. By 2013 Google's ad revenues surpassed those of both newspapers and magazines. This shift has been devastating not only to older media but also to traditional advertising agencies, whose revenues have been lost in this shift of platforms, both in print and in television. Google also has the power to further consolidate its dominance; although it has barely one-third the number of employees as the largest ad firm, Publicis Omnicom, its market cap in 2014 was roughly ten times as large.[82]

This shift also previews a shift in geographic power from centers such as New York and Los Angeles and to the centers of tech influence, most notably Silicon Valley/San Francisco, as well as the Puget Sound area. Even as the new software-based media expanded over the last decade, the newspaper, music, and publishing industries have endured massive losses that are many times larger than the gains made by social media firms. Since 2001, for example, book, periodical, and newspaper publishing—all traditionally concentrated in the New York area—have lost some 250,000 jobs, while Internet publishing and portals generated some 70,000 new positions, many of them in the Bay Area or Seattle.[83]

To the new Oligarchs, older industries are holdovers from what one venture capitalist derisively called "the paper economy" that is destined soon to be swept away by the new digital aristocracy.[84] As relatively young people—even Bill Gates is barely sixty—they will have the money, and the time, to disseminate their views to the public, both the mass market and the influential higher echelons.[85] Another new $250 million venture, First Look Media, with a specific mission to support largely left-of-center investigative reporting, is being backed by another Oligarch, eBay founder Pierre Omidyar.[86]

One way to consolidate such influence—previously used by Gilded Age moguls like William Randolph Hearst—has been to buy up the former bastions of the old media. Facebook billionaire and Obama tech guru Chris Hughes[87] has bought the venerable *New Republic*. Perhaps more importantly, the purchase of the *Washington Post* by Amazon's Jeff Bezos has brought not only resources to that struggling, still influential paper but also technical savvy and a certain entrepreneurial aura. Moreover, it places the tech Oligarchy at the center of the media in the nation's capital.[88]

Yet over time the purchase of existing media may prove to be just a sideshow. Far more critical will be the growth of their own Oligarch-controlled news media. Yahoo is now the top news site in the United States with 110 million monthly viewers, and Google News isn't far behind, in fourth place with 65 million users. The Valleyites are also moving into the culture business with both YouTube (owned by Google) and Netflix beginning to develop original entertainment content. Given the often limited skills of tech people in terms of writing, music, or fashion, the Oligarchs may need to source from more established vendors on the East Coast or Hollywood, but they increasingly will control the financial purse strings as well as the critical pipelines.[89]

The intrusion of tech firms into media is likely to become even more pervasive as the millennial generation ages and the older cohorts begin to die off. Among those over 50, only 15 percent get their news over the Internet, according to a Pew report; among those under 30, the number rises to 65 percent.[90]

Should the New Oligarchs Rule?

"We're the best thing happening in America," one tech entrepreneur told the *Los Angeles Times* in 2012.[91] Some, on both right and left, believe that the Valley's geeks should reform the nation and recreate the government in their image.[92] This view, not surprisingly, is frequently embraced by the tech hegemons, who sometimes even propose the idea of creating their own country outside the control of the federal government, or at least of separating themselves from the poorer regions of California.[93]

"We need to run the experiment, to show what a society run by Silicon Valley looks like," venture capitalist Chamath Palihapitiya recently argued.[94] The notion here is that Silicon Valley might do best detached from the limitations of American citizenship, with firms essentially running their own countries out of islands or man-made offshore facilities.[95]

However bloated and distorted their self-image may seem to outsiders, oligarchs, past and present, generally see themselves as huge assets to society. They rarely see themselves as crowding out competition, restraining innovation, or fleecing their customers. In this, as in many ways, they resemble the old industrial oligarchs of the late nineteenth century. Edward Harriman, the great railway financier, once insisted that it would be "suicidal" for the firms under his control, supported by his minions in government, to gouge their customers. Yet this "discriminating monopolist," in the words of economic historian Jonathan Hughes, could not resist raising rates that ended up "transferring money en masse from railroad users to railroad owners."[96]

Historically, such brazenly monopolistic power-mongering might have been looked down upon in Silicon Valley. But in recent years, the tech elite has established a powerful presence in the Washington lobbying community, hiring many of the professional parasites that Valley denizens used to demean.[97] "Something new has come about," said Reed Hundt, a former chair of the Federal Communications Commission turned technology consultant. "The new generation of leaders in the valley is much more interested in public policy than their predecessors."[98]

Facebook's lobbying budget, for example, grew from $351,000 in 2010 to $2.45 million just in the first quarter of 2014. The commitment to "progressive" ideals may prove less compelling when in conflict with an aggressive, dominating business culture that, outside of social policy, seems more akin to the laissez-faire right than the anti-capitalist left.[99]

This represents more than a traditional bid for mere political influence by a new industry. It is also driven by the notion that technology firms should reshape the entire structure of government. One tech booster foresees a new era in which the old "nexus" between Wall Street and Washington is replaced by a supposedly more productive one between the Valley and the Federal leviathan, which "will usher the world into a new age of abundance, connectivity, innovation and sharing."[100]

The Green Age

This reflects a shift from the traditionally conservative or libertarian ethos of the entrepreneurial class to one more in line with the nominally populist Democratic Party and its regulatory agenda. The Bay Area, particularly the Silicon Valley–San Francisco corridor, has become one of the most solidly and reliably liberal regions in the country, with leading tech companies sending four-fifths of their contributions to Democratic candidates.[101] Along with the public sector, they present California as "the spiritual inspiration" for modern "progressives"—that is, reliable backers of President Obama and the mainstream Democratic Party—across the country.[102]

Energy and the environment represent arguably the most critical part of the tech political agenda. In their embrace of a strong opposition to fossil fuels, the Oligarchs are facing off against some of the nation's most powerful, long-established plutocratic interests and wealthiest individuals. This assault on traditional energy reflects in part the relative lack of sensitivity by many tech firms to high electricity prices. If California electricity is too unreliable or expensive, firms such as Google or Yahoo can shift their power-consuming server farms to places with cheap electricity, such as the Pacific Northwest, Utah, or the Great Plains.[103]

Some of this shift is also driven by legitimate concerns about climate change. Eric Schmidt of Google believes not only oil and coal but even natural gas should be terminated.[104] Similarly San Francisco hedge fund manager Tom Steyer has spent millions of dollars attacking the Keystone pipeline for being environmentally unfriendly, even if he made some of his fortune in oil and natural gas.[105]

Besides climate change, there are other reasons why these firms embrace the hyper-regulatory regime.[106] For one thing, the Oligarchs have also sought to directly benefit from policies that favor renewable energy. They have developed a great self-interest in assuring a safe, and guaranteed, market through mandates and subsidies for generally high-cost "renewable" energy companies, including such failed ventures as Solyndra and Fisker Automotive.[107] Google alone has invested $1 billion in renewable energy developments.[108]

And finally, they have been primary backers of California legislation, passed in 2006, that has imposed strict regulatory powers over both fossil fuel and suburban development. A 2010 attempt by fossil fuel firms to overturn this effort was repulsed in large measure by contributions from eBay and TechNet, a technology-led lobbying group that includes Apple, Google, and Yahoo, venture capitalist John Doerr, and billionaire Vinod Kholsa, formerly of Sun Microsystems.[109]

Do No Evil, but Leave My Private Jet Alone

The very rich, as F. Scott Fitzgerald once put it,

> are different from you and me. They possess and enjoy early, and it does something to them, makes them soft where we are hard, and cynical where we are trustful, in a way that, unless you were born rich, it is very difficult to understand. They think, deep in their hearts, that they are better than we are because we had to discover the compensations and refuges of life for ourselves. Even when they enter deep into our world or sink below us, they still think that they are better than we are.[110]

Despite the its patina of bohemian anti-establishment "coolness," Jay Gatsby would not be totally out of place in Silicon Valley. Like their early twentieth-century counterparts, or today's Russian oligarchs, those at top of the tech upper class live very well, occupying some of the most expensive and attractive real estate in the country. They travel in style: Google maintains a fleet of private jets at San Jose airport, making enough of a racket to become a nuisance to their working-class neighbors. The top executives have even proposed an $85 million flight center, called Blue City Holdings, which would manage airplanes belonging to Google's founders, Larry Page and Sergey Brin, and its executive chairman, Eric Schmidt, who also enjoys numerous estates.[111] Similarly John Doerr, a major venture capitalist and strong advocate of green policies, owns his own Gulfstream and resides in a spacious manor in tony Woodside.[112]

The fact that Google executives, between 2007 and 2013, have burned the equivalent of upwards of 59 million gallons of crude oil on these jets—at subsidized federal rates—seems somewhat less than consistent from a company that touts its green agenda.[113] Of course, the wealthy of the past, and more traditional plutocrats today, also consume at a high level, but they at least do so without lecturing everyone else to cut their consumption.

Essentially there appear to be two sets of rules, one for Oligarchs and another for everyone else. Yahoo's Marissa Mayer, a former Google executive, banned telecommuting options for many of her employees— particularly critical for those unable to house their families anywhere close to ultra-pricey Palo Alto. Yet Mayer, herself pregnant at the time, saw no contradiction in building a nursery in her own office.[114]

But perhaps nothing so mimics the arrogance and hubris of the old oligarchs than the successful efforts of tech firms to avoid taxation. Rather than "share the pain," tech firms are notorious for not paying much in the way in taxes, including on their property.[115]

To be sure, the very wealthy have long found ways to lower or even avoid taxes through various dodges, such as trusts, and this pattern of avoidance has not changed under the tech-led regime. Individuals like Bill Gates have voiced public support for higher taxes on the rich. Yet at the same time, the individual companies and organizations in Silicon Valley have bargained and evaded paying their own taxes while the higher taxes fall on the heads of the middle class.[116] Founders of even newer companies, such as Twitter, have developed elaborate plans to avoid taxation and protect their suddenly vast estates as their companies went public.[117]

Facebook, for example, paid no taxes in 2012, despite making a profit of over $1 billion.[118] Apple, which the *New York Times* recently described as "a pioneer in tactics to avoid taxes,"[119] has kept much of its cash hoard abroad to help avoid taxes.[120] Microsoft has shaved nearly $7 billion off its U.S. tax bill since 2009 by using loopholes to shift profits offshore, a Senate panel said in a recent report.[121]

People: "Flies in the Ointment"

"People are the flies in Moore's Law's ointment," notes Jaron Lanier, referring to the oft-cited principle of inexorably greater computer power.[122] Technological change has had a devastating effect on many workers, yet the Oligarchs have not, at least until recently, faced any strong criticism for how they deal with their own employees.

Ironically, one reason lies with the nature and relatively small size of their workforce. Unlike the moguls of the last century, they do not employ large numbers of poor domestically based workers (those whom they employ abroad often labor in harsh conditions).[123] Andrew Carnegie and Henry Ford mostly exploited workers in Pittsburgh or Detroit, not in Chengdu or Guangzhou.

As a result, the elite tech firms have never had to deal with such problems as factory fires or employees working themselves to exhaustion or even death—except in occasional exposés about their plants in China and other developing countries.[124] Keeping the worst exploitation far away, firms like Apple have avoided the kind of domestic scrutiny—and labor activism—that has plagued automakers, petrochemical processors, port operators, and, in the past, the more industrially oriented firms that created Silicon Valley in the first place.

A critical difference with traditional industries has been the almost total absence of organized labor. Not so much anti-union as post-union, the new Oligarchs have lived in an atmosphere untroubled by the labor activism that has cast firms such as Walmart and McDonald's in a negative light. "Remaining non-union is an essential for survival for most of our companies," Intel founder Bob Noyce said over two decades ago. More recently, venture capitalist Marc Andreessen declared that "there doesn't seem to be a role" for unions in the modern economy because people are "marketing themselves and their skills." Amazon, which has the kind of warehouse facilities that could be organized, has battled unions not only in the United States but also in more union-friendly Europe as well.[125]

The good news for the tech sector is that they need less people than ever before. Between 1959 and 1971, the Valley produced 100,000 tech jobs; by 1990 it generated 150,000 more, and during the 1990s boom, another 170,000. But between 2000 and 2008, the industry lost over 108,000 high-tech jobs. Even the social media boom has created perhaps a net of no more than 20,000 to 30,000 new positions since 2007. Overall, even amidst the social boom, the Valley in 2012 has 40,000 fewer jobs than it had in 2001.[126]

The reasons for this drop-off vary. Certainly offshoring is a factor. Only 30 of the about 16,000 production workers for the iPod are based in the United States.[127] The Valley's shift from a production to a software orientation, as well as its growing dependence on social media, has changed its character, with much of its remaining industrial equipment already carted off to other parts of the country and the world.[128]

The Rise of the Technocoolies

The lack of reliance on large numbers of workers reflects the realities of the tech industry, which increasingly resembles that of the "gold rush," where some people make fortunes and far more are periodically displaced from their jobs, as occurred most dramatically after the first dot-com crash.[129] One way to avoid laying off workers has been to look abroad, not only for factory operations but for skilled labor as well.

This can be seen in the tech Oligarchy's practice of importing temporary programmers from Asia. They claim that the use of what Indians have called "technocoolies"[130] is necessary to offset a critical shortage of skilled computer workers. Yet this notion may be exaggerated, if it is not entirely specious. A 2013 report from the labor-aligned Economic Policy Institute found that the country is producing 50 percent more IT professionals each year than are being employed. Another report, this one from the economic consulting firm EMSI, estimates that there are now three times as many new IT graduates as job openings.[131]

But many in the Valley, notes EPI, would rather hire "guest workers," who now account for one-third to one-half of all new IT job holders, than recruit Americans. Some of this reflects a preference for hiring younger workers. Even as thousands of older, American-born workers have lost jobs in the Valley's transformation, firms seek out young workers, frequently from abroad, who don't have families here and don't need the affordable housing or expensive health plans of mature workers. This is particularly true for social media firms.[132] "I want to stress the importance of being young and technical," said Mark Zuckerberg at a Stanford University event in 2007. "Young people are just smarter. Why are most chess masters under 30? I don't know. Young people just have simpler lives. We may not own a car. We may not have family. Simplicity in life allows you to focus on what's important."[133]

This approach also has an impact on wages. Even amidst a powerful tech bubble, programmer salaries have not skyrocketed but have risen only modestly over the past few decades, notes the Economic Policy Institute. The new, young, heavily immigrant tech workforce, unlike many middle-class Americans, are often willing to live in crowded apartment complexes or to buy or rent a house in an almost absurdly distant periphery of the region.[134]

In the end, technocoolies may prove as valuable today as Chinese and Irish railway workers were to the railroad builders or as New England farm girls were to the early textile mills: they provide a largely compliant and cheap labor force to complement the swelling numbers overseas.[135] But what they do not seem to do is add much to the upward mobility of the vast majority of Americans, including those in Silicon Valley itself.

The Two Valleys: Precursors of the American Future?

Tech industry boosters such as U.C. Berkeley's Enrico Moretti extol the broad societal virtues of the new tech Oligarchy, claiming they constitute the key to a growing economy and greater regional well-being. This is also the widespread conventional wisdom in both parties, among both left and right, and throughout the media.[136]

Yet in reality, high-technology industries have long been characterized by what one researcher described as "a highly unequal structure of employment," with sharp divisions between the top employees and low-wage workers in retail and other service industries such as janitors, clerks, and cashiers.[137] Valley boosters speak of the "glorious cocktail of prosperity" they have concocted, but they have been very slow to address the social problems festering at their feet, apparently out of their line of sight. In terms of philanthropy, with some exceptions, notes E. Chris Wilder, executive director of the Valley Medical Center Foundation, Silicon Valley "underperforms when it comes to giving."[138]

This social divide has expanded greatly as the Valley has de-industrialized, losing over 80,000 jobs in manufacturing since 2000.[139] The social impacts of this process have been so severe, even amidst a boom, that some parts of the Valley—particularly San Jose, where manufacturing firms were clustered—look more like "Rust Belt" cities than exemplars of tech prosperity, observes geographer Jim Russell.[140]

"The job creation has changed," notes longtime San Jose economic development official Leslie Parks. "We used to be the whole food chain and create all sorts of middle-class jobs. Now, increasingly, we don't design the future—we just think about it. That makes some people rich, but not many."[141]

Rather than the old somewhat egalitarian culture, the Valley is now increasingly bifurcated. Employees at firms like Facebook and Google enjoy gourmet meals, childcare services, even complimentary house-cleaning that is supposed to create, as one Google executive put it, "the happiest most productive workplace in the world," something of a techie Disneyland.[142] With all of these well-paid and largely male geeks around, there's even a burgeoning sex industry, with rates upwards of

$500 an hour, providing that which the company cannot be reasonably expected to provide.[143]

And despite their progressive image, many large tech firms are also notoriously skittish about revealing their diversity data.[144] A *San Jose Mercury News* report found that the numbers of Hispanic and African American employees, already far below their percentage in the population, have actually been declining in recent years. Hispanics, roughly one-quarter of the local workforce, account for barely five percent of those working at the Valley's ten largest companies. The share of women, despite the rise of high-profile figures in management, also showed declines.[145]

The mostly white and Asian geeks in Palo Alto and San Francisco may celebrate their IPO windfalls, but wages for the region's African American and large Latino populations, roughly one-third of the population, have actually dropped, down 18 percent for blacks and 5 percent for Latinos between 2009 and 2011, notes a 2013 Joint Venture Silicon Valley report.[146] Overall, most new jobs in the Valley, according to an analysis by the liberal Center for American Progress, earn less than $50,000 annually, far below what is needed to live a decent life in this ultra-high cost area.[147]

This situation reflects the reality faced by many of those who inhabit the bottom rungs of the Valley economy. Part-time security workers often have no health or retirement benefits, no paid sick leave, and no vacation. Much the same applies to the janitors who clean up behind the tech elites.[148]

So, despite record prosperity at the top, poverty rates in Santa Clara County since 2001 have soared from 8 to 14 percent, a 75 percent jump. By 2013 one out of four people in the San Jose area is underemployed, up from a mere 5 percent just a decade ago. The food stamp population in Santa Clara County, meanwhile, has mushroomed: from 25,000 a decade ago to almost 125,000 in 2013. San Jose is also locale of the largest homeless camp, known as "the Jungle," in North America.[149] As Russell Hancock, president of Joint Venture Silicon Valley, admitted: "Silicon Valley is two valleys. There is a valley of haves, and a valley of have-nots."[150]

Even in San Francisco, where Silicon Valley companies provide free and more luxurious transport for the privileged few, the *San Francisco*

Chronicle observes that the Google buses have become a "daily reminder" of the growing segregation between rich and poor. This might seem "nonsensical" to the Oligarchs and their supporters in the media and financial community. Indeed, they seem oblivious to the fact that the "growth" created by the tech firms increasingly has little benefit to the middle- or working-class people who have long lived in the city. It also make San Franciscans "resentful about the technology industry's lack of civic and community engagement," the *Chronicle* concludes. Yet tech power in the city has continued to rise, in part precisely because they have invested in local politics and walked away, not surprisingly, with some nifty tax breaks.[151]

Increasingly, large sections of the Bay Area—with an economy as large as that of Switzerland—resemble a "gated" community, where those without the proper academic credentials, and without access to venture funding, are forced into a kind of marginal nether-existence. They live in crowded houses and even in their cars, or they commute huge distances to jobs that serve the Valley's upper crust. With the highest real estate prices of any American region, it has become almost impossible for any but the wealthiest to afford a house, while many working-class neighborhoods face enormous rent pressure on their residents.[152]

There is no denying that the Valley does play a critical role in the American economy. The country similarly benefited from the often ruthless actions of the industrial moguls. But at some point, the public has to weigh how much power and money can be concentrated in a relative handful of companies and people without undermining upward mobility and the health of the political system.

Innovation and entrepreneurship remain critical values that contribute mightily to the overall vitality of a society. But given their dangerous hubris, disdain for privacy rights, low rates of tax compliance, and minimal ability to create middle-class jobs, the Valley Oligarchs should not be held up as the supreme role models of the Republic, any more than the Gilded Age moguls were early in the last century. That is, unless we have decided that we wish to live in a high-tech, twenty-first century version of a highly ossified, stratified society.

CHAPTER THREE

The New Clerisy

With the rise of knowledge-based industries, expertise, and education in the economy, Daniel Bell, in his landmark study *The Coming of Post-Industrial Society* (1973), prophesied the inevitable "pre-eminence of the professional and technical class." This emergent new "priesthood of power" would eventually overturn the traditional hierarchies based on land, corporate, and financial assets.

The aim of this "priesthood," Bell suggested, would be the rational "ordering of mass society." Although some of the new priestly class are directly tied to the tech Oligarchy, others inhabit the realms of governmental institutions, universities, the mainstream media, law firms, and major foundations. If property and wealth serves as the coin of the realm for the more traditional Oligarchs, knowledge and authority are the basis for power of this rising class, although they also often seek to translate these assets into property, capital, and social status.[1]

This new class resembles the old clerical First Estate in pre-revolutionary France, which in the words of the historian George Lefebvre "possessed a control over thought in the interests of the Church and king." Like today's Clerisy the medieval church exercised considerable economic power, owning vast tracks of land, maintaining "a monopoly" in education and poor relief, and, to a large extent, censoring unapproved thoughts.[2] This is not to suggest that anything quite like such a monopoly exists today, although, as will be shown below, there are certain orthodoxies that seem to have gained semi-universal embrace throughout the modern Clerisy.

The very term *clerisy* has its origins somewhat later, appearing first in 1830 in the work of Samuel Taylor Coleridge, who described this group as bearers of the highest ideals of society, charged in part with transmitting them to the less enlightened orders.[3] They played a central role in maintaining social order amidst the chaos of the industrial revolution, adopting the notion of *noblesse oblige*, which sometimes included taking steps to mitigate the worst impacts of the new economic order, primarily through charitable works.

Unlike aristocrats and bishops of the Middle Ages, or even the pastier nineteenth-century version of Coleridge's "clerisy," today's version obtains the right to rule not so much from God or King but from their assumed superior command of science and information. There remains, of course, a still potent conservative camp in the Clerisy, including some important think tanks, such as the Heritage Foundation, and a host of publications and broadcasters, most notably the media empire controlled by the Murdoch family.

But although the conservative movement took an early lead in the policy debates in the 1970s and 1980s,[4] over the past decades the vast preponderance of the Clerisy has coalesced on the "progressive" side of the political divide. Educated along similar ideological lines at major universities, the Clerisy is concentrated in very "progressive," albeit rich, places, and embraces a socially liberal, environmentally self-conscious, and globally oriented perspective.[5] As such, they live, as analyst Walter Russell Mead suggests, "within a cocoon." Inside that cocoon, they operate from a "thoroughly absorbed and internalized...set of beliefs and behavioral norms" that follow "the standard upper-middle-class gentry American set of progressive ideas."[6]

This ideological tilt matters greatly in terms of the future direction and culture of the nation. In much the same way as its predecessors, today's Clerisy attempts to distill for the masses today's distinctly secular "truths" on a range of issues, including economics, justice, race, gender, and the environment. This is particularly critical in persuading large sections of the middle or working class to accept policies that, in some cases, work against their material interests or traditional beliefs.

Even as the American economy and employment levels have lagged, two of the critical linchpins of the Clerisy—academia and the federal bureaucracy—have grown enormously. Since 1990, the number of government workers has expanded by some five million to some twenty million, four times the number who were employed by the government at the end of the Second World War, a growth roughly twice that of the population as a whole.[7]

Similarly, academia has also expanded rapidly in recent decades. In 1958 universities and colleges employed under 370,000 people. By 2014 that number had expanded to roughly 1.7 million, and they currently serve roughly twenty million full- and part-time students. Each year they influence a growing number of young Americans, as the percentage of people over 22 with four-year degrees has tripled since 1970.[8] This makes the ideological tilt among academics more critical as they increasingly regulate speech along politically correct lines and indoctrinate the young.

Although they share many ideas, particularly on the environment and social issues, with the tech Oligarchs, large portions of the Clerisy—especially academia and the regulatory bureaucracy—are divorced from the worst rigors of the capitalist system itself. Tenured faculty enjoy close considerable immunity from economic downturns, while public sector workers enjoy pension protections that, at least to date, have survived even the Great Recession. This separation from economic reality can be seen in those causes that have animated campus protests, which for the most part are centered on either social or environmental issues, or in some cases on special causes such as tuition. In contrast, the class-conscious Occupy Wall Street movement gained remarkably little traction on college campuses compared to other protest movements in the past, or, for that matter, the 2008 presidential campaign of Barack Obama.[9]

To be sure, many in the Clerisy share attitudes toward the economy that differ from those of traditional business leaders and, on occasion, even those of the tech moguls. For example, some elements of the Clerisy, notably in academia and the media, are less sanguine about technological change than many among the new Oligarchs. There remains some sentiment, reminiscent of the 1960s hippie movement, of nostalgia for aspects of the pre-industrial past. The Clerisy, for example, often object to things like genetically modified foods, while the new Oligarchs are more sympathetic, naturally, to the imperatives of a science-led future. In this way, suspicion of technology remains a significant force dividing parts of the Clerisy from each other, and even more so from the Oligarchs.[10]

But the mainstream Clerisy also shares many basic beliefs with the new Oligarchs—particularly on social and environmental issues—even though motivations and interests are different. This class reflects Karl Polanyi's notion that many people act not primarily to protect their money but "to safeguard" their "social assets" and their status. But the Clerisy still help to confirm the position of the new Oligarchs, much as the bishops and parish priests did for the rulers of medieval Europe, or as the public intellectuals, university dons, and Anglican worthies of early nineteenth-century Britain justified the ruling classes of their day.

The attempts by the Clerisy to distill today's secular "truths" often appear to restrict discussion on the matters they address, such as gay marriage, climate change, and race and gender issues. Those who dissent from the "accepted" point of view may not suffer excommunication, but they can expect their work to be vilified, or in some cases simply ignored.[11] In some Clerical bastions, such as San Francisco, an actress with unsuitable views can be pilloried and a campaign launched to remove her from work.[12] Rather than embrace the traditional liberal ideal of diversity of viewpoint, the Clerisy appears increasingly like the old church establishment—ironic given that its ideology, particularly in the elite universities, ranges from secular to openly anti-religious.[13]

From Religious to Scientific Faith

Throughout history, class structures have been held up not only by economic forces but also by patterns of belief. "One person with a belief," observed John Stuart Mill, "is a social power equal to ninety-nine who have only interests."[14]

In the past, this notion of belief—for example, in the ancient Mediterranean world—was built around religious ideas, as well as those of the home and hearth. In the medieval period, the Church often influenced the political realm, making alliances with powerful princes; they could at times bolster some political leaders or undermine them. But overall, great power stemmed from control of thought. As late as the seventeenth century, notes historian William Gibson, "philosophy, science, religion, and politics could still be treated as a unity."[15]

As the old moral and economic order of the Middle Ages declined and faded, belief systems became less religiously based but also more inclusive of figures from the literary, journalistic, and academic worlds.

Rather than the unique bearers of celestial order, the Protestant clergy served, as one historian noted, "as a group of professional men not unlike lawyers and doctors." But like their medieval counterparts, Coleridge's more broadly based clerisy also played an important social role; in this case, they helped defend and justify, but at times also challenged, the emerging capitalist order.[16]

In the Victorian era, public intellectuals, university dons, and Anglican worthies not only espoused ideals supportive of the values of emergent capitalism, but they also provided theological support for colonialism and even in some cases the expansion of slavery. The late nineteenth-century clergymen Josiah Strong, for example, embraced what he described as "a race of unequaled energy"—that is, the white Anglo-Saxon—to conquer lesser races and bring with them the blessings of Christianity.[17]

Yet as the vestiges of the feudal order collapsed, new, more secularly derived ideas emerged to take the place of the divinely based ones. As early as the nineteenth century, secular-minded reformers such as Henri de Saint-Simon advocated the formation of a multi-national European state, whose prime directive would be to follow a "corporate will" for self-improvement. Saint-Simon believed the clergy's belief system had been made irrelevant by advances in scientific and technical knowledge. The ideal future state—what he saw as the impending "Golden Age of the human race"—would be shaped, in large part, by an elite corps of scientists, administrators, businesspeople, and magistrates.[18]

This technocratic approach appealed to the early Progressive reformers, who also saw the need for what H. G. Wells envisioned as "the New Republic," in which the most talented and enlightened citizens would work to shape a better society. They would function, he suggested, as a kind of "secret society," reforming the key institutions of society from both within and without. Wells was prescient in maintaining that the biggest challenge facing these secular clerics would be to find ways to relieve the sufferings of the poor, what he labeled "the Abyss," made up of what he called "the sweepings of Europe," as well as the brown and yellow races.[19]

Wells's notions appealed particularly to rapidly modernizing societies, such as the United States, where highly materialistic culture conflicted with traditional spiritual ideals of piety and self-abnegation.

Americans regularly embraced a "religion of action," and this admixture of Christianity and reform was common among progressives like Theodore Roosevelt. In some senses Christianity appealed to reformers in part because it "ran counter to the acquisitive drift in American life" and offered some alternative beyond materialism.[20]

Economic Roots of the New Clerisy:
The Social-Industrial Complex

In a commercial and individualist society like America's, Tocqueville noted, voluntary association, family, and religion were necessary to moderate egoism and serve community needs. He marveled at the ability of Americans to meet challenges without state interference.[21] But as these bulwarks have weakened, many traditional functions of family and community began to be taken over, first by the corporations, including for their top executives, and then increasingly by the state starting in the 1960s.[22]

This may have brought some benefits to the most beleaguered part of society, although poverty rates eventually returned to close to pre-1960s levels.[23] Yet the role of government has increasingly blurred into attempts to regulate even the most personal of behaviors, not to achieve some spiritual goal, or even to improve material wealth, as was common in the past, but to shift behavior in order to achieve some perceived social "good."

To be sure, efforts to influence some behaviors, such as cigarette smoking and obesity, should continue, but the expansion of government fiat on a whole range of social behaviors extends the state into areas that were once primarily the province of families, churches, and various communal associations. This shift in influence to the wisdom of government-sanctioned regulators and media has been critical to the increasing power and influence of the Clerisy and its constituent parts.

The emergence of a "politics of happiness," as one British author puts it, has proven a boon for the public sector and those parts of the private sector that work with government.[24] Just as the Second World War sparked the growth of federally funded science for defense purposes, the onset of the Great Society two decades later gave birth to what the socialist writer Michael Harrington would dub "the social-industrial complex."[25]

Harrington, whose writings, notably *The Other America*, helped usher in the "war on poverty," lived to witness the extraordinary expansion of the social welfare state. Between 1950 and 1980, social welfare spending grew twentyfold, ten times the rate of the population increase. Such spending may have ameliorated some of the worst results of poverty and discrimination, but Harrington perceived that the largest beneficiaries were not the poor but those—both inside and outside government—who serviced them.[26]

In essence, the private sector increasingly sought to make addressing social problems "the new business of business," as one top IBM executive put it. Developers seeking housing subsidies, or in some cases building new cities, all rushed to feed at the trough, and they have continued to do so. Harrington, although supportive of many of these initiatives, plainly saw the dangers of "private alliances between self-interested executives and ambitious bureaucrats."[27]

This commingling of private and public sectors, John Kenneth Galbraith suggested, was a natural expression of technology—"the enemy of the market is not ideology but the engineer." In his mind, and those of many contemporaries, this applied as much to capitalist America as the Soviet Union. The technostructure made up of private firms, governmental institutions, and universities would evolve, he predicted, beyond a primary concern with "pecuniary motivation" and focus more on meeting social goals. Rather than ownership, as Ralf Dahrendorf suggested, "authority" is what matters—and authority is the very essence of the Clerisy's power.[28]

Yet this optimistic view, believing that the well-trained would also be naturally selfless, ignores the realities of both history and human nature. For example, the legal profession, whose influence over daily life and business has risen with the regulatory regime, now clearly benefits from an expanding state. Although some lawyers are linked with conservative causes, as a group they have emerged as strong backers of an expanded government, which tends to create demand for their services; as such, roughly three-quarters of all contributions by lawyers go to the Democratic Party.[29]

But arguably the biggest beneficiaries of expansive government have been those at the highest levels of the bureaucracy. The number of workers, particularly at the federal level, continued to rise even at the height of the Great Recession. Between late 2007 and mid-2009, the number of U.S. federal workers earning at least $150,000 more than doubled. Even as private sector and state government employment fell, the ranks of federal *nomenklatura*—including many private contractors—have swelled so much that by 2012 Washington, DC, replaced New York as the wealthiest region in the country, with the average top lobbyist earning in excess of $2.3 million.[30] Much of this has been sparked by a large increase in expenditures by private firms, notably tech companies, as well as by increased spending by nonprofits on lobbying.[31]

This regulatory state has grown also at the local levels, expanding sixfold since 1980. In California, where the public sector is particularly dominant, state workers are allowed such special privileges as having their Department of Motor Vehicle records kept confidential— a sensible precaution for those, like police, who deal with criminals, but which has now expanded to cover a vast array of public servants, including supervisors and social workers. Naturally, as beneficiaries of an expanded government, public sector unions have been among the strongest backers of regulatory growth and governmental privilege as well as ever more social services. Their political power has also been on the rise; since 1989, public sector unions have accounted for two of the top three donors to political candidates.[32]

The regulatory state administered by government workers has expanded rapidly in recent decades, greatly enhancing the power of the Clerisy and its generally uniform ideology. By 2013, the over 300 federal independent and regulatory agencies publish more than 75,000 pages of new and proposed rules every year. The current edition of the Code of Federal Regulations is more than 200 volumes in length, far larger than the U.S. Code, which contains all the laws passed by Congress and signed by the president, and is roughly 35 volumes.[33]

These agencies at the various levels of government, notably in areas such as planning and the environment, often stand apart from traditional political constraints. This has given them the power to undermine unfriendly conservative organizations, as with the IRS's targeting of Tea Party groups, or to monitor the populace's private conversations, as with the NSA's domestic spying program. This has been reflective of a growing militarization of police power as well as a gradual expansion of surveillance that has concerned both liberals and conservatives.[34]

Increasingly, where persuasion is insufficient, some well-placed members of the Clerisy have advocated greater power of the state to enforce their views. Indeed, many of its leading figures, such as former Obama budget advisor Peter Orszag and *New York Times* columnist Thomas Friedman, argue that power should shift from naturally contentious elected bodies—subject to pressure from the lower orders—to credentialed "experts" operating in Washington, Brussels, or the United Nations. This reflects the view that the general populace is lacking in scientific judgment and societal wisdom.[35]

The Creative Elite

Not all of the Clerisy exists primarily by clinging to the regulatory teat. It is also includes a significant part of the upper-middle classes, particularly those with elite educations or who are engaged in culture-based industries. Arnold Toynbee identified the "creative genius" as the historic leader and savior of society, the person who sustains the current order or creates new social paradigms.[36]

In modern times, this "creative" element has grown as media has become ever more pervasive, often at the expense of family, ethnicity, local community, and religion, which some consider to be in an inexorable decline. The notion of media and culture as profitable, as opposed to dependent on plutocratic patronage, is itself a product of modern times. "An industrial culture," noted sociologist Norman Birnbaum, "rests on the industrialization of culture." Not all cultural workers can be considered to be part of the Clerisy, but their largely homogeneous worldview fits the pattern that they share with the public sector bureaucracy and academia.[37]

With this increased reach, the media has become ever more influential in shaping popular perceptions. Artists, writers, fashion designers, and actors have achieved enormous status in our society, and a handful have become very wealthy. More important still has been the rise of media Oligarchs, some tied to the tech establishment, who now rank among the wealthiest Americans. Indeed of the world's 25 richest people, a majority come from either the information sector, the fashion industry, or the media. Combined with the tech Oligarchy, they could well emerge as the dominant part of the twenty-first century's economic elite, pushing aside fortunes made in energy, manufacturing, or housing.[38]

At the same time, the media itself, particularly in its most visible manifestations, is increasingly populated by the children of prominent politicians and by those who come from the ranks of the plutocracy. These include the offspring of the Reagans, GOP standard-bearer John McCain, various Kennedys, and Nancy Pelosi. In Hollywood, meanwhile, some of the new powerful producers come from the ranks of the ultra-rich, including heirs to the Pritzker fortune and the daughter of Oracle founder Larry Ellison, one of the world's ten richest men.[39]

This creative community, as Daniel Bell observed over half a century ago, now serves as something of a permanent conscious "avant-garde."[40] As Thomas Frank has shown, even the term "hip," once seen as anti-materialistic and hostile to the establishment, has devolved into an advertising technique. Today, the values of the alienated bohemian have been transformed into a marketing strategy that creates "powerful imperatives of brand loyalty and accelerated consumption." Frank notes that "hip consumerism" solves the problem, identified by Bell in the 1970s, of the disjunction between mass society and the artistic avant-garde.[41]

The Academic State: The Real College of Cardinals

The expanding university system has provided the Clerisy with enormous power over elite jobs and professions, and their power as a central institution has waxed even if doubts about its effectiveness for many students have grown. Even in tough times, high-level academics are something of a protected class, enjoying tenure that insulates them from job cuts.

As seen in so many realms, time has eroded the democratic intent of higher education. Initially, U.S. universities, particularly the land-grant colleges, were designed for popular needs, providing practical solutions to the problems of newly formed states while offering valuable training to middle- and working-class youngsters.

But as higher education expanded rapidly, the role of the university enlarged even further. This confluence was central to the ideal of the "multiversity" that Clark Kerr developed in California. In his estimation, universities would play the role of solving societies' problems, creating a more prosperous and democratic future.[42]

This commingling of interests has also been embarrassing at times. Various universities, for example, have been involved in trials of new drugs with patients, some of which had disastrous effects on the patients. Whether over pharmaceuticals, the climate, planning, or a host of other issues, the confluence of government and business interests with the university has a tendency to weaken the traditional notion of the University as a neutral and objective research institution.[43]

The influence of universities, particularly large research institutions, has been enhanced by their ties to the burgeoning tech industry. Over the past half century, the technical aspects of the university have grown as demand for engineers exploded. Between 1930 and 1986, the number of engineers grew by 350 percent, seven times the growth of the over-all workforce. The role of universities such as MIT and Stanford in the evolution of the tech Oligarchy, first around Boston and then in Silicon Valley, has influenced many business and political leaders to support universities for largely economic reasons.[44]

Yet increasingly, despite its patina of egalitarian beliefs, the academic world now epitomizes the new hierarchical class order as much as any major institution. There are roughly 1.4 million instructors in the university system, but they are divided along what one writer calls "the great stratification" between roughly 500,000 largely older tenured "alpha" professors and a vast "beta" of low-paid teaching assistants, contingent faculty, and those working in extension programs. Between 1975 and 2011, these generally poorly paid instructors grew from 30 to 51 percent of all faculty.[45]

At the same time, the bureaucracy of the university, like that of the government, has exploded, even more so at elite (and tax-favored) private schools than among public ones. Whereas there were about 250,000 administrators and professional staff members in 1975, about half the number of professors, by 2005 there were over 750,000, easily outnumbering tenure-stream professors. As the university has gained in power, it has increasingly taken on the trappings of an institution whose primary mission is self-preservation, a pattern that would not have been absent in the upper reaches of the European clergy.[46]

The class nature of the university also extends to the student body. Recent studies reveal that even land-grant colleges are providing less aid to students from needy families and more to wealthier students; the latter are often judged as better prepared and also as better prospects for future fundraising. As both conservative social critic Charles

Murray and leftist economist Thomas Piketty have observed, this has helped make universities, particularly the elite ones, less a means to upward mobility and more a determinant of class status. The average income of parents of Harvard students, estimates Piketty, now surpasses $450,000.[47]

At the same time, the returns on education are falling, particularly for those largely less affluent students attending what are often referred to as second-tier institutions. The long-heralded education bonus started to decline in 2006, narrowing the gap between college and high school graduates. This trend will be discussed at length in the chapter that addresses the challenges facing the new generation.[48]

The Enforcers of Orthodoxy

As its utility as an engine of upward mobility has waned, the university's role as an enforcer of orthodoxy has waxed. Mid-century intellectuals such as Galbraith and Bell optimistically believed that educated people would be, by nature, both objective and open to skepticism. But this ignores the tendency, as the Beards noted over eighty years ago, for science to become "a kind of dogmatic religion itself whose votaries often behaved in the manner of theologians, pretending to possess the one true key to the riddle of the universe."[49]

In recent times this has been particularly notable in the area of climate change, where serious debate would seem prudent not only on the root causes and effects but also on what may present the best solutions.[50] Similarly, orthodoxies can be seen in issues such as gender, sexual preference, and urban planning. Issues of great import, for example, generally are deemed "settled," and those who do not agree are simply ignored or pilloried.[51] Indeed, this closing of debate is so strong that a 2010 survey of 24,000 college students found that barely a third thought it "safe to hold unpopular views on campus."[52]

Various studies of the political orientation of academics have found that liberals outnumber conservatives by between eight and fourteen to one. Whether this is simply a reflection of the natural preferences of the well-educated or at least partially a sign of blatant discrimination remains debatable, but some research suggests that roughly two out of every five professors would be less well-inclined to hire an evangelical or conservative colleague than a more conventionally liberal one.[53]

A remarkable 96 percent of all presidential donations from the nation's Ivy League schools went to Barack Obama, something more reminiscent of Soviet Russia—or the rightward tilt in donations made by the Clerisy's enemies among white Christian evangelicals[54]—than a properly functioning pluralistic academy. Nor is there any sign that this trend is slowing: between 2007 and 2010, a University of California study revealed, "far left" and liberal views grew from 55 percent to almost 63 percent of full-time faculty, while the conservative segment dropped from roughly 16 percent to less than 12 percent.[55]

This tendency is, if anything, greater at the most elite institutions. Academia may have long had a "progressive" tilt, but in recent years this has spawned an increasingly political cast. This reality is reflected by the very high, and unprecedented in recent history, proportion of Ivy Leaguers, as opposed to graduates of state or regional private colleges, within the Obama administration. A *National Journal* survey showed that the administration had more graduates of Oxford (United Kingdom) in key positions than any U.S. public university.[56]

In the future, some university partisans envision an expanded role for their institutions in the further shaping of society. The authors of the visionary text *Planet U* see schools as the new center of a "post-modernist" perspective committed to a series of basic beliefs common among the Clerisy—concerning the environment, the wickedness of the suburbs, ambivalence about economic growth, and acceptably progressive views of gender, race, and sexual orientation. This agenda has been increasingly applied not only at the university level but down to grade schools as well.[57]

The Culture of the Media

A similar, if less uniform, Clerical consensus suffuses the entire media culture, led by the networks and the major newspapers. In fact nearly half of all Americans consider the media too liberal, more than three times as many as those who see it as too conservative. Overall, the percentage who feel news is tilted to one side has grown dramatically, from 53 percent in 1985 to 77 percent in 2011, according to a Pew study.[58]

There remain many important exceptions to this rule, notably Fox News, talk radio, and the editorial pages of the *Wall Street Journal*. Sadly they, too, tend to follow news in a "party line" manner, albeit from the right. On the whole, the media shows little desire to look at both sides of the issues. Like their conservative counterparts, the traditional mainstream media like to proclaim their "objectivity," but in practice they maintain the basic Clerical bias that follows a fairly predictable progressive line. A detailed UCLA study found that of the twenty leading news outlets in the country, eighteen were left-of-center, including not only the *New York Times*, NPR, and the *Los Angeles Times* but also, surprisingly, the news pages of the *Wall Street Journal*.[59]

This reflects not just management but the personal preference of those who do the reporting and editing. Despite the journalistic embrace of diversity, notes a recent Indiana University study, journalists themselves have become less so; they are far more likely to be college educated than journalists in 1970, and, surprisingly, there are fewer minorities than just a decade ago. But the biggest similarity has been an ideological one: barely seven percent in 2013 were Republican, compared to nearly a quarter in 1971.[60]

Indeed, it is almost impossible to find a major news outlet, outside the Murdoch empire, that is not largely committed to this basic agenda: support for even draconian steps to battle climate change, opposition to suburban lifestyles, social liberalism, and the politics of racial redress. These positions are all reflected in, among other things, the almost lockstep support for President Obama. Over sixteen prominent journalists joined the Obama administration, which was something of a record, and in 2012 employees at the major networks contributed almost eight times as much to President Obama as they did to his Republican opponent.[61]

Longtime Democrats like Pat Caddell have observed how media coverage in the election amounted largely to running interference for the administration. "This press corps," notes the former Carter pollster, "serves at the pleasure of this White House and president."[62] This tendency for the press to follow the lead of the administration has led one wag to suggest that we are entering an era of "secretarial journalism," where reporters essentially shill for their preferred ideologies, right or left.[63]

The fact that Republicans continue to maintain considerable power in both Washington and the states suggests that this alliance is not yet determinative. And certainly, the development of Internet-based media has allowed for the growth of alternative news sources.[64] Yet in most of the centers of power for media and culture, the secular trend tilts clearly, and increasingly so, to the progressive side.[65] Even Arnold Brisbane, the former ombudsman of the country's premier news source, the *New York Times*, has noted the group-think that now overshadows objectivity, long cherished by that most important of America media outlets. Brisbane observed that "so many share a kind of political and cultural progressivism—for lack of a better term—that this worldview virtually bleeds through the fabric of the *Times.*"[66]

Indeed, in the last days of the 2012 presidential campaign, Obama appeared to campaign more with cultural icons, like Bruce Springsteen, than with the often less appealing figures from his own party. His most widely covered fundraisers featured such figures as Anna Wintour, the editor of the fashionista bible *Vogue*, movie moguls such as Dreamworks principal Jeffrey Katzenberg, and stars like George Clooney and Sarah Jessica Parker. Obama's success reflected not just on his views but on his persona, which Ishmael Reed characterized as "the president of the Cool." This cultural linkage also proved decisive in communicating with younger "low information" voters, who turned out overwhelmingly for both the president and his party.[67]

After President Obama leaves office, the power of the Clerisy may be temporarily diminished, but its ability to set the social and political agenda on a host of issues will likely persist. Entertainment and media firms have already shown their ability to push favored issues—such as steps to combat climate change—on the public. As the liberal author Jonathan Chait suggests, the media increasingly reflects the values of the progressives. The screen now reflects not just commercial values but "a vast left-wing conspiracy": "You don't have to be an especially devoted consumer of film or television (I'm not) to detect a pervasive, if not total, liberalism," writes Chait.

Sadly, this trend impacts how we discuss the weightiest public issues. In the case of climate change, even mild skeptics of the Clerical consensus have been banned from key website forums, while papers such as the *Los Angeles Times* refuse to publish their letters. Whatever one's feelings about the issue, it seems fairly clear that coverage has been tilted toward the conventional thesis that the planet is getting hotter, with humans being the primary cause. Even nuanced discussion of such topics as the decade-long "plateau" of temperatures, acknowledged by the United Nations, has been sparse outside of conservative media, which, to be sure, has its own energy industry–oriented biases, extending also to financing.[68]

The Ascent of the Trustifarians

In the coming decades, the power of the Clerisy will likely be further enhanced by the growth in inherited money. As the "Greatest Generation" dies off, they are set to pass on $8.4 to $11.6 trillion to the "baby boomer" generation, according to a study by MetLife. This inheritance will likely accelerate class divisions, as the top decile will inherit upwards of a million while those in the lower class will at best count their bequests in the thousands. Boomers who will receive an inheritance that will be highly concentrated, with the top 10 percent receiving more than every other decile combined.[69]

The millennial generation is set for an even greater inheritance. The Social Welfare Research Institute at Boston College estimated that a minimum of $41 trillion dollars would pass between generations from 1998 to 2052. This huge transfer, the researchers believe, will usher in what they call "a golden age of philanthropy." As the bulk of younger Americans struggle to obtain decent jobs and secure property, the Social Welfare Research Institute concluded that America is moving toward an "inheritance-based economy," where access to the last generations' wealth could prove a critical determinant of both influence and power.[70]

This can already be seen in the rise of nonprofit foundations, which have been growing rapidly in size and influence since the late 1960s, paralleling the expansion of other parts of the Clerisy like the universities and government.[71] Between 2001 and 2011, the number of nonprofits increased 25 percent to over 1.5 million today. Their total employment has also soared and at 10.7 million in 2010 was larger than that of the construction and finance sectors combined, expanding far more rapidly, adding two million jobs since 2002, than the rest of the economy.[72] By 2010 the nonprofit sector accounted for an economy of roughly $780 billion and paid upwards of nine percent of wages and ten percent of jobs.[73] Nonprofits, due to their accumulated wealth, are able to thrive in tough times, adding jobs even in the worst years of the Great Recession.[74]

The direction of this rapidly expanding part of the Clerisy will be increasingly important in the future. Historically, much inherited wealth followed the old notions of *noblesse oblige*; they supported traditional aid to the poor, such as scholarships and food banks. But this has been changing for decades, with many of the largest foundations— Ford, Rockefeller, Carnegie, and MacArthur—veering far toward a left social action agenda, ironic since their founders were conservative, or even reactionary, and many held strong, sometimes fundamentalist religious beliefs.[75]

Much of this shift reflects the social phenomena of inheritors in general. Not involved with, or even embarrassed by, how their fortunes were made, the new generation of "trust-fund progressives" often adopt viewpoints at odds with those of their founders; they sometimes even "see what they have received as unfair."[76] This trend is likely to accelerate as millennials—who will inherit the most money and may be the most inheritance-dominated generation in recent American history— enter adulthood.

Agendas are increasingly common among nonprofits. This includes some well-known conservative groups, such as the Koch brothers, who wield their fortunes for highly partisan causes. But roughly seventy-five percent of the political contributions of nonprofits tend more to the left, green, or progressive direction. In some cases, this has been described as "philanthropy for show," with a larger impact on generating positive media than delivering concrete results.[77]

Author Chrystia Freeland sees the emergence over time of "the Silicon Valley school" of philanthropy, which stresses technocratic, data-driven solutions to complex social problems, even though it may not appeal very much to a majority that may be suspicious of help that "arrive[s] in a wrapper of remote benevolence." Coming from atop an ever sharper pyramid, their solutions may help in incremental ways but, as essentially beneficiaries of the new class order, they are unlikely to challenge the fundamental chasm now dividing society.[78]

Endgame: The Technological Religion

As befits a technological age, the new Clerisy also enjoys the sanction of what Bell defined as the "creative elite of scientists." Often the scientific community has had a strong case to make, particularly in countering some notions among the religious and extreme right on issues such as evolution, the critical nature of protecting the environment, or even the relevance of natural history.

Whether their views are right or wrong on a particular issue, the scientific community has taken on a partly theological character, with top scientists achieving something of the role of supreme clerics.[79] This approach ignores the reality that widely held "truths" are often found to be, if not untrue, significantly flawed. The numerous assumptions made by prominent academics, such as the MIT team behind the 1972 *Limits to Growth* study, turned out to be far off-base, as new technologies both made more resources available and increased the efficiency of their use. Similarly the bold predictions of mass starvation due to overpopulation made by the then celebrated Paul Ehrlich in the late 1960s also provided remarkably inaccurate. His call for draconian birth control, including the introduction of sterilants into the water supply, fortunately never was applied.[80]

This is occurring at a time when science is increasingly the domain of specialists, whose knowledge cannot be widely shared and is difficult for laymen to challenge. As early as 1900, Henry Adams noted that the rapid pace of change was making knowledge of many topics indecipherable for even well-educated people. In this respect, science takes on the cloak of mystery, like "a religious order," since only its adherents can understand its secrets.[81]

This drift toward what might be called a theology of science has been so marked that a British judge in 2014 ruled that scientific beliefs—specifically about climate change—can now be accorded the same protections of religion. There is a growing embrace of what one writer has called the "sacralization" of particular lifestyles that are approved by the Clerisy and sanctified as reflecting the values of science.[82] The once proud role of the French First Estate as the arbiter of values and beliefs has been transferred from the church and its mysteries to the precepts of the practitioners of official science.

Clerical Dreams: A High-Tech Nirvana

For at least a century or more, some scientists have dreamed of a society that was driven by the imperatives of technology, as opposed to the often messy, frequently irrational dynamics of mass democracy. This notion was noted in 1950 by the early computer designer John von Neumann, who saw that "the ever accelerating progress of technology...gives the appearance of approaching some essential singularity in the history of the race beyond which human affairs, as we know them, could not continue."[83]

In this new formulation, technology essentially supplants divinity, community, and family as the driving force in history. This viewpoint embraces the notion of a relentlessly improved society, powered and shaped by ever more intrusive technology, and, as a result, dominated by those who design or control them.

Perhaps the most advanced voice for this new vision is Ray Kurzweil, a longtime entrepreneur and inventor. Now the director of engineering at Google, he predicts the ever more rapid evolution of humanity through technology, with the end being the merging of biological and machine intelligences. Eventually, he predicts, "the entire universe will become saturated by our intelligence."[84]

Kurzweil promotes "the singularity" not only as allowing for the perfectibility of mankind—long a goal of theological speculation—but also as a step toward immortality, with our brain patterns imprinted as software and preserved permanently. This "transhumanist" vision also reflects an almost obsessive concern to the aging inventor, who takes around 150 vitamin supplements a day in the hopes of delaying his own demise.[85]

This may sound like something for the far-off future, but we are clearly on a path that could lead to this objective. Google, along with other companies, has already moved heavily into "biological computing," which seeks to duplicate the brain's functions in machine language.[86]

There is little question that such research could have powerful, and often positive, impacts, but the insistence on seeing information technology as the solution to human problems is troubling in part because it diverts resources from things that may improve the material lives of people today. Increasingly, notes one Yale computer scientist, the new vision of humanity is wrapped up with computer intelligence as determinative. In contrast, the importance of subjective notions tied to emotions and sentiments fades with the embrace of the idea that "we are machines." Following this logic, all questions of human behavior have objective answers—except perhaps those that violate the belief systems of the Clerics.[87]

More disturbing are the potential class implications of Kurzweil's "transhumanist" project. The agenda of melding human and machine intelligence has within it the potential to create a kind of high-tech feudalism, in which technology replaces faith or civic virtue as the justification for an increasingly stratified society. As media, technology, and ideology merge, we could be headed to a greater chasm between the scientific "elect" and those destined to inhabit the subsidiary realms.

In the foreseeable future, the drive toward ever longer lives or even immortality will not be easily achieved by those beyond the very rich, who will have access to these technologies arguably decades before the others. Kurzweil suggests this gap between first adopters and later ones will shorten over time. But those who refuse or are incapable of cybernetically augmenting themselves are described by the scientist as Mostly Original Substrate Humans, or MOSHs. "Humans who do not utilize such implants are unable to meaningfully participate in dialogues with those who do," writes Kurzweil.[88]

These technologies could exacerbate class divisions in unique and disturbing ways. "Due to improved techniques the elite will have greater control over the masses; and because human work will no longer be necessary the masses will be superfluous, a useless burden on the system," predicts futurist Bill Joy, a founder of Sun Microsystems. The priesthood could choose to eliminate or systematically cull the unneeded masses; or, "if the elite consists of softhearted liberals," they could play the role of "good shepherds to the rest of the human race." But under any circumstance, he predicts, the mass of humanity "will have been reduced to the status of domestic animals."[89]

CHAPTER FOUR

The Proletarianization of the Middle Class

From early in its history, the United States rested on the notion of a society based upon a large class of small proprietors and owners. "The small landholders," Jefferson wrote to his fellow Virginian James Madison, "are the most precious part of a state." To Jefferson and Madison, both the widespread dispersion of property and limits on its concentration—"the possession of different degrees and kinds of property"—were necessary to a functioning republic.

Jefferson, admitting that the "equal division of property" was "impractical," also believed "the consequences of this enormous inequality producing so much misery to the bulk of mankind" that "legislators cannot invent too many devices for subdividing property."[1] The notion of a dispersed base of ownership became the central principle around which the Republic was, at least ostensibly, built. As one delegate to the 1821 New York constitutional convention put it, property was "infinitely divided," and even laborers "expect soon to be freeholders," which was a bulwark for the democratic order.[2]

This notion of American opportunity has ebbed and flowed, but generally gained ground well into the 1960s and 1970s. The very fact that the United States was more demographically dynamic, notes Thomas Piketty, naturally reduced the role of inherited wealth compared to Europe, especially France, where population growth was slower. Mass prosperity hit a high point in America in the first decades after the Second World War, the period when the country achieved its highest share of world GDP at some forty percent. By the mid-1950s the percentage of households earning middle incomes doubled to 60 percent compared with the boom years of the 1920s. By 1962 over 60 percent of Americans owned their own homes; the increase in homeownership between 1946 and 1956, notes historian Stephanie Coontz, was greater than that achieved in the preceding century and a half.[3]

But today, after decades of expanding property ownership, the middle orders—what might be seen as the inheritors of Jefferson's yeoman class—now appear in a secular retreat. Homeownership, which peaked in 2002 at nearly 70 percent, has dropped, according to the U.S. Census, to 65 percent in 2013, the lowest in almost two decades. Although some of this may be seen as a correction for the abuses of the housing bubble, rising costs, stagnant incomes, and a drop-off of younger first-time buyers suggest that ownership may continue to fall in the years ahead.[4]

The weakness of the property-owning Yeomanry comes at a time when other classes, notably the Oligarchs and the Clerisy, have gained power and influence. Over twenty years ago, Christopher Lasch argued that a "new class" was arising that "begins and ends with the knowledge industry." For this group, the rest of society, he suggested, exists only "as images and stereotypes."[5] Progressive theorists, such as Ruy Teixeira, have suggested that, in the evolving class structure, the traditional middle and working classes are of little importance compared to the rise of a mass "upper-middle class" consisting largely of professionals, tech workers, academics, and high-end government bureaucrats.[6]

The Economic Decline of the Yeomanry

All this suggests what could be seen as the proletarianization of the Yeoman class. In the four decades since 1971, the percentage of those earning between two-thirds and twice the national median income has shrunk, according to Pew, from over sixty to barely fifty percent of the population. While middle-class incomes have fallen relative to the upper-income groups, house prices and the costs of health insurance, utilities, and college tuition have all soared.[7]

This reflects some very dramatic changes in the nature of the employment market. For over a decade, job gains have been concentrated largely in the low-wage service sector, such as in retail or hospitality, which alone accounted for nearly sixty percent of job gains; in contrast middle-income positions actually have been declining. Meanwhile, taxes on corporate profits, which are at an all-time high, have fallen to near historic lows.[8]

This trend has continued even in the recovery. Between 2010 and 2012, the middle sixty percent of households did worse than not only the wealthy but even the poorest quintile during that period. In the years of the recovery from the Great Recession, the middle quintile's income dropped by 1.2 percent while those of the top five percent grew by over five percent. Overall the middle sixty percent have seen their share of the national pie fall from 53 percent in 1970 to barely 45 percent in 2012.[9] Roughly one in three people born into middle-class households, those earning between the 30th and 70th percent of income, now fall out of that status as adults.[10]

This decline, not surprisingly, has engendered a dour mood among much of the Yeomanry. For many, according to a 2013 Bloomberg poll, the American dream seems increasingly out of reach. This opinion was held by a margin of two to one among all Americans, and three to one among those making under $50,000, but also a majority earning over $100,000 annually.[11] By margins of more than two to one, more Americans believe that they enjoy fewer economic opportunities than their parents, and that they will have far less job security and disposable income. This pessimism is particularly intense among white working-class voters and large sections of the middle class.[12]

Many people who once had decent incomes, and who may have owned or hoped to own a house or start a business, have slipped to the lower rungs of the economy. In the past decade, the number of people working part-time and receiving such benefits as food stamps has expanded well beyond inner cities and impoverished rural hamlets. Many of the long-term unemployed are older and often well-educated workers who have fallen from the middle class over the past decade. The curse of poverty has also expanded further into suburban locations—a development widely cited by the urban-centric Clerisy, but which nevertheless further confirms the Yeomanry's stark decline.[13]

The Assault on Small Business

Perhaps nothing reflects the descent of the Yeomanry better than the fading role of the ten million small businesses with under 20 employees, which currently employ upwards of forty million Americans.[14] Long a key source of new jobs, small business startups have declined as a portion of all business growth from 50 percent in the early 1980s to 35 percent in 2010.[15] Indeed, a 2014 Brookings report revealed that small business "dynamism," measured by the growth of new firms compared with the closing of older ones, has declined significantly over the past decade, with more firms closing than starting for the first time in a quarter century.[16]

Instead of stemming from the grassroots, the recovery after the latest crash was led, unlike in previous expansions, by larger firms while small company hiring remained relatively paltry. Self-employment rose, but increasingly this took the form of sole proprietorships as opposed to expanding smaller companies with employees.[17] By 2013, smaller firms with under one hundred employees added far fewer jobs than in the prior decade. Unlike prior postwar recoveries, since 2007, grassroots companies did not lead the way out of recession and continued to lose ground compared with larger companies that could either afford the costs or avoid the taxes imposed by the Clerical regime.[18]

This decline in entrepreneurial activity marks a historic turnaround. In 1977, Small Business Administration figures show, Americans started 563,325 businesses with employees. In 2009, they launched barely 400,000 business startups, long a key source of new jobs, which have declined as a portion of all businesses from 50 percent in the early 1980s to 35 percent in 2010.[19]

There are many explanations for this decline, including the impact of offshoring, globalization, and technology. But in part it reflects the impact of the ever more powerful Clerical regime, whose expansive regulatory power undermines small firms. Indeed, according to a 2010 report by the Small Business Administration, federal regulations cost firms with less than 20 employees over $10,000 each year per employee, while bigger firms paid roughly $7,500 per employee. The biggest hit to small business comes in the form of environmental regulations, which cost 364 percent more per employee for small firms than for large ones. Small companies spend $4,101 per employee, compared to $1,294 at medium-sized companies (20 to 499 employees) and $883 at the largest companies, to meet these requirements.[20]

The nature of federal policy in regard to finance further worsened the situation for the small-scale entrepreneur. The large "too big to fail" banks received huge bailouts, yet they have remained reluctant to loan to small business. The rapid decline of community banks, for example, down by half since 1990, particularly hurts small businesspeople who have depended historically on loans from these institutions.[21]

The Descent of the Yeomanry, with Cheers from the Clerisy

Despite America's egalitarian roots, the prospect of mass downward mobility has been embraced widely by some business Oligarchs and much of the Clerisy. The future being envisioned is one dominated by automated factories and computer-empowered service industries that will continue to pressure both jobs and wages. In this scenario, productivity will rise but wages may stagnate or decline.[22] This leads some to propose that the American middle and working classes have become economically passé. Steve Case, founder of America Online, has even suggested that future labor needs can be filled not by current residents but by some thirty million immigrants.[23]

Arguably the first group to feel the downward pressure has been blue-collar workers, whose lot has declined over the past few decades. After World War II, as the United Auto Workers' Walter Reuther noted, "the union contract became the passport to a better life" and was creating "a whole new middle class." But with the shifting of industry overseas and the decline of private sector unions, the path for blue-collar workers to enter the middle class has become more difficult.[24]

Although they often claim to defend the middle class, the political stance adopted by the Clerisy, as well as by the tech Oligarchs and investors, tends to worsen this trajectory. Environmental concerns impose themselves most against basic industries such as fossil fuels, agriculture, and much of manufacturing. These employ many in highly paid blue-collar fields, with average salaries of close to $100,000. In the last decade, top U.S. firms, notes the liberal Center for American Progress, have cut almost three million domestic jobs. Automation also leads to the diminution of traditional white-collar professions as well as the shift of high-end service jobs offshore.[25]

Overall, it has become increasingly common to regard the middle class as threatened and even doomed. Indeed, as early as 1988 *Time* magazine featured a cover story on the "declining middle class," which at that time was considerably healthier than it is today. After the Great Recession, the American blue-collar worker has been pitied, but certainly not helped, by the Clerisy, many of whom believe that there is no hope for manufacturing or similar outmoded jobs in an information age. Blue-collar workers were described in major media as "bitter" and "psychologically scarred," and even as an "endangered species." Americans, noted one economist, suffered a "recession," but those with blue collars endured a "depression."[26]

This perspective extends across ideological lines. Libertarian economist Tyler Cowen suggests that an "average" skilled worker can expect to subsist on little but rice and beans in the future U.S. economy. If they choose to live on the East or West Coast, they may never be able to buy a house and will remain marginal renters for life.[27] Left-leaning *Slate* in 2012 declared that manufacturing and construction jobs, sectors that powered the Yeomanry's upward mobility in the past, "aren't coming back."[28] Rather than a republic of Yeoman, we could end up instead, as one left-wing writer put it, living at the sufferance of our "robot overlords," as well as those who program and manufacture them, likely using other robots to do so.[29]

Contempt for the middle orders is often barely concealed among those most comfortably ensconced in the emerging class order. *Financial Times* columnist Richard Tomkins declared that the middle class, "after a good run" of some two centuries, now faces "relative decline" and even extinction. This historical shift toward mass downward mobility elicited only derision, not concern: "Classes come and classes go," and when the middle orders disappear the only ones who will be sorry to see them go might be the "middle classes themselves. Boo hoo."[30]

The Rise of the Yeomanry

This reversal in class mobility and the slowing diffusion of property ownership in America, if not addressed, threaten to undermine the country's traditional role as a beacon of opportunity. Equally important, the diminution of the middle orders threatens one of the historic sources of economic vitality and innovation.

The roots of America's middle class reflect the critical role such smallholders have played throughout history. Dynamic civilizations tend to produce more than their share of "new men." But nowhere was this middle-class ascendency more dramatic than in Europe, first in Italy and later in northern Europe.

Initially, this was a comparatively small group, with much of the activity conducted by outsiders such as Jews and, later, Christian dissenters.[31] They were the driving force of the expanding capitalist market, the creators of cities, and among the primary beneficiaries of economic progress. Peter Hall quotes a historian of fifteenth-century Florence:

> Apprentices became masters, successful craftsmen became entrepreneurs, new men made fortunes in commerce and money-lending, merchants and bankers enlarged their business. The middle class waxed more and more prosperous in a seemingly inexhaustible boom.[32]

These "new men," who included some landless peasants, gradually overthrew the older traders and eventually even superseded the aristocracy. They were also among the first commoners to seek out land, often in the periphery, in part as a business decision but also to mimic the lifestyles of the traditional aristocracy.[33]

As occurs in every economic transition some benefited at the expense of others. Some "new men" from peasant and artisan backgrounds rose, but others became part of an impoverished proletariat.[34] Many urban artisans lost their jobs to machines, but many others used their expertise to move into the middle class, often through technical innovations that, in the words of the French sociologist Marcel Mauss, constituted "a traditional action made effective," notably in agriculture, metallurgy, and energy.[35]

As a colony of Britain, America reflected that island's rapid ascendancy of smallholders in the seventeenth and eighteenth century, which linked liberation from feudalism with a less hierarchical order and the dispersion of ownership.[36] The rise of the yeoman class in Britain was particularly critical in foreshadowing the evolution of America. These small landowners played a critical role in the overthrow of the monarchy under Cromwell, and they consistently pushed for greater power for those outside the gentry.

Yet ultimately many paid a great price for liberal reform, such as laws allowing for enclosures of what had been communal pastures. In the process productivity rose. Some benefited, becoming gentry themselves, while many smallholders lost their lands and flowed into the towns, where they joined the swelling proletariat. Others, notably large merchants, bought political influence and marriage into old families. By 1750, according to Marx, the yeomanry had disappeared, a claim denied by some who believed this class persisted, albeit weakened, well into the nineteenth century.[37]

The American Model

Many of these displaced yeoman found a more opportune environment in America, where diffusion of ownership, as both Jefferson and Madison noted, remained central to the very concept of the nation. Smallholders served, in the words of economic historian Jonathan Hughes, as "the seat of Republican government and democratic institutions."[38]

America's focus on dispersed ownership was further enhanced by government actions throughout the country's history. In contrast to their counterparts in Britain, the yeomanry in the United States enjoyed access to a greater and still largely economically underutilized land mass, as well as a persistently growing economy. "In America," Tocqueville noted, "land costs little, and anyone can become a landowner."[39]

The Homestead Act was signed by President Lincoln in 1862. By granting land to settlers across the Western states, Lincoln was extending the notion of what historian Henry Nash Smith described as an "agrarian utopia" ever further into the continental frontier.[40] Yet in reality the Homestead Act, which offered 160 acres for a $1.25 per acre fee, proved more symbolic than effective, impacting at most two million people in a nation of over 30 million. Railways, using their land grants, actually sold more land than the government gave away.[41]

The westward expansion of the Republic created huge opportunities for expansion of land ownership. Jefferson wanted the land sold to the public to be a source of one-time revenue and a permanent holding for the buyer. In many ways, at least until the 1890s, a far higher proportion of Americans owned land—almost 48 percent—than in countries such as Britain, where ownership was far more concentrated.[42] These lands, not surprisingly, also became the source of often wild speculative booms and busts, both on the agricultural frontier and the burgeoning cities.[43]

Many factors ultimately undermined the first old agrarian Jeffersonian dream. Capitalist-led industrial growth shifted the proportion of the population living in cities. Only 5 percent in 1790, the urban population rose to almost 20 percent in 1850 and nearly 40 percent by 1900.[44] The new order, as in England, also weakened the position of the old artisanal professions, which often made up the ranks of the small-scale owners. In many cases they were replaced by women, children, and new migrants from the countryside or from abroad. They became, as the British reformist paper *The Morning Star* wrote, "our white slaves, who are toiled into the grave, [and] for the most part silently pine and die."[45]

The movement into cities, as well as the industrial economy, turned many workers from owners to renters. In the new industrial centers, it became far harder to start a business or own property. Even white-collar workers often lost out, as the instrumental economic rationality of capitalism displaced a more locally focused economy based on tradition, religion, and small-scale production.

In the United States, conditions were generally less gruesome than in Britain or the rest of Europe, but this did not slow the tendency toward ever greater concentration of ownership. The rise of great entrepreneurs like Morgan, Vanderbilt, and Carnegie drove parts of the economy into the hands of a relatively small number of people. This concentration of power and land ownership engendered a powerful protest in both rural and urban areas. Henry George's influential *Progress and Poverty*, published in 1879, maintained that "the ownership of land" was the "fundamental fact" determining the social, political, and "moral condition of a people." Land, he asserted, should be owned by the public and government funded by rents.[46]

George's approach appealed to a population that was seeing land ownership slipping from their grasp. Even on the land, as farming itself modernized, there was a gradual shift toward tenancy as farms mechanized and markets became more global; by 1900 one in three American farmers were landless tenants. The concentration of property ownership continually grew from the 1870s on well into the 1920s.[47]

By the early twentieth century, as the original rustic yeoman dream was weakening, there was increased pressure for change from the growing urban population. Much of the pressure came from a middle and upper-middle class who felt threatened by the concentration of ownership and political power in the hands of the industrial and financial oligarchies.[48]

The Homeownership Revolution

As the nation moved from its agricultural roots, the Yeoman class interest in property would find a new main expression in the form of homeownership. This would represent an opportunity either to escape the crowded city or, for the migrant from rural areas, to live in a less dense urban environment.[49] This drive was supported by both conservatives and New Dealers, who promulgated legislation that expanded homeownership to record levels. "A nation of homeowners," Franklin Roosevelt believed, "of people who own a real share in their land, is unconquerable."[50]

The great social uplift that occurred then, coming to full flower after the Second World War, saw a working class—not only in America but in Europe and parts of East Asia—enjoying benefits previously available only to the affluent. In 1966, author and *New Yorker* reporter John Brooks observed in *The Great Leap: The Past Twenty-Five Years in America* that the "middle class was enlarging itself and ever encroaching on the two extremes—the very rich and the very poor."[51] Indeed, in the middle decades of the twentieth century, the share of income held by the middle class expanded while that of the wealthiest actually fell.[52]

New Deal legislation—the National Housing Act of 1934, the Federal Housing Administration (FHA), and the Federal National Mortgage Association (Fannie Mae)—set the stage for the great housing boom of the 1950s. This was further augmented by the GI Bill, which also provided low-interest loans to returning veterans. The success of the private financial and construction interests who benefited from this boom, suggests author Eric John Abrahamson, was largely fostered by what he describes as a "planned" economy that consciously sought to expand ownership both during the New Deal and particularly in the ensuing decades. Almost half of suburban housing, notes historian Alan Wolfe, depended on some form of federal financing.[53] This egalitarian impulse was in part driven by people returning from World War II and Korea, many of whom benefited from the GI Bill.

This resulted in an unprecedented dispersion of property ownership. This process was aided by a strong economy and the expansion of automobile ownership, which greatly enhanced the Yeomanry's mobility.

Increasing numbers of the middle class and even working-class people became homeowners, sparking an enormous surge in homebuilding. By 1953, the number of Americans owning their own homes climbed to twenty-five million, up from eighteen million in 1948. A country of renters was transformed into a nation of owners. Between 1940 and 1960 non-farm homeownership rose from 43 percent to over 58 percent. It was an accomplishment of historic proportions, notes historian Abrahamson, of "a transformed Jeffersonian vision."[54]

New Class Conflict over the Form and Nature of Growth

In recent decades, this vision of widening prosperity and property ownership has become increasingly threatened, as most evidenced by the housing bust of 2007–8. It also has come under increased attack from among the ranks of the Clerisy. To be sure, many of those who bought homes in the last decade were not economically prepared, as some analysts suggest.[55] But in the wake of the housing bust, the attack on homeownership expanded to include not only planners and pundits but also parts of the investment community, who have seen the Yeomanry's decline as an opportunity to expand the base of renters for their own developments.

The ideal of homeownership, particularly in the suburbs, has long raised the ire of many academics and intellectuals in particular. Some have sought to de-emphasize increased wealth and seek instead to embrace what they consider a more moral, even spiritual standard. This movement, not so far from old feudal concepts, had its earliest modern expression in E. F. Schumacher's influential *Small Is Beautiful* (1973) and in the writings of the London School of Economics' E. J. Mishan.

Both writers rightly criticized the sometimes cruelly mechanistic nature of much technological change, but they also revealed a dislike of the very kind of expansive growth that lifted so many into the Yeoman class after the Second World War. "The single-minded pursuit of individual advancement, the craving for material success," Mishan wrote, "may be exacting a fearful toll in terms of human happiness."

In the search for an alternative, both writers looked not forward but backward. Schumacher described "the good qualities of an earlier civilization," that is, the old rural English society identified not so much with progressivism or socialism but with the old Tory class order.[56]

More recently, many advocates of slow or no growth are finding inspiration in even less enlightened settings than old England. Some point to the small Himalayan kingdom of Bhutan, the site of a 2014 pilgrimage by Oregon Governor John Kitzhaber. This "happiness" poster child makes an odd exemplar for the twenty-first century. In contrast to the praise heaped on the tiny nation by Kitzhaber, one Asian development expert recently described the country as "still mired by extreme poverty, chronic unemployment and economic stupor that paints a glaring irony of the 'happiness' the government wants to portray." In this "happiest place on earth," one in four lives in poverty, nearly forty percent of the population is illiterate, and the infant mortality rate is five times higher than in the United States. It also has a nasty civil rights record of expelling its Nepalese minority from the country.[57]

Bhutan, of course, is a pastoral country, but some urbanists also increasingly apply their "happiness" ideal to cities, particularly poorer ones. Canadian academic Charles Montgomery, for example, celebrates what he sees as high levels of happiness in the city slums of developing countries. Montgomery points to impoverished Bogotá, for example, as "a happy city" that shows the way to urban development. If we can't replicate a Bhutanese village, maybe we can be compelled to evacuate suburbia for the pleasures of life in a setting that resembles a crowded favela.[58]

Although this emphasis on happiness certainly has its virtues, and should be a consideration in how a society grows, lack of economic growth, along with low levels of affluence, seems an unlikely way to make people more content. Recent research, in fact, finds that, for the most part, wealthier countries are not only richer but happier than those assaulted by poverty. Indeed the happiest countries are not impoverished at all, according to the Earth Institute, but highly affluent countries, led by Denmark, Norway, Switzerland, the Netherlands, and Sweden, while the countries ranked least happy were all very low-income countries in Africa.[59]

The argument against growth has gained currency with the rise of environmentalism, long focused, often with justification, on the negative impacts of economic expansion. This has engendered an understandable search for an alternative method to measure societal well-being. Climate change campaigners, such as the *Guardian*'s George Monbiot, propose "a battle to redefine humanity," essentially replacing the era of "expanders" with one of "restrainers." Some economists, particularly in Europe, have embraced the notion of what they call "de-growth," that is, a planned ratcheting down of mass material prosperity.[60]

Winners and Losers in the "Happiness" Game

In any conflict over the preferred shape of society, there are usually winners and losers. The shift from a focus on growth to one on what is fashioned as sustainability has proven a boon both for the public sector, particularly those working in regulatory agencies and politicians who now have new ways to elicit contributions, and for those parts of the private sector that work most closely with government. Other beneficiaries include connected investors, such as the many who benefit from "green" energy subsidies, which, particularly when measured by their production of energy, are considerably higher than those secured over the past century by oil and gas interests.[61]

The downsizing of growth, naturally, also appeals to many who already enjoy wealth, such as Ted Turner, who then promote anti-growth policies[62] through their foundations and, as a bonus, get to feel very good about themselves. Other winners include the media Clerisy, notably in Hollywood—who propagandize such views while living in unimaginable luxury—as well as academics. The successful and well-compensated producer and director James Cameron complains about "too many people making money out of the system" and warns that growth must stop to save the planet.[63]

So who loses in the new anti-growth regime? Certainly these include large parts of the working class—farm workers, lumberjacks, factory operatives, oil field workers, and their families—who work in the extractive industries most subject to regulatory constraints and higher energy prices. Particularly hard hit may well be young families who, perhaps forsaking the "slacker" life, now find their aspirations of a house and a decent job blocked by the generally older, and better off, advocates for "happiness."

Wall Street and "Progressives" Find Common Ground

The rise of neo-feudalism and the decline of the Yeomanry are best understood as the consolidation of ownership in ever fewer hands. This process has been greeted with enthusiasm by financial hegemons, who have stepped in with billions to buy and then rent out foreclosed homes. In some states this has accounted for upwards of twenty percent of all new house purchases. Having undermined the housing market with their "innovations," notably subprime and zero-down loans, they now look to profit from the middle orders' decline by getting them to pay the investment classes' mortgages through rents.

In the wake of the housing bust, and the longer than expected weak economy following the Great Recession, many financial analysts insisted that we were headed toward a "rentership society," as homeownership rates plunged from historic highs in the three years following the crash.[64] Part of this shift has been exacerbated by the movement of large investment groups like Blackstone to buy up single-family houses in order to rent them, representing a kind of neo-feudalist landscape, where landlords replace owner-occupiers, perhaps for the long term.

The impact of the investor move into housing has had a negative effect on potential middle- and working-class buyers, who find themselves frequently outbid by large equity firms. In a 2013 *Washington Post* article, Jack McCabe, a Florida real estate consultant, remarked, "There is the possibility that Wall Street and the banks and the affluent one percent stand to gain the most from this.... Meanwhile, lower-income Americans will lose their opportunity for the American Dream of building wealth through owning a home."[65]

But however convenient these developments may prove to investors on Wall Street, for society, and for the future of the democracy, the concentration of ownership in fewer hands is highly problematic. Rather than the Yeoman with his own place, and the social commitment that comes with it, we could be creating a vast, non-property-owning lower class that is permanently forced to tip their hats—and empty their wallets—for the benefit of their economic betters.[66]

One would expect that this diminution of the middle class would offend those on the left, which historically supported both the expansion of ownership and the creation of a better life for the middle class. Yet some progressives, going back to the period before the Second World War, have disliked the very idea of dispersed ownership; many intellectuals, notes Christopher Lasch, found a society of "small proprietors" and owners "narrow, provincial, and reactionary."

Increasingly, the media and many urbanists, who see a new generation of permanent renters as part of their dream of a denser America,
also embrace this vision as being more environmentally benign than traditional suburban sprawl.[67] The very idea of homeownership is widely
ridiculed in the media as a bad investment, and many journalists, on
both the left and the right, deride the investment in homes as mis-
placed. Instead, they suggest that people invest their resources on Wall
Street, which, of course, would be of great benefit to the plutocracy. One
New York Times writer even proposed that people should buy housing
like food, largely ignoring homeownership's societal benefits to children
and the stability of communities. Traditional American notions of independence, permanency, and identity with one's neighborhood are given
short shrift in this approach.[68]

This odd alliance between the Clerisy and Wall Street works directly
against the interest of the middle and aspiring working class. After all,
the house is the primary asset of the middle orders, who have far less
in terms of stocks and other financial assets than the highly affluent.[69]
Having deemed high-density housing and renting superior, the confluence of Clerical ideals and Wall Street money has the effect of creating
an ever greater, and perhaps long-lasting, gap between the investor class
and the Yeomanry.[70]

This shift toward renting also is widely portrayed in the media, and
by some pundits, as something that people actually want. Yet in reality,
the desire for homeownership has not ebbed. Research for the Woodrow Wilson Center indicated a continuing aspirational preference for
homeownership. In fact, homeownership was generally considered
more important even after the housing bubble than before. Indeed the
desire to own becomes more important as people get older and richer.
If homeownership were not preferred, it would be expected that as people become more affluent the rates of homeownership would decline, or
would be rejected as they matured.[71]

The First Great Social Unraveling

The pressures placed on the Yeoman class, exacerbated by technological changes and globalization, also have exacted a social cost that could
accelerate their downward trajectory. Traditionally, the middle orders
were characterized by a high degree of family and community cohesion.

When the old feudal order worked against the interests of the rising class of smallholders, the coherence of their families and religious communities gave them an edge over the often less morally upright aristocracies. The early capitalist enterprises tended to be built around strong kinship ties, and generally this worked best in cultures that embraced the ethic of moral regulation, particularly in the Protestant world.

As has occurred in the new technological age, the onset of the industrial era undermined many of these values, displacing male bread-winners from their place in the family, turning proud artisans into a proletariat dependent on wages and locked in ferocious competition not only with other men but with women and children as well. In Brit-ain, the homeland of the industrial age, pauperism surged more than four-fold as a percentage of the population between 1760 and 1818. The industrial revolution, as one late nineteenth-century historian noted, could "produce wealth without producing well-being."[72] It would take decades before the benefits of the new economic paradigm reached the working classes.

One reason for this slow progress lay in how the new paradigm impacted the social conditions of the emerging proletariat in particular. Part of this can be seen in the decline of religion; by the 1850s, religious attendance in Britain fell to below 50 percent,whereas in earlier times it had been nearly universal. It was lower still in the major industrial cit-ies, such as Manchester.[73]

In *The Condition of the Working Class in England*, Engels portrays the impact of the early industrial revolution on family and moral life. In the first half of the nineteenth century, there was a marked increase in crime, drunkenness, and dysfunctional family life, with children fre-quently abandoned, abused, and left to their own devices. Since they lacked any sense of security, asked Engels, "why on earth should they be provident in any way?"[74]

This breakdown of family life—along with old kinship-based trades and agriculture—raised the specter of an excessive individualism pro-pelled by capitalism. For his part, Tocqueville saw American family and religious culture as the key means to curbing the excessive greed and individualism inherent in our culture. Through the "natural bonds and legitimate pleasures of home," the aspirational American would be con-strained from socially destructive behavior.[75]

As in Britain, family and religious ties were undermined by the industrial transformation that broke down the social mores of the old middle class and, perhaps even more so, that of immigrants, many of whom arrived from far less developed countries. In a world where household authority was being supplanted by economic forces, the sociologist Max Weber suggested, the family lost its historic role as "the bearer of cultural values."[76] The number of children living in fatherless homes grew 25 percent during the period of rapid industrialization in the 1870s. Divorce rates also soared from one in twelve in 1900 to one in seven in 1924.

To a large extent, this decline reversed in the years after the Second World War. Although the influence of the traditional extended family ebbed with greater prosperity, the 1950s and 1960s were "a profamily period if there ever was one," according to historian Stephanie Coontz. The percentage of children living with unmarried mothers actually declined by nearly a quarter from the 1880 levels. Many factors underpinned this development, such as the expansion of the welfare state, longer lifespans, and powerful unions, all of which nurtured a moral and familial climate far more secure than in the early industrial era.

There were, of course, numerous negative aspects to this era, notably the consignment of women to the home, the exclusion of African Americans and other minorities, and, at times, what could be seen as a certain stultifying conformity. Yet despite these limitations this period ushered in a unique boom for the middle-class family, including those rising from the working class, notably industrial workers, who also were able to buy homes in the very suburbs now so widely detested by the Clerisy.[77]

The Rise of Post-Familialism and the Decline of the Yeomanry

Clearly broad-based economic growth brought significant benefits for the Yeoman class and their families. As Coontz has argued, the heyday of the nuclear family in the 1950s and 1960s was predicated on widespread economic growth; it created a peculiar social environment that was seen neither in the past nor since. Indeed, the decline of the economic position of the middle class has accompanied, and paralleled, a deterioration of such social indicators as crime and divorce, not only in the United States but also Europe. By the 1980s, non-family households surpassed family households, a trend that continued through much of the following decades.[78]

For the better part of a half century, this breakdown has been a core concern of social conservatives, who regard themselves as waging a desperate war to defend "family values." However well-intentioned, this effort has to be written off as something of a failure, in part due to the unfortunate concentration of religious fundamentalism on divisive issues such as school prayer, gay marriage, and absolute bans on abortions. These views are increasingly marginal in an era where the real issue is not so much theology but the dynamic, particularly in economic terms, of class relations.[79]

Yet if the tactics of the right have been ham-handed, the connection between the changing economic order and the fate of the middle orders cannot be easily dismissed. After the period of stability in the postwar era, we have seen a ratcheting up of social dysfunction through the middle and working classes. The number of children from single mothers continues to soar. In 1970, 11 percent of births were to unmarried mothers; by 1990, that number had risen to 28 percent. Today, 41 percent of all births are to unmarried women. Most frightening of all, for mothers under 30, the rate is 53 percent.[80]

This has long-term implications for both the unmarried parents and their progeny. As Charles Murray, among others, has noted, conditions once associated with minorities are now becoming commonplace among large swaths of the Yeoman class. Rates of illegitimacy among the white working and lower classes, he notes, have reached the levels experienced by African Americans a half century ago. This could have disastrous social consequences. Murray points out that the deterioration of family life—as measured by illegitimacy and low marriage rates—now has reached particularly high levels among white American women with only a high school education: 44 percent of births are out of wedlock, up from 6 percent in 1970.[81]

Looking backward, the parallels with the first era of proletarianization are fairly chilling. As during the industrial revolution, religious affiliation, if not in a free fall, is clearly on the downward trend, most dramatically among white working- and lower-class Americans.[82] Declining job prospects and financial security also affect marriage stability.[83] With incomes dropping and higher unemployment, Murray predicts the emergence of a growing "white underclass" in the coming decade.[84]

Much of this decline can be ascribed to the economic conditions that have made what was once seen as normal family life more difficult. Households with steady incomes, a degree of security, and a stronger sense of a better future have a greater propensity to stay together. Similarly, family dysfunction grows with economic insecurity, loss of property, and in some cases the decline in blue-collar unionization.

"Working-class people with insecure work and few resources, little stability and no ability to plan for a foreseeable future become concerned with their own survival and often become unable to imagine being able to provide materially and emotionally for others," notes Sarah Corse, an associate professor of sociology in University of Virginia's College of Arts and Sciences and author of a 2013 study on declining family structure in the working class.[85]

Such dysfunction is, if anything, more profound in minority communities, particularly among immigrants and, most critically, the next generation. The foreign-born and their offspring have accounted for one-third of the nation's population growth over the past three decades, but the longer they stay, the more marriage and childbearing decline over time. Even more seriously, 44 percent of all millennials think marriage is becoming "obsolete"; among the baby boomer parents, the number is 35 percent. And fewer young people think childbearing is even important in a marriage.[86]

Is Mass Serfdom the Future?

Given these trends, what is the future for the Yeoman class? Some see a growing role for the state as the ultimate replacement for the family or the traditional community. If you want to glimpse the worldview of the progressive Clerisy, watch the inane online slideshow called "The Life of Julia," presented in 2012 by the Obama campaign. In "Julia," virtually every step in life is predicated on some government service. She "decides" to have a child although a man is never mentioned (it's dubious that progressive Clerics accept the notion of immaculate conception), and the child, once sent off to government-funded preschool, never reappears. Although hardly a stunning embrace of strong family structure, *Ms.* magazine hailed Julia as "a future standard for women."[87]

Such an approach threatens to continue pushing the Yeoman class toward something closer to serfdom, with the state supplanting the role of the medieval Church and the *noblesse oblige* of the upper classes. To be sure, the role of government in alleviating poverty—as occurred with the war on poverty—was dramatic, particularly for seniors and minorities.[88] It is equally clear that increasing dependence on public assistance, as opposed to family reliance, has helped create the kind of semi-permanent underclass unforeseen a half century ago. As economist Robert Samuelson has noted, the "safety net" has rescued millions from the worst abject poverty but has proved "a failure as an engine of self-improvement."[89]

In the future, large swaths of what might have once been parts of the Yeoman class, both Anglo and minorities, may become more like the traditional poor, whether in the inner city or outside, living paycheck to paycheck. Their descendants may enjoy far fewer opportunities for property ownership, or any form of economic independence. As with the poor, government subsidies can help relieve the pain and the worst aspects of poverty—the American poor live much better than their counterparts in many parts of the world—but greater dependency works against upward mobility.[90]

The devolution of society under a slow-growth regime—or growth that benefits essentially the most well-placed and affluent citizens—suggests a further intensification of class divides. Unless broadly based economic growth is restored, large parts of an emergent middle class—including immigrants and minorities—are in danger of turning into something of a permanent class of low-wage proletarians, with some falling into the lumpenproletariat or underclass. If so, it would spell the end of what has been the American dream, ushering in a new era of vast inequality utterly at odds with the nation's historic role as a society driven by aspiration.

CHAPTER FIVE

Geography of Inequality

From early on in the settlement of North America, class relations have been defined in large part by the generosity of its geography. This was particularly different from the more constrained land areas in Europe. The French geographer Paul Vidal de la Blache,[1] visiting the United States in 1912 and 1913, observed how rapidly American cities were expanding outward, and tending away from a mono-centric to a multi-centric pattern of employment as well. "Swarming all around, indefinitely expanding its urban districts, the city is a perfect expression of Americanism," he wrote.[2]

Every surge of empowerment for the middle orders and the working class has been accompanied by an expansion of occupied land area, from the earliest settlements east of the Appalachians and the Homestead Act to the great suburban boom of the 1950s. In contrast, when obstacles to the availability of land arose, class barriers also increased. Most notably in the South, this was in large part due to a preponderance of large farms, dependent heavily on European-centered export trade with the Caribbean and West Africa and the institutions of English penal transportation, European indentured servitude, debt bondage, and slavery. In the antebellum South the top one to two percent possessed more wealth than the rest of the population combined.[3]

Class barriers also rose during the initial phase of American industrial development. As they huddled in cities, many new immigrants as well as migrants from the countryside ended up in denser housing owned by others, a reversal of the great American yearning for more space. "The Homestead Act failed," concluded Henry Nash Smith, "because it was incongruent with the industrial revolution."[4] By the

1870s, city dwellers tended, then as now, not to own property; but those who did own property in larger cities were far richer than their counterparts elsewhere.[5]

The City as Luxury Product

Today we may be on the verge of yet another expansion of class barriers. This reflects market forces, but also the attempts by the Clerisy and urban developers to concentrate people and companies within the centers of core cities, an idea that gained momentum in the 1970s as part of the environmental movement's anti-sprawl campaigns. This approach is widely cheered by commentators on both the right and the left. "The new American dream is a condo in the city," argues Fox News commentator Kate Rogers in a very typical media statement.[6]

The "back to the city" movement increasingly relies on a new model of urbanism that is less about creating opportunity for the aspirational class and more about offering what former New York Mayor Michael Bloomberg calls "a luxury product," a place that focuses on the very wealthy.[7] This approach has a simple economic formula: if you please and lure the ultra-rich, you can serve the rest of the population from their surplus. "If we can find a bunch of billionaires around the world to move here, that would be a godsend," Bloomberg, himself a multi-billionaire, suggests. "Because that's where the revenue comes to take care of everybody else."[8]

This approach has transformed the urban economy into what Citigroup analysts have labeled a "plutonomy": an economy and society driven largely by the investment behavior and spending of the über-rich.

The rise of the plutonomy has been greatly enhanced by the nature of the recovery from the Great Recession, which overwhelmingly has benefited the very rich, and their stock and real estate holdings, and priced the vast majority out of the market, especially in the most desirable cities. It has particularly benefited those with inherited wealth, as the returns on capital have surpassed those of labor.[9]

The growth of the foreign oligarchy has further contributed to this process. Fifty percent of buyers in some urban areas are foreigners seeking pieds-à-terre in what is increasingly an exclusive global club. This concentration of wealth begins to change everything in the political realm as well. In New York, as Fred Siegel, among others, has noted, the finances of the country's largest municipality are now "entirely at the mercy" of a few thousand very rich taxpayers.[10]

This process marks an enormous transformation of the function of urban communities. Since the late Enlightenment, great cities, often built around markets, were typically places not only for the rich and their servants but also for the aspirational middle and lower classes. A great city, wrote René Descartes in the seventeenth century, represented "an inventory of the possible,"[11] a place where people could create their own futures and lift up their families. In early nineteenth-century New York, artisans and small shopkeepers provided the "reservoir of people" who rose to the landowning class and could afford spacious places to live.[12] The ability to rise in cities from North America and Europe to Asia—through what historian Peter Hall calls "this unique creativity of great cities"[13]—stands as one of the great social achievements of modern times.

But increasingly, in this era of Oligarchs, certain cities are not so much centers for upward mobility as preferred locales for the successful, talented, and wealthy. The strangely popular thesis that the luxury city is a desirable outcome has been defined by author Aaron Ehrenhalt as the "Great Inversion,"[14] a return to nineteenth-century urbanism, where the rich cluster in the center and the *hoi polloi* serve them from the dull, dreary periphery.[15]

Indeed, some metropolitan areas—particularly larger ones—at least partially fit this description, becoming in the process increasingly bifurcated between a wealthy elite and a lower class. These are places like San Francisco, New York, and Chicago, which receive much of the attention of the media. At the same time many others, like Detroit and St. Louis have continued to shrink even as increasingly self-sufficient suburbs thrive. Still others—Raleigh, NC, Columbus, OH, Houston—thrive as opportunity cities, with generally lower density and relatively affordable areas.

Not surprisingly the luxury cities—as well as the upscale retirement centers in Florida—tend to boast the areas with the highest concentrations of inherited and other rentier wealth in the nation. According to an analysis of Census data by Mark Schill of Praxis Strategy Group, New York County, Manhattan, was one of the leaders among nation's core cities in asset-based wealth while the Bronx, just across the Harlem

River, ranked at the absolute bottom.[16] This inherited wealth is increasingly diffused among multiple cities as members of the expanding ranks of the ultra-rich purchase apartments in numerous locations.[17]

Increasingly, New York, San Francisco, London, Paris, and other cities where the cost of living has skyrocketed are no longer places where one goes to be someone; they are where one lives when already successful or living on inherited largesse. They increasingly constitute, as journalist Simon Kuper puts it, "the vast gated communities where the one percent reproduces itself."[18]

The Changing Economy of Cities

Compared to the early capitalist cities of the early nineteenth century, or the industrial city or the postwar mass-market cities, the primary sectors now driving key urban areas—high technology, media, and financial services—are far less reliant on the mass mobilization of labor, both skilled and unskilled.[19] At the same time, formerly higher-wage blue- and white-collar employment has shifted to the suburbs or smaller cities.[20]

In the wake of the middle-class exodus, many urban areas now have a two-tier salary structure: the high-wage sector at the top and the generally low-wage service sector. The great winnowing of the less affluent caused by ultra-high prices and the proliferating use of unpaid interns has even affected the creative class itself. Musician Patti Smith laments, "New York has closed itself off to the young and the struggling. New York City has been taken away from you."[21]

But it's not just artists who are affected; even professionals like airline pilots generally avoid postings in New York (only Detroit does worse in this respect) due to the high cost of living. New York's middle class has been in decline for decades, and as early as 1989 its economy was declared to be "hollow in the middle."[22]

The most profound level of inequality and bifurcated class structure is found in the densest and most influential urban environment in North America—Manhattan. In 1980, Manhattan ranked seventeenth among the nation's more than 3,000 counties in income inequality; by 2007 it ranked first, with the top fifth of all households earning 52 times that of the lowest fifth, a disparity roughly comparable to that of Namibia.[23] Manhattan's GINI index now stands higher than that of South Africa before the apartheid-ending 1994 election. If Manhattan were a country, it would rank sixth highest in income inequality in the world out of more than 130 for which the World Bank reports data.[24]

Amid the upper-tier affluence, in part due to the impact of bailouts of the great financial institutions concentrated in the city, New York's wealthiest one percent earn a third of the entire city's personal income—almost twice the proportion for the rest of the country.[25] This makes all the more understandable how, despite the city's relatively strong recovery from both 9/11 and the recession, the strident populist campaign of Mayor Bill de Blasio was so strongly supported.[26]

The same patterns can be seen, albeit to a lesser extent, in other major cities, notes a recent analysis of 2010 Census data by the Brookings Institution. In many of these core cities, notes Brookings, the percentage of middle-income families has been in a precipitous decline for the last thirty years.[27] Using more recent data, University of Washington demographer Richard Morrill has demonstrated that the highest levels of inequality tend to be in larger metropolitan areas such as New York, Los Angeles, Houston, and Miami.[28]

The role of costs is critical here. A 2014 Brookings study found that big cities—with the exception of Atlanta—that suffer high costs also have the most pronounced inequality: San Francisco, Miami, Boston, Washington, DC, New York, Oakland, Chicago, and Los Angeles. The lowest degree of inequality was generally found in smaller, less expensive cities like Fort Worth, TX, Oklahoma City, Raleigh, NC, and Mesa, AZ. Nor does the wide income gap in signature luxury cities reflect a rising tide for all, even less so at the bottom. Income inequality has risen most rapidly in the very symbol of luxury progressivism, San Francisco, where the wages of the poorest 20 percent of all households have actually declined amid the dot-com billions.[29]

The Persistence of Poverty

Manuel Castells, writing as early as the 1980s, believed that an "informational city" would generate nodes of prosperity that increasingly communicated with themselves while shunning the rest of the metropolitan areas.[30] Most of the metropolitan population, historically a key source of customers and workers for major businesses, would have a "decreased relevance" for the more elite nodes. In such a society, the benefits of "post-industrialism" would, unlike in prior periods of growth, concentrate in selected metropolitan areas as opposed to throughout the country as a whole.[31]

This may be one reason why the much celebrated urban renaissance has done little to reduce poverty. In many of the most celebrated new urbanist cities, middle- and working-class employment has faded, leaving the Yeomanry and the poor struggling to make ends meet, even in the most successful, but high-cost, urban regions. Indeed, when average urban incomes are adjusted for the higher rent and costs, the middle classes in metropolitan areas such as New York, Los Angeles, Portland, Miami, and San Francisco have among the lowest real earnings of any metropolitan area.[32]

Core cities have also not been too kind to the working-class minorities and immigrants who historically migrate to the metropolitan area in search of economic opportunity. Advocates of the creative class, including Richard Florida, worship mightily at the altar of ethnic diversity.[33] Yet as the Urban League points out, the very cities most praised as exemplars of urban revival—San Francisco, Chicago, and Minneapolis—also suffer the largest gaps between black and white incomes.[34]

Indeed, in some of the most heralded "creative class" cities, both struggling ethnic newcomers and African Americans not only are economically marginalized but are becoming a smaller percentage of the population as costs have risen and good job opportunities have shrunk. Cities such as New York, Chicago, Philadelphia, and Boston, notes a 2013 Urban Institute study, are generally also the places where African American and Latino incomes most lag those of whites. Notwithstanding the rhetoric, much of the "hip and cool" world increasingly consists of monotonic "white cities" with relatively low, and falling, minority populations.[35] San Francisco, Portland, and Seattle, for instance, achingly political correct in theory, are actually becoming whiter and less ethnically diverse as the rest of the country diversifies.[36]

In larger cities like New York, Chicago, and Los Angeles, where the minority population remains large, this separation between rich and poor, minority and white, can be seen geographically. In the Bronx, New York's most heavily Latino county, roughly one in three households lives in poverty, the highest rate of any large urban county in the nation.[37] Even in nouveau hipster and increasingly expensive Brooklyn, nearly a quarter of residents—mainly African American and Latino—are below the poverty line. While the wealthy gentry shop at artisanal cheese shops and frequent trendy restaurants, one in four Brooklynites receives food stamps. New York has, in fact, experienced the biggest rise in the numbers of homeless in the nation, and the number of children sleeping in shelters rose steadily even as the elite economy "boomed."[38]

New York, of course, has unique assets that continue to attract the very rich, as well as the young and ambitious. Conditions in other core cities with less assets are often even worse. Indeed, the average poverty rate in the historical core municipalities in the 52 largest U.S. metro areas was 24.1 percent, more than double the 11.7 percent rate in suburban areas—despite a considerable urban turnaround in this period. To be sure, the heavy urban core population losses of the 1960s through the 1980s are generally no longer occurring. Yet, between 2000 and 2010, more than 80 percent of the new population in America's urban core communities lived below the poverty line, compared with one-third of the new population in suburban areas. The majority of poor people, like the largest chunk of the overall metropolitan population, live in the suburbs, but on a percentage basis the concentration of poverty remains far greater in the central cities.[39]

Uncool Cities

These statistics undermine the optimistic spin on urban renaissance, as the rise of the creative-class strategy has proven ineffective in reversing urban poverty. University of British Columbia's Jamie Peck has described the current fashion of focusing on hipsters and the affluent as a "biscotti and circuses" approach that exacerbates poverty and inequality in urban centers.[40] "To put it in political speak," notes urban thinker Aaron Renn, "the creative class doesn't have much in the way of coattails." The new urbanism is a new, and equally ineffective, form of "trickle-down economics." Even Florida, the guru of the "creative class," admits that the benefits of the urban strategies he advocates "flow disproportionately to more highly-skilled knowledge, professional, and creative workers." Yet many cities, including some unlikely cultural centers such as Detroit or Cleveland, have adopted the idea that sponsoring artists and "hip" urbanism are the keys to civic success.[41]

It seems clear that the current recipe for urban growth is destined to preserve and expand inequality, largely ignoring the needs of the lower and working classes. The most fundamental problem is the limited scope of the largely childless, well-educated, and young urbanistas who are now the targets of city developers. The vast majority of all people, and particularly those in their twenties and thirties, do not live in urban core districts.[42] Often as little as one or two percent of a city's population lives in the densest urban core, but these urbanites receive outsized attention from governments as well as the media, often with the support of urban developers.[43]

Worse still, the number of cities that can reasonably join the ranks of the "hip and cool" cities is extremely limited. Former Michigan governor Jennifer Granholm famously proclaimed that the key to turning around Rust Belt cities like Detroit lay in becoming "cool" by cultivating the "creative class" and subsidizing the arts. Detroit and other Michigan urban areas failed to grow, notwithstanding the hype. "You can put mag wheels on a Gremlin," commented one long-time Michigan observer, "but that doesn't make it a Mustang."[44]

Mindful of these lessons, Cleveland-based urban analyst Richey Piiparinen now suggests that many cities simply don't appeal primarily to trendy hipsters, most of whom have the financial wherewithal to live somewhere cooler. As the *American Prospect* noted, many down-at-the-heels burgs like Cleveland, Toledo, Hartford, Rochester, and Elmira, NY, have tried to reinvent themselves as hipster-oriented, but they have largely failed to do so.[45]

Piiparinen, however, believes that most urban communities would do better to focus on affordability, improving the existing housing stock, and building from their remaining industrial resources. In places like Cleveland, cultivating their essentially Rust Belt roots makes far more sense rather trying to compete with cities like San Francisco. Most urban dwellers need high-wage middle-skill jobs, better infrastructure, and education.[46] For them, the "cool cities" approach tends to have very uncool results, at least for the modestly educated and much of the middle class.

California Latifundia

The pathologies of the luxury urban economy are most apparent in California, which now epitomizes the evolving geography of inequality, just as in the past it served as an exemplar for middle-class aspiration. The Golden State is now home to 111 billionaires, by far the most of any state. In total, California billionaires personally hold assets worth $485 billion, more than the entire GDP of all but 24 countries in the world.[47]

At the same time, California also suffers the highest poverty rate in the country (adjusted for housing costs)—above 23 percent—and a leviathan welfare state. With roughly 12 percent of the population, California now accounts for roughly one-third of the nation's welfare recipients. This burgeoning underclass exacerbates the demand for public services, deprives the state of potential taxpayers, and puts enormous pressure on the private-sector middle class to come up with revenue.[48]

The contemporary social trajectory of the Golden State can be best described as "back to the future" in its regressive character. In the nineteenth and early twentieth century, as Carey McWilliams noted, "unpleasant realities," including a highly feudalistic rural society controlled by Anglos that largely replicated the pattern of land-grant feudalism generated by the Spanish conquest.[49]

This contrasts with the period, starting with the New Deal, where government spending—water projects, military bases, aircraft manufacture, shipbuilding, freeways—helped underpin rapid growth. Postwar California then experienced a period of largely unparalleled upward mobility, as a vast, middle-class, and largely suburban culture of small homesteads grew throughout the state. Despite massive in-migration from other states, California enjoyed a remarkably diverse economy that maintained relatively low rates of unemployment well into the late 1980s.[50]

Today, due in part to globalization and shifts in technology, but also related to no-growth policies favored by the planning Clerisy and their developer allies, opportunities for the state's minority and working-class population have been largely depressed. Increasing numbers of Californians, particularly Latinos, are downwardly mobile and doing worse than their parents; native born Latinos actually have shorter lifespans than their parents, according to one recent report.[51]

Unemployment in many of the state's largest counties—Sacramento, Los Angeles, Riverside, San Bernardino, Fresno, and Oakland—remains above the national average. By the end of 2013, California was home to eleven of the twenty largest U.S. counties with the highest rates of unemployment. The vast expanse of economic decline in the midst of unprecedented, but very narrow, urban luxury has been characterized as "liberal apartheid." The well-heeled, largely white and Asian coastal denizens live in an economically inaccessible bubble insulated from the largely poor, working-class, heavily Latino communities in the eastern interior of the state.[52]

Public policies have helped reduce working- and middle-class opportunity by discouraging industrial, logistics industry, or construction growth—all linchpins of the state's once flourishing blue-collar economy. The state's "green energy" initiatives, supported by most tech and many financial Oligarchs, have raised electricity rates well above the national average, making it difficult for firms in traditional fields like manufacturing, fossil fuels, agriculture, or logistics.[53] Similarly, "green" policies designed to preserve or encourage certain fish species have worked to reduce agricultural production, causing further distress in many interior and rural areas. Calls for increased water storage for the inevitable dry years have been muted, due in part to a belief that the state's droughts, long a feature of its geologic history, are in fact the inevitable result of relentless climate change.[54]

At the same time many of the traditional means by which Californians ascended economically have deteriorated. Some may blame funding, teachers' unions, or demographics, but the state's basic education system has been deteriorating for decades. California was ranked 48th in high school attainment in 2009. In 2000 it was ranked 40th. In 1990 it was tied with Illinois for 36th place.[55]

Young Californians, notes one study, are now less likely to graduate from college than their parents. "At present," long-time California economist Bill Watkins observes, "California completely fails its lower-class population. It begins with an educational system that many don't complete, while most of those who do [graduate] are often unprepared to participate in a twenty-first century economy. It ends up with a lack of opportunity and upward mobility."[56]

At the same time, the state's middle class continues to decline. Since 1999, according to research at the California Lutheran University forecast project, the state has seen a far more dramatic drop in households earning between $35,000 and $75,000 than the national average. As late as the 1980s, the Golden State was about as egalitarian as the rest of the country and roughly sixty percent of its population was middle class. But now, for the first time in decades, the middle class is a minority.[57]

One key to these discouraging trends is reduced access to landownership, in part a result of draconian regulations[58] that push home prices well above what all but the wealthy, or those who have inherited wealth, can afford.[59] These regulations make very difficult any new single-family house construction, which has the effect of pushing the remaining stock of single-family houses ever more out of reach.[60] Many Californians live as modern-day land serfs, renting and paying someone else's mortgage; if they seek to start a family, they increasingly look to settle elsewhere. Ironically they turn to locations like Oklahoma and Texas,[61] places that historically sent eager migrants to the Golden State, whose appeal was not just economic opportunity but the mild climate and spectacular scenery.

The high prices hit all across the spectrum, from the poor to the relatively affluent. In 2012, four California housing markets—San Jose, San Francisco, San Diego, and Los Angeles—ranked as the most unaffordable metropolitan areas relative to income in the nation. According to the Center for Housing Policy, 39 percent of working households in the Los Angeles metropolitan area spend more than half of their income on housing, as do 35 percent in the San Francisco metro area—a higher proportion than the 31 percent level in the New York area and well above the national rate of 24 percent.[62]

A recent study done for National Core, a low-income housing company, by demographer Wendell Cox found that even skilled workers, such as an Orange County biomedical engineer earning well above $100,000 a year, could not afford to buy a home there. California's hold on aspirational families, previously fueled by the dream of homeownership, is rapidly fading for all but the most affluent, even those whose incomes would be more than sufficient in other regions.

The Real Geography of Opportunity

Cities in what Fernand Braudel described as "the core of a world-economy" have always had higher costs, and sometimes they have suffered in competition with other, less expensive locales.[63] But for most of the country's population, the best hope for upward mobility and a better life does not lie in ultra-pricey, dense, crowded, and often highly praised urban areas, or, for that matter, in pricey faux-dense developments in smaller towns.

In the coming decades, the bulk of the nation's economic and demographic growth likely will to continue to occur where the cost of housing is more reasonable and regulatory restrictions and taxes fall less heavily on the working- and middle-class economy. While much the media has been infatuated with Wall Street and Google, the geography of opportunity over the past decade has largely favored often derided locations like Texas, the South, and parts of the Great Plains.[64]

Ever since the Great Recession ripped through the growth-driven economies of the Sunbelt, America's urban-focused pundit class has been giddily predicting the entire region's demise.[65] Some have even resorted to the claim that due to climate change, people will flock north and away from "the once great Sunbelt of America." Strangled by high energy prices, cooked by global warming, rejected by a new generation of urban-centric millennials, the vast southern region is, in the words of the *Atlantic*, where the "American dream" is now "dead."[66]

Yet over the past thirty years, virtually all of the fastest-growing American metropolitan areas were located in the Intermountain West or the South. This is not primarily due to a newfound desire for life in Tombstone or Mayberry, although many small towns in these regions are doing well, but is rather the result of an alternative form of urban development. In 2012, nine of the ten fastest-growing large metropolitan areas in America were in the Sunbelt, including the biggest Texas cities—Austin, Houston, Dallas–Fort Worth, San Antonio—as well as Denver, Orlando, Raleigh, Phoenix, and Charlotte.[67] In 2013, Houston alone had more housing starts than the entire state of California.[68]

The Sunbelt's continuing expansion is being generated in large part by middle-class movement away from the coastal states infatuated with the luxury city idea and toward other urban areas that offer a much better chance of owning a home and far more economic opportunity. Immigrants—traditionally seekers of upward mobility—are flocking to lower-cost metropolitan areas such as Houston, which saw the second largest growth in foreign born after New York. Once largely immigrant-free, locales such Charlotte and Nashville saw their foreign-born populations double as immigrants increasingly beat a path to these and other Sunbelt cities. This has occurred despite the fact that these locations may offer a less extensive safety net than more established immigrant hubs.[69]

Death to the Suburbs

The shift to the Sunbelt parallels a longer-standing movement among the aspiring middle and working classes to the suburban periphery, including those regions in the periphery of older, more central cities.[70] Robert Bruegmann has pointed out that the urban wealthy have always had the option of choosing a large city apartment, as opposed to a crowded one in a less appealing area, as was the usual fate for the working and even middle classes. They also had the option of settling in very low-density exclusive suburbs; in addition to their in-town residences, they often purchased country houses that could provide them with a break from the urban pressures.

In contrast, Bruegmann argues, suburbia offered the "surest way" for the broader portions of the population "to obtain some of the privacy, mobility and choice that once were available only to the wealthiest and most powerful members of society."[71] It was also in the suburbs that many long-term urban renters could at last buy their own residence.[72]

Occasionally attacked, with some justification, for restrictions against minorities, suburbs in recent decades have become bastions of relative economic equality. American Community Survey data for 2012 indicates that the suburban areas have considerably less household income inequality than the core cities. Among the 51 metropolitan areas with a population of more than 1 million, suburban areas were less unequal (measured by the GINI Coefficient) than the core cities in 46 cases.

Despite its egalitarian promise, the suburbs traditionally have been disdained by large parts of the academic, media, and policy communities. The American intelligentsia, notes historian Michael Lind, has been "all but united in its snobbish disdain for America's working-class and middle-class suburbs." They included, Lind suggests, the children of the affluent, who "could afford to live and play" in what he calls "the expensive bohemias in New York, San Francisco, and other big cities."[73]

As early as 1921, Lewis Mumford described the emerging "dissolute landscape" as "a no-man's land which was neither town nor country." Decades later urban author Robert Caro described the new rows of small houses at the edge of New York as "blossoming hideously," as families fled venerable, but dirty and crowded, parts of Brooklyn and Manhattan for more spacious tree-lined streets further east, west, south, and north.[74]

These early critics saw suburbs as often largely homogenous and spiritually stultifying. Jane Jacobs, who famously detested suburban Los Angeles, also considered the bedroom communities of Queens and Staten Island "the Great Blight of Dullness."[75] The 1960s social critic William Whyte denounced suburbia as hopelessly conformist and stultifying. Like many of today's density advocates, he predicted in *Fortune* that people would tire of such dull places and move back toward the city core.[76] Of course, there were always those who did indeed return to the urban center, but most, as the Census trends show, did not.

Part of this intellectual disdain arises from a neo-feudal belief that mass landownership destroyed environmental attributes that only the refined and wealthy could appreciate. It was easy enough to decry many of the early suburbs, built by mass production and lacking much in the way of aesthetic or environmental values. As early as 1948, William Vogt believed that "excessive breeding" and the resulting "abuse of the land"—both widely identified with early suburbia—were the primary threats to the planet's future.[77] Many environmentalists, of course, argue that suburbs will be undermined by the higher energy prices that their commuting patterns generate. Just in case, though, other environmental activists like Vice President Al Gore have long been ready to directly "control" suburban sprawl.[78]

"The American way of life—which is now virtually synonymous with suburbia—can only run on reliable supplies of cheap oil and gas," thundered James Howard Kunstler in his 2005 jeremiad *The Long Emergency*. "Even mild to moderate deviations in either price or supply will crush our economy and make the logistics of daily life impossible."[79]

Small wonder that he and other environmentalists view suburbs as "the greatest misallocation of resources in the history of the world," one that, fortunately, "has now entered a state of terminal decline."[80]

In what resembles a kind of religious certainty, much of the Clerisy, particularly among architects and planners, has divined a direct relationship between climate change and U.S. housing patterns. "What is causing global warming is the lifestyle of the American middle class," says new urbanist architect Andrés Duany, a major developer of dense housing himself.[81] Densification, claims influential architect Peter Calthorpe, is no less than "a climate change antibiotic."[82] Yet these statements ignore the fact that American carbon emissions are falling and that much of the world's increase is occurring in densely packed places like India and China.[83] To be sure, we should work to control emissions here in the United States. But the real driver of increased emissions is now in the developing world and may not require the kind of radical remaking of metropolitan life being demanded throughout much of the Clerisy.[84]

In reality, densification and related strategies have been found to provide little in greenhouse gas emissions reduction, while the costs are exorbitant. The most effective approaches involve not reshaping lifestyles but incorporating new technologies. For example, the Environmental Protection Agency indicates that its fuel economy standards will reduce greenhouse gas emissions at a minus cost of $200 to $300 per ton.[85] This compares to costs of $1,000 or more for densification strategies and a current market price for carbon offsets of under $15.[86] A McKinsey and Company study concluded that sufficient greenhouse gas emissions reductions can be achieved with shifts in technology, such as greater use of natural gas or better mileage cars, that require "no change in thermostat settings or appliance use, no downsizing of vehicles, home or commercial space and traveling the same mileage" and no "shift to denser urban housing."[87]

And if the looming climate apocalypse was not reason enough, others contend that suburban life and homeownership are doomed by demographic factors. For example, Chris Leinberger at Brookings argues as follows: As people age, and as the percentage of traditional family households drop in the nation as a whole, demand for single-family houses—largely stimulated by young families with children—will also drop. The replacement generation, the millennials, won't have much use for large-lot homes on the leafy cul-de-sacs that their parents once occupied. Exurbia, he predicts, will largely be populated by poor families crowding into dilapidated, bargain-priced former McMansions in the new "suburban wastelands" that demographic forces will create. Suburbs, not inner cities, will be the new epicenter of inequality, even though the percentage of poor people, as shown above, has remained far higher in the urban core.[88]

The Coming Conflict over Land Use

Real-world behavior, however, is overwhelmingly inconsistent with such fervently held expectations of the coming wave of density. Single-family homes are still preferred, notes a survey by Smart Growth America, by 80 percent of all households over denser, multi-family living spaces, or even townhomes. Numerous surveys, including from Pew and the University of California at Irvine, have consistently found that suburbanites are much more satisfied with their communities than their urbanized counterparts, even those living in small towns. Suburbs have much lower poverty rates and a greater degree of income equality than urban communities, notes demographer Richard Morrill.[89]

Indeed, the decennial Census further shows something contrary to the beliefs of the Clerisy. Rather than flock to the cities, Americans are still decisively moving away from dense urban areas, no mater how luxurious, and toward the suburban periphery. Today, barely six percent of all Americans live in locations with densities of over 10,000 people per square mile. Between 2000 and 2010 the fastest growing central cities in the country—including Raleigh, Charlotte, and Austin—were markedly less dense than New York or San Francisco.

Overall, domestic migrants are moving away from metropolitan areas with denser urbanization—such as New York, Los Angeles, Boston, San Francisco, and Chicago—to less dense ones. Between 2000 and 2009, a net 1.9 million people left metropolitan New York, 1.3 million left Los Angeles, 340,000 left the San Francisco area, and 230,000 left San Jose and Boston. In contrast, the largest net in-migration over the past decade, and again since 2010, has occurred in the generally "sprawling" locations much despised by the Clerisy, such as Houston, Dallas, Fort Worth, Tampa–St. Petersburg, Atlanta, and Nashville.

By waging war on suburbia, the Clerisy, particularly the planning profession, academia, and much of the media, is intrinsically lobbying against the unequivocal interests and preferences of the middle class. "On the surface," notes New Mexico journalist Jeffry Gardner, "the smart-growth advocates appear to be focused on evil developers. But their true targets are the lower to middle income families who don't want to live á la Soho."[90]

Steps to make suburban areas more energy efficient—through such measures as developing amenities close to housing, dispersing work to the periphery, promoting home-based businesses, and planting trees— are necessary and important. But the real challenge will be to find ways to achieve those environmental goals without undermining middle-class aspirations, both in the more urbanized and, as we shall soon see, in rural areas as well.

The Forgotten Country

The Clerisy's war on suburbia resonates with themes that go back to the earliest periods of our history. Opposition to an expansive frontier by those in the centers of power and influence has been a recurring theme in American history, dating back to the country's origins, as Frederick Jackson Turner noted. They start with the early attempts of the British imperial authorities, and later those of the tidewater South and the mercantilist Northeast, to constrain the movement west. These efforts failed in earlier periods, including pre-revolutionary efforts of America's British overlords. As Edmund Burke observed, largely because of the continental scale of the United States: "If you drive the people from one place," they will simply move themselves to another.[91]

Today this attempt to hem people in, and restrict opportunity, extends into the countryside as well. This is particularly true in states such as New York, California, and Oregon, where the gentry and Clerisy dominate culture and politics. In these states, policies that disfavor energy, agriculture, and manufacturing might cripple urban opportunity, but they also destroy rural economies facing competition from other similarly situated, but lower-cost, regions of the country and the world.

Contemporary rural decline and impoverishment can even be seen in states such as Oregon, where the influence of relatively small luxury urban communities, centered on Portland, has produced economic conditions that one top state official says are now "dire" and may be close to irreversible.[92] Unemployment and underemployment in many rural Oregon counties reach well into the double digits. People in the interior regions of the state, much like their counterparts in California, complain that Portland's strict control over such things as energy and land use makes economic development all but impossible, even where these resources are far more plentiful.[93]

Another example of this dichotomy, perhaps best described as the dilemma of being a "red state" economy in a "blue state," can be seen in upstate New York, where by virtually all the measurements of upward mobility—job growth, median income, income growth—the region ranks below long-impoverished southern Appalachia. Yet when the opportunity to open natural gas drilling seemed to provide a wholly unanticipated way out of poverty for economically depressed south-western New York State as well neighboring northern Pennsylvania, it was rejected by New York's powerful gentry and green constituen-cies, who increasingly favor an accelerated, but very expensive, shift to renewable energy.[94]

Few dispute, at least outside those with an interest in exploiting these resources, that natural gas drilling should be safely regulated, due largely to potential impacts on water quality. But intelligent compromises can be delivered, as has been attempted in Colorado under the tutelage of Democratic Governor John Hickenlooper, working with both environ-mental and energy interests.[95]

But in other states, such as New York, which lacks Colorado's long history of energy development, the conflict over this new industry reflects not so much a battle over policy as a conflict between classes and differing geographies. Much of the opposition to shale gas, notes urban historian Fred Siegel, comes from wealthy core city residents—including celebrities such as Yoko Ono—and from the pockets of the Clerisy, notably in the local universities, who religiously oppose mod-ern gas extraction, or fracking, even in a region that has been in chronic economic decline. Those supporting development include local busi-nesspeople and landowners, who have no real share of the urban elite economy.

The anti-gas movement, in fact, increasingly resembles the social class structure of the anti-industrial Tory ethos of mid-nineteenth-century England. Adelaide Gomer, the Duncan Hines heiress who directs the Park Foundation of Ithaca and finances much of the local anti-gas and fracking movement, bases her opposition on the belief that energy development would ruin "the ambience, the beauty of the region."

But whereas British Tories also felt they had a paternal obligation to look after the well-being of the peasants they governed, today's liberal gentry express few common concerns. The fact that parts of rural Pennsylvania have seen a significant rise in per capita income between 2007 and 2011—providing jobs for truckers, riggers, engineers, welders, pipefitters, and all the auxiliary workers needed to support the drillers—means very little to those who want to preserve the land near their upstate estates as a private playground while making their living in the core city that few others can afford.[96] As Dick Downey of Otego, NY, a former history teacher and a supporter of fracking, notes, "the class divide in the argument over drilling in New York is the elephant in the living room. Everyone's aware of it, but no one is talking about it."[97]

The New Enclosures

Ultimately the new planning regime—with its abhorrence of both mass suburbia and rural development—has adopted policies that in many ways resemble the period of land consolidation in Britain during the period of the enclosure acts. As in Britain at that time, the masses are expected to move into crowded core cities, where only the wealthy can afford to own property or enjoy sufficient space.

Some critics of suburbanization openly embrace a return to the early, but highly disruptive and exploitative, model of urban development. Planners such as Britain's Richard Rogers speak directly to the ideal of "medieval" cities and towns. He holds up the ideal of a permanent, configured community with planned, understood boundaries and rigid regulations. Such a conception could not be more foreign to the ever changing nature of cities.

This archaic, backward-looking vision has little room for the development of suburbs. Rogers regards its often ungainly structures and lack of aesthetic character as having "no community." Rogers also views suburban communities as aesthetically unpleasant and socially destructive.

"Do you really want to be living in the suburbs with five cats, four dogs, a cabbage patch and five rooms?" he blithely asks,[98] apparently oblivious to the fact that most Britons, like most Americans, in fact prefer suburban living to the kind of urban cramming their betters insist they accept.

As in Victorian England, support for policies that limit options for the middle class often comes from above. Al Gore, trustifarians like Prince Charles, and their patrician allies (e.g., Richard Branson) do not "live small" even as they urge the Yeomanry to do so, forcing them either into dense cities or, at best, crowded neo-medieval villages like the Prince's beloved Poundbury.[99] Blissfully unaware of the hypocrisy, many leading advocates for forced densification themselves consume land and resources at levels far above those of the lower orders for whom they desire to reduce their consumption and access to land. Al Gore's gargantuan carbon imprint is just one example. An examination of where high-profile "smart growth" advocates in Los Angeles live, for example, found that almost all lived in large houses, on suburban- or even exurban-sized lots, a few even in gated communities, and none were located anywhere near the public transit lines they want everyone else to use.[100]

Cramming for Profit

The future that is being planned and designed suggests a radical return to ways of life that were once thought of as belonging to a different time. If the Clerisy does not exactly envisage a return to the tenements that housed Depression-era families, the much smaller, less communal arrangements they advocate come close enough to this long-forgotten, and hardly desirable past. For the hip and cool young urban crowd, the new rage among planners is "micro-units"—modern tenements, as one observer noted, of 200 to 300 square feet. These are either being built or planned in such cities as Seattle, New York, San Francisco, Santa Monica, and Portland.[101]

Such units have appeal to developers for whom cramming, especially with an urban subsidy in hand, may be particularly profitable. Yet a considerable amount of research shows that life in ultra-small apartments has a depressing effect on people. "Sure, these micro-apartments may be fantastic for young professionals in their 20s," notes Dak Kopec, director of Design for Human Health at Boston Architectural College.

"But they definitely can be unhealthy for older people, say in their 30s and 40s, who face different stress factors that can make tight living conditions a problem."[102]

According to Kopec, the space-saving trend of tiny apartments can lead to increased claustrophobia, domestic abuse, and alcoholism. The shift to ever denser living also reduces birthrates and family formation. Families do not make up the prime market for dense housing; married couples with children constitute barely 10 percent of apartment residents, less than half the percentage for the population overall.[103]

Such "anti-sprawl" policies ultimately seek to feudalize even the suburban landscape. If new suburban single-family living options are not developed, the cost of houses everywhere becomes ever more expensive. Desirable and wealthy areas like Silicon Valley, particularly in locations like Atherton, are now among the most expensive zip codes in the country. But even in the more modest traditionally middle-income areas, small houses routinely approach the one million dollar level, not only in San Francisco but in entire suburban counties such as San Mateo and Marin.[104]

Is Density the Key to Growth and Upward Mobility?

Our perceptions of density are often distorted by the nature of media coverage, which tends to focus heavily, even obsessively, on the central core. To be sure, many downtown areas have experienced recent growth, often rapid, which seems all the more remarkable in part because these areas performed so poorly in the past. The urban core, however, accounted for less than one percent of the 27 million population increase between 2000 and 2010 in the United States as a whole. In reality, almost all of the country's net population growth took place in counties with under 2,500 persons per square mile, rather than in Manhattan or downtown San Francisco, where densities are far higher. The total population increase in counties with under 500 people per square mile was more than 30 times that of the increase in counties with densities of 10,000 and greater.[105]

Much of the current justification for density lies with the notion that packing people together makes for a more productive and "creative" economy, as well as a better environment for upward mobility.[106] A 2013 Harvard study widely cited as supportive of this notion, actually found the highest rates of upward mobility not in the largest metropolitan areas, like New York or Los Angeles, but in lower-density areas such as Salt Lake City and the small cities of the Great Plains, such as Bismarck, Yankton, SD, and Pecos.[107]

Rather than an ode to bigness, notes demographer Wendell Cox, the study found that commuting zones (similar to metropolitan areas) with average populations of less than 100,000 have the highest average upward income mobility.[108] This reinforces the findings of the University of Washington's Richard Morrill, who found the least inequality in highly dispersed, largely smaller communities in the Intermountain West, the northern Great Lakes, and parts of rural New England.[109] And we shouldn't forget the success story of the oil town Bakersfield, CA, a metropolitan area with high levels of upward mobility in the Harvard study. Columbia University urban planning professor David King wryly labeled the California city "a poster child for sprawl."[110]

These findings contrast with the common assertion that density leads to innovation and upward mobility. Urban boosters like Bruce Katz at Brookings, for example, contend that technological innovation will now be focused in the urban core—say, San Francisco—as opposed to the largely suburban Silicon Valley that gave birth to the computer and Internet age. Yet the vast majority of the tech jobs in the region, and most major corporate headquarters, remain far from the city. As urban analyst Jim Russell notes, it is other factors—migration, openness to outsiders, friendliness to entrepreneurs—that make the difference far more than simply density.

Some of the most respected urban research also has been mischaracterized to suggest an association between higher densities and greater metropolitan productivity. Yet one such mischaracterized study, by the prestigious Santa Fe Institute, specifically indicated that it found no such association.[111] Indeed, over the past half century it has been largely suburban areas—notably Boston's Route 128, various job centers of Los Angeles, and most of all Silicon Valley—that have driven much of the country's innovation, and in the past much of its job growth.

Even today Silicon Valley remains very much a suburban area. It hardly adheres to the idea that high-density urban areas are the ultimate founts of creativity and economic progress. Transit carries a one-quarter smaller share of commuters in Santa Clara County than the national average for urban areas, while more than two-thirds of households live in single-family houses. Much the same can be said, to some degree, about other burgeoning tech hubs, such as Raleigh, Austin, or Orange County, CA.

Places for People

The group with the most at stake in this shift toward neo-feudalism is the new generation, and those who follow them. Much of contemporary urban theory rests on the idea that weakening family connections, less marriage, and lower birthrates will decrease the appetite for lower-density housing.

Indeed, the places that most attract the "creative class" are also the ones with the fewest families and children, led by San Francisco, Seattle, Manhattan, and rapidly gentrifying Washington, DC. The very high housing and office prices, celebrated by urban real estate boosters, have made it hard not only on the poor but on middle- and even upper-middle-class families. This is not to mention how having children changes your view of the ways society should operate. It is hard to imagine being a parent in a place like San Francisco, where there are raging debates about the right of people to walk around naked in restaurants, markets, and other public places.[112]

Studies of migration patterns by age show this pattern. The San Francisco area does very well among younger people, according to an analysis of government migration data, but poorly once people enter their 30s, as they begin to move either to the suburbs or to less dense, more affordable areas outside the country. By the time people enter their 30s, they move decisively to lower cost, less dense places like Nashville, Houston, Austin, San Antonio, and Oklahoma City. This migration is particularly marked among parents of young children.[113]

This flight from density among families is not merely an American phenomenon. Other national census data shows far higher percentages of families with children in the suburbs of Tokyo, London, and Toronto than within inner urban areas. The ultra-dense cities of East Asia—Hong Kong, Singapore, and Seoul—have among the lowest fertility rates on the planet. Tokyo and Seoul now have fertility rates around 1 while Shanghai's has fallen to 0.7, among the lowest of any city ever recorded, well below China's "one child" mandate, and barely one-third the level required to replace the current population.[114]

The Battle for the Future

The notion that Americans should follow the cramming model seems certain to emerge as a source of class—and generational—conflict in contemporary America. Some have suggested that the Obama administration is conspiring to turn American cities into high-rise forests. But the coalition favoring forced densification—greens, planners, architects, developers—well predates Obama.[115] The result seems, wittingly or not, to make life increasingly difficult for the middle class, particularly families, and to cut off permanently the road to upward mobility for those below the more enlightened elite.

Sadly, there seems little interest in trying to achieve environmental goals in ways that do not so strongly interfere with aspirations. Faced with their inability to change conditions for the poor, some progressives see poverty not as something explainable by deficiencies in their programs, but as a reflection, in the words of California Governor Jerry Brown, of his state's "incredible attractiveness and prosperity."[116]

It would be much less disruptive to people's aspirations, and likely more effective, to reduce greenhouse gases by boosting work-at-home rates and reducing the cost of lower-emissions cars. These steps would allow for the continued expansion of traditional suburbs and preserve lower-density urban neighborhoods from Queens to the San Fernando Valley while also cutting carbon emissions.[117]

But such approaches undermine the Clerisy's drive to rein in the traditional desire for Americans to own land and spread themselves out as they wish. This could shape class dynamics, as we already see in California. Such impacts may not be their intention, but it will likely be the effect, as we see the highest levels of inequality in dense cities.

Over the longer term, the prospect that more Americans should become renters, largely in apartments, represents nothing less than an attempt to reverse the class gains of the postwar era and return us to a more stratified society. This should be of concern to anyone who cares about the future of the nation and most especially those of the next generation, who are being asked to give up the traditional American dream and to live instead in a new, more stratified class order, as demanded by their more "enlightened," and often far more affluent, superiors.[118] It is not clear how conflict over such opportunity and freedom may be resolved.

At a minimum, the density agenda needs to be knocked off its perch as the *summum bonum* of a planning policy that tends to regard density as a virtue in itself. These policies may not hurt older Americans, like me, who bought their homes decades ago, but they will weigh heavily on the already hard-pressed next generation. All this for a policy that, despite its progressive support, will make more Americans more unhappy and less well-positioned to improve their condition in life.

CHAPTER SIX

A Screwed Generation?

Perhaps no single group is more challenged by America's emerging class order than the young generation. Pummeled by decreasing opportunity and high costs for everything from education to housing, the new generation has been called many things—millennials, generation Y, and, perhaps most insultingly, "echo boomers." Yet, the best moniker for Americans under 35 may well be the "screwed generation."

This a long way from the triumphant tone widely applied to the rise of the millennials, born after 1983 and the largest group in American history. Some, such as generational theorist Neil Howe, who, with William Strauss, was the prime architect of generational theory, described them as "the next great generation" who could transform the country in profoundly positive ways. Indeed the future for the young has been generally cast in very optimistic tones, as President Obama suggested when he stated, "We are the ones we've been waiting for."

Yet this conceit of a new "great generation" conflicts with the bitter economic reality faced by most millennials.[1] Although incomes have dropped for those under 55 over the past quarter century, the largest declines by far were for households under 34. The median net worth of people under 35, according to the U.S. Census, fell 37 percent just between 2005 and 2010; those over 65 took only a 13 percent hit.[2]

Those just entering the workplace now are particularly hard-pressed. Teen unemployment currently exceeds 24 percent; in 2011 in the nation's 100 largest metropolitan regions, it stands at roughly twice the rate in 2000.[3] Americans aged 18 to 19 are unemployed at the highest percentage in three decades.[4]

The harsh conditions they face are leading many of this generation not to "launch." Large numbers moved back home with their parents during the Great Recession and its aftermath; according to the 2013 Pew Study, 56 percent of 18-to-24-year-olds live with their parents. Almost one in three young people (between ages 18 and 34) has put off getting married or having a baby because of the weak economy and wages that have been dropping even for college graduates.

Perhaps more worrisome still, some, such as Aaron Renn, suggest that many millennials avoid work that they consider "McJobs" and may remain outside the labor force for a prolonged period. Rather than work in a fast food restaurant, many prefer simply to stay unattached to the labor force. By 2013, the labor participation rate among workers 16 to 19 had dropped to 35 percent from over 50 percent in 2000; those aged 20 to 24 saw their rate drop from 80 to 70 percent at the same time.[5]

What the new generation faces, at least in the immediate future, is not greatness, or even great relevance. Indeed their biggest challenge may be avoiding downward mobility. The wealth gap today between younger and older Americans now stands as the widest on record. The median net worth of households headed by someone 65 or older is 42 percent higher than in 1984, while the median net worth for younger-age households was $3,662, down by 68 percent from a quarter-century ago. Poverty among households under 35 is nearly twice that of those over 55.[6]

The Codger Economy

The older generation, particularly the boomers, notes a recent Pew study, were "the beneficiaries of good timing" in everything from a strong economy and a long rise in house prices to pensions and relatively inexpensive educations. In contrast, quick prospects for improvement are dismal for the younger generation. This can be seen in the results as the economy began to recover from the Great Recession. By 2013, income levels had returned for older Americans over 55, but remained 30 percent lower for households under 40, many of whom are members of generation X, the group between the boomers and the millennials.[7]

One key reason: many boomers are not leaving the workforce, forcing younger people to put careers on hold. Indeed, people over 55 are now the fastest-growing portion of the U.S. employed population and by 2020 will constitute 25 percent of the workforce, up from 19 percent in 2010.[8]

Some of this reflects choice among older workers but also the difficulties faced by less affluent boomers in saving for retirement. Nearly half of middle-class workers said they are not confident that they will be able to save enough to retire comfortably, according to a Wells Fargo survey of 1,000 workers between the ages of 25 and 75 with household incomes between $25,000 and $100,000. As a result, 34 percent said in 2013 that they plan to work until they're at least 80—that's up from 25 percent in 2011. An even larger percentage, 37 percent, said they will never retire and plan to work until they either get too sick or die.[9]

This trend can be seen in the shift of employment away from the young, which also reflects, to some extent, the growing numbers enrolled in higher education. Since 2008, the percentage of the workforce under 25 has dropped 13.2 percent, according to the Bureau of Labor Statistics, while that of people over 55 has risen by 7.6 percent. Among high school graduates in the classes of 2009–11, only 16 percent had full-time work, 22 percent worked part-time, with most wanting a full-time job.[10] Between 2000 and 2011, notes Brookings, both unemployment and underemployment among workers 20 to 24 roughly doubled. These trends, according to the U.S. Department of Labor, will continue, particularly for workers between 20 and 24, and will likely accelerate over the next decade.[11]

Overall, the young suffer stubbornly high unemployment rates—and an even higher incidence of underemployment. The unemployment rate for people between 18 and 29 is 12 percent in the United States, nearly 50 percent above the national average. That's a far cry from the fearsome 50 percent rate seen in Spain or Greece, the 40 percent rate in Italy, and the over 20 percent rate in France or the United Kingdom, but still well above the 8 percent rate in Germany.[12]

The screwed generation also enters adulthood loaded down by a mountain of boomer- and senior-incurred debt that spirals ever more out of control. Indeed, some, like Neil Howe, suggest that the "greed, shortsightedness, and blind partisanship" of the boomers, of which he is one, has "brought the global economy to its knees" and left the millennials holding the bag.[13]

Part of the problem lies with huge public debt. This constitutes a toxic legacy handed over to offspring who will have to pay it off in at least three ways: through higher taxes, less infrastructure and social spending, and, fatefully, the prospect of painfully slow growth for the foreseeable future.[14]

The pattern of indebtedness extends to local and state governments as well. The huge public employee pensions now driving many states and cities toward the netherworld of bankruptcy represent an extreme case of intergenerational transfer from the young to a retired population. Providing guaranteed generous benefits to older public workers while handing the financial upper echelon an opportunity to invest and manage their pensions constitutes what Walter Russell Mead has aptly called a "Wall Street boondoggle."[15]

The implications of low birth rates and a largely disengaged younger workforce can be seen in other advanced countries. In Japan, the red ink for the next generation comes in at over $95,000 a person. One nasty solution to pay for this growing debt is to increase taxes on both workers and consumers. Both Germany and Japan, which has considered steps to double its VAT rate, have been exploring new taxes to maintain the government, much of it due to the burdens of paying off boomer pensions.[16]

The Limits of Education

For generations, education has provided the key to upward mobility, but many coming of age today face both a rising burden for education and diminishing returns. The average student, according to *Forbes*, already carries $12,700 in credit card and other kinds of debt. But far more worrisome is student debt, which has grown consistently over the last few decades to an average of $27,000 per student and which now totals well over a trillion dollars. This indebtedness impacts a growing proportion of the youth population; the percentage of 25-year-olds with school debt has risen from roughly 25 percent in 2004 to close to 40 percent in 2012.[17]

At the core of the crisis facing the new generation lie two seemingly contradictory factors: the rising price of college and its increasingly poor returns. From the 1940s to the 1980s, tuition was relatively stable and a good investment. At a tuition cost of $750 ($7,200 current value) in the 1940s and $3,440 ($9,733 current value) in the 1980s, college was a viable option for even families of modest means. Today, four-year private colleges cost, on average, $129,700, while public in-state universities cost $38,300. The cost of college since 1978 has gone up three times faster than the rate of general inflation, and far more even than medical care. This has been worsened by lower levels of state support for public higher education, shifting more of the burden to students and their families.[18]

This debt often results from the conviction that only more and increasingly expensive education can guarantee a decent living for the young. And certainly having an education remains an important determinant of future earnings.[19] "Our generation decided to go to school and continue into even higher forms of education like Masters and PhD programs, thinking this will give us an edge," notes Lizzie Guerra, a recent graduate from the University of San Francisco. "However, we found ourselves incredibly educated but drowning in piles of student loans with a job market that still isn't hiring."[20]

Yet if education still pays a dividend, and it does, the payback for this expensive education seems increasingly limited given the costs. Over 43 percent of recent graduates now working, according to a 2012 report by the Heldrich Center for Workforce Development, labor at jobs that do not require a college education. Some 16 percent of bartenders and almost the same percentage of parking attendants, notes Ohio State Economics Professor Richard Vedder, have earned a Bachelor's degree or higher. Others have taken jobs as nannies.[21] Although a college education is clearly no requirement for such a job, the fact that so many graduates feel compelled to take them clearly reflects the dearth of high-paying jobs in the marketplace.

Particularly hard hit are those from less prestigious schools or with majors in the humanities and fields like law, notes a recent Pew study. In 2007, over 90 percent of law school graduates found jobs and salaries were soaring; by 2011, roughly half could find a job after finishing school. Indeed, many leading law firms have either reduced staff or stopped hiring, and several have gone out of business.[22]

The lack of opportunities for college graduates affects not only lawyers. Overall the incomes earned by graduates have dropped over the last decade by 11 percent for men and 7.6 percent for women. No big surprise, then, that the class of 2013 suffered the highest level of stress on record, according to an annual survey of college freshmen taken over the past quarter-century.[23]

As for the returns on education, a recent Rutgers University report found that barely half of all college graduates since 2006 had full-time jobs. And it's not getting better: those graduating since 2009 are three times more likely not to have found a full-time job than those from the classes of 2006 through 2008.[24]

This relative decline in the educational dividend, although made much worse by the Great Recession, also predates it. Since 1967, notes one 2010 study, the percentage of underemployed college graduates—those working well below their level of qualifications—has soared from roughly 10 percent to over 35 percent.[25]

The glut of college graduates reflects the difficulties facing a generation that, growing up in an era of relative prosperity, now finds the realities of life far more challenging than they were led to believe.[26] The millennials have frequently been told that they could pursue the fields that they "loved" and somehow make a living at it. Yet for many this has turned out to be a fairy tale, a life that can be afforded only by the rich. "'Do what you love' disguises the fact that being able to choose a career primarily for personal reward is a privilege, a sign of socioeconomic class," notes one observer.[27]

The disjunction between career choice and reality, then, is particularly intense for those who receive degrees from second- or third-tier institutions. What happens to the ever expanding crop of Latino studies majors, postmodern English graduates, and art historians? These kinds of degrees are, as the New York Times reported, ones that tend to earn graduates the least, while those that offer the most are largely at schools aimed at technology, mining, and other "hard skills."[28]

Confronting the grittier reality requires more emphasis on training for jobs that have significant and even growing demand. Even President Obama has poked fun of the proliferation of "art history majors."[29] Others might see in a more "basics"-oriented approach a suggestion of the infamous "tracking" system that was used to steer the most academically gifted minorities and working-class whites into manual professions.

Some progressives believe the solution lies in further subsidizing the current system, which after all helps maintain and expand the Clerisy. Yet in reality such an approach will only continue the current failures, with fewer students graduating with needed skills and more years of wasted effort. Replacing the financial burdens of parents and students by shifting them onto business and the taxpayer does not seem the best way to boost public support for education.[30]

Even worse, the more "enlightened" approach of stuffing more students into a system that, in the end, fails to prepare young people for the future, and lands them in debt, makes little sense. Today a record one in ten of recent college borrowers has defaulted on their debt, the highest level in a decade. With wages for college graduates on a downward slope, one has to wonder how many more will join them.[31]

Education and the Future of Class

Among its many effects, college debt seems likely to exacerbate the class divides in the future. Student debt is much more common in less affluent households; those whose parents could afford to pay for their education, at the very least, enter their careers unencumbered by the weight of obligations. "If you graduate with a B.A. or doctorate and you get the same job at the same place, you make the same amount of money," said William Elliott III, director of the Assets and Education Initiative at the University of Kansas. "But that money will actually mean less to you in the sense of accumulating assets in the long term."[32]

The proliferation of those graduate degrees also will be felt among those without such educations. Today, high school graduates increasingly find themselves competing with college graduates for basic jobs in service businesses. In 2011, almost sixty percent of recent college graduates were underemployed, notes the New York Fed. Many of them are taking jobs that previously went to high school graduates or even dropouts. In the long run this will create a crisis at the bottom end of the labor market. By 2020, notes McKinsey, there will be six million more high school dropouts than jobs for them.[33]

But it's not just the dropouts who are in peril. By 2013, the unemployment rate for recent high school graduates not enrolled in school was 34.4 percent, compared with 17.7 percent for recent graduates. Many of these non-college-educated youths only work part-time where much of the employment gain has taken place. Many younger people, particularly without college degrees, have to wonder if gainful full-time employment is in their future.[34]

This could presage the expansion of a class of permanently unemployed or underemployed young people, never a good development for society as a whole. One early harbinger, observes author Walter Russell Mead, may be the recent rise of random criminality, often racially tinged, taking place in American cities such as Chicago, Milwaukee, and Philadelphia.[35] This phenomenon is not just seen in inner cities or in areas where the economy has been in decline for decades.[36]

The End of Intergenerational Optimism?

Once known for their optimism, many millennials, not surprisingly, are becoming somewhat less sanguine about the future, particularly in comparison with their parents. According to a Rutgers study, 56 percent of recent high school graduates feel they would not be financially more successful than their parents; only 14 percent thought they would do better. College education does not seem to make a difference: 58 percent of recent graduates feel they will not do as well as the previous generation; only 16 percent thought they would do better.[37]

The rise of pessimism about the future—even greater among the parents of millennials, as shown earlier—marks a break with the historic notion of intergenerational mobility that has animated the more vibrant societies even in the earliest times. In ancient cultures, the desire to place one's children—historically boys—in a more socially and economically secure place drove much of what accounted for human progress. In Roman society, law fostered the growth of the patriarchal land-owning class, which spearheaded the spread of the empire. The importance of kinship and securing a better place for the next generation shaped social development from China to the Middle East.[38]

This sense of intergenerational responsibility was present in other cultures as well. The great Arab historian Ibn Khaldun saw an ebb and flow in "the shadow and power of group feeling"—lodged in clan and kinship relationships—as shaping powerful dynasties, some linked directly to the family of the prophet.[39] Three of Confucianism's five key relationships were familial, led by the all-important father-son tie.[40] Individual achievement and struggles were encapsulated within the context of the family; one never took credit or shouldered blame alone.[41]

The notion of passing on one's fortune, or preparing the next generation for the future, was also among the animating features in the emergence of early capitalism and the passing of feudalism. In the Middle Ages, when opportunity for upward mobility was sharply limited, many sought out lives as priests or nuns. As many as one in ten women in sixteenth-century Florence were celibate.[42] In contrast, the modern European concept of family arose with the rise of capitalism and the Protestant Reformation; strictures on marriage to cousins helped moved society from clan to the slimmer nuclear family.[43] The family, united by mutual affection and with the active presence of women and children, emerged in the late sixteenth and early seventeenth centuries.

This reality was painted lovingly by Rembrandt and the other Dutch masters. Here, Phillipe Aries notes, "the child has taken a central place in the family."[44] The family stood at the center of enterprise, and raising children for a better future evolved into a task undertaken by striving families in what Simon Schama labeled "the Republic of Children."[45]

In the emergence of capitalism, the family firm, united by what two historians characterize as "internal loyalties," was the incubator of the first great trading companies. Those who drove Britain's "Age of Ambition" in the sixteenth century were particularly concerned with "family feeling" and the advancement of their heirs and relations.[46] Much the same can be said of Britain's offspring in the early United States, where, as Tocqueville noted, sentiment about family was one of the primary restraints on excessive individualism, and where the lack of aristocratic privilege and set class positions granted to family relations "an energy and sweetness" unseen in European nations.[47]

The notion that things will improve for the next generation—and that parents would work to assure that result—has been intrinsic to the American experience.[48] This ethos survived the disruptions of the Industrial Age, the Depression, and the Second World War, as well as the entrance, en masse, of women into the workforce. After dropping in the 1950s, starting in the 1960s more families began to depend on women's earning. In 1967, for example, barely a third worked outside the home but by 2000 barely one-third of children under six in married households had a stay-at-home mother.[49]

The Decline of Marriage and the Failure to Launch

Although the entrance of women into the workplace made it possible for families to support their children's education, the institution of marriage has also begun to weaken. Recent decades have seen what European scholar Angélique Janssens has described as "the deinstitutionalization of marriage." This has resulted in "the emancipation of individual members from the family" but also in parents feeling a less keen sense of responsibility for their children—and has led many others not to have children at all, notes the Center for Work-Life Policy. Indeed, for many unmarried women, according to a 2008 Wisconsin study, the very fact of having a child increases a woman's chances of being poor.[50]

At the same time, many in the current generation do not have to give up their sex lives if they remain single. Middle-class women—and their male counterparts—in their twenties and thirties, suggests Stanford sociologist Michael Rosenfeld, can enjoy "a second adolescence," seeking "new experiences" with a series of partners of considerable diversity.[51] Kate Bolick, writing in the *Atlantic*, believes that many of these accomplished women will do without long-term committed relationships, choosing instead "a room of one's own," a place where a single woman can live and thrive as herself.[52]

Of course single men can enjoy the same lifestyle of what may be seen as permanent adolescence. Yet surprisingly, perhaps, women may be even more likely than men to view childlessness favorably, suggests a University of Florida study.[53] According to the study's author, Assistant Professor of Sociology at the University of Florida, Gainesville, Tanya Koropeckyj-Cox, this is particularly true among educated women who regard the costs related to childbearing as "potentially lost income, promotions, and opportunities for career advancement."[54]

To these existing social trends, the weak economy has led many millennials to delay their transition into adulthood. By Census estimates the percentage of young adults living at home has more than doubled to over 20 percent, and by 2020, according to some projections, it will increase even more.[55]

A Generation of Serfs

Not surprisingly, the millennial generation also has the lowest percentage of homeowners of any generation in recent American history. Since

1970, according to the Census, the percentage of households under 34 who own their home has dropped from 41 to 32 percent, with most of the drop coming after 2007.[56]

Some "new economy" theorists insist that detaching the young from property ownership will lead to a more flexible and buoyant economy, allowing these young workers a greater degree of personal flexibility and geographic mobility.[57] In the so-called "creative age," homeownership is regarded as "overrated" and the proper aspiration is to live in a dense, expensive city, such as San Francisco or Manhattan, where only a fraction of the population can conceivably own their place of residence.[58]

This marks a significant shift from previous generations. Since World War II the expectation of each generation has been to own property, preferably a single-family house. The large majority of boomers became homeowners during the Reagan–Clinton era.

Yet it is increasingly fashionable to insist that this "dream" must be expunged. Instead, suggests Morgan Stanley's Oliver Chang, we could see the emergence of a "rentership" society, which sees a long-term decline in personal homeownership and fulfills an almost Marxian dialectic in which ownership of property concentrates in ever fewer hands.[59]

As seen earlier, much of the advocacy for delaying or abandoning homeownership comes from the gentry class. As one Texas architect points out, they "have the least to lose" from higher housing prices and forced densification, as they already live large, in spaces that can accommodate families if they wish to have them.[60]

In contrast, present economic conditions have forced many younger people to delay or even abandon the old middle-class dream.[61] The boomers, chief beneficiaries of rising home prices, have contributed, albeit unconsciously, to this phenomenon. Many, particularly in places like California, have supported regulations that make new home-building difficult. "In large part," writes one southern California analyst, "boomers in their golden sarcophagus have forgotten about their offspring."[62]

The long-term implications for class relations of this shift from ownership could be profound. In the future, it is not inconceivable that, in many markets, only the affluent—and those who inherit—who will be able to own homes. This has been the predominant way that the Yeomanry develops assets and establishes its independence. Without property, they essentially work to pay someone else's mortgage. In many cities, affordable apartments can be had if your parents bought early or, in places like New York, you are able to use your parent's rent-controlled units, which are often several times cheaper than market-rate ones.

For those who don't have such advantages, some have proposed a return to the boarding house, suggesting that we hurl away "middle-class norms of decency" governing housing and go back to the ad hoc ways in which many were forced to live during the nineteenth and early twentieth centuries.[63] If current trends continue, when millennials move out of their parents' houses, many may be forced to live in apartments they do not own, and probably never will have the chance to own. "I'm hoping that the Millennial Generation doesn't set its sights on home-ownership as a benchmark of economic stability," sociologist Katherine Newman suggests, "because it's going to be out of reach for so many of them."[64]

A Coming Birth Dearth?

Unable to afford a home or get a good job, more young people, wherever they live, are postponing marriage and childbearing as well.[65] Despite a total rise in population of twenty-seven million, there were actually fewer births in 2010 than there were ten years earlier.[66]

Over time, this "failure to launch" among millennials could lead historically fecund America to experience, albeit to a lesser degree, the kind of demographic disaster already evident in parts of Europe and Japan. The millennial generation's trajectory is particularly trou-blesome since the decline in births has been especially severe among women in their mid- and late 20s, while older women have increased their birth rates. But as families start later, they also tend to have fewer children, and it is, after all, the young who are able to bear the most children.[67]

This reluctance to have children—including the common choice to have none—could impact millennials in the coming decades. For one thing, there may not be the sort of support for education and other crit-ical services that occurred both in the original baby boom as well as in the second "echo" boom when that large generation started to have children. If the percentage of people who have children at home con-tinues to decline, it could effect all sorts of policy choices. As Austrian demographer Wolfgang Lutz has pointed out, the shift to an increasingly childless society creates "self-reinforcing mechanisms" that make child-lessness, singleness, or one-child families increasingly predominant.[68]

Perhaps more disturbing, it is largely individuals with higher incomes and skills who are the ones most frequently putting off having kids. The birthrate for those making under $10,000 is almost twice as high as for those with incomes over $75,000.[69] By having kids, these poorer and less prepared parents all too often doom the next generation by passing on poverty to them. In this way "generation screwed" could end up adding to the next wave of the American proletariat.

Prospects for Millennials

Unlike previous generations, who were often able to look forward to a better and more independent future, the millennials are faced with the prospect of inhabiting a country where the Yeomanry shrinks, family fades, poverty expands, and the power of inherited wealth grows. This world is already taking shape and could worsen due to the huge increase in government debt, which all but assures both higher taxes and the likelihood of reduced services.[70]

This prospect conforms to the mainstream economic view of the American future. Since the financial panic of 2008, "the new normal" has become the conventional wisdom. Coined by former PIMCO executive Mohamed El-Erian, the term has become a widely accepted description of the future. Bill Gross, the company's Managing Director, has characterized "the new normal" as one "of muted western growth, high unemployment and relatively orderly delevering."[71] Another key mainstream writer, economist Robert Samuelson, believes we are in the midst "a generational war" in which the young are destined to be losers in the "withering of the affluent society." As he puts it: "For millions of younger Americans—say, those 40 and under—living better than their parents is a pipe dream. They won't."[72]

Some financial experts believe that future generations, by lacking stable employment or any kind of financial equity, will become more dependent on the kinds of instruments, such as prepaid credit cards and payday loans, that have historically been associated with the poor.[73] The future facing this generation, suggests the *American Prospect*, is an unemployment rate twice the national average and "flat or declining wages."[74]

American Herbivores

Some commentators on millennials suggest that these downwardly mobile trends are accepted, and even embraced, by the new generation. Whereas previous generations of adults wished for their children to do better than themselves, many pundits increasingly have pushed a more déclassé vision, with fewer families, more singles, and less focus on upward mobility. Indeed some, particularly some among the environmental community, actually embrace the idea that most people in richer countries should adopt this vision. Millennials, by not buying homes and cars, and perhaps also not growing into family life, are portrayed by the green magazine *Grist* as "a hero generation"—one that will march willingly, even enthusiastically, to a downscale future.[75]

In one article, a writer wrote hopefully of the rise of a generation that will not, as did previous generations, get on with their lives, buying cars or anything outside of electronic gadgets. They will do this, they note, for not just economic but environmental and philosophical reasons.[76] "We know the financial odds are stacked against us, and instead of trying to beat them, we'd rather give the finger to the whole rigged system," the millennial author concludes.[77]

This diminished worldview recalls the devolution that has already taken place in Japan, particularly among that country's younger male generation. Growing up in a period of tepid economic growth, a declining labor market, and a loss of overall competitiveness, Japan's "herbivores" are more interested in comics, computer games, and socializing through the Internet than in a career or a relationship with the opposite sex.[78] Marriage and family have increasingly little appeal to them.[79]

The figure is even higher (59 percent) for females in the same age group. The percentage of sexually active female university students, according to the Japanese Association for Sex Education, has fallen from 60 percent in 2005 to 47 percent last year. There's a bigger issue here than overly tame libidos, suggests sociologist Mika Toyota. Once intimate relationships are now being replaced by ad hoc arrangements based on common interests. Not surprising then that passion is replaced by peer relationship among unattached singles. A survey in 2013 by the Japan Family Planning Association (JFPA) found that 45 percent of women aged 16 to 24 "were not interested in or despised sexual contact."[80]

Although some hail the rise of herbivores as a model for a less aggressive existence,[81] the long-term prognosis for such a society is not a good one. Japan is a country where sales of adult diapers exceed those of child diapers, and the workforce and consumer market is destined to fall dramatically over the coming decades. By 2050, according to government projections, the country may have more people over 80 than under 15.[82]

What Do Millennials Want?

But will young Americans prove ready to move away from the economic playing field and onto the herbivore pastureland? Although they differ in many ways from previous generations, most millennials clearly do not aspire to the ideal of singleness and childlessness embraced by more radical boomer enthusiasts. Nearly four in five millennials still express a desire to have children, and close to 80 percent, according to some recent estimates, will have offspring while a vast majority will get married in their lifetimes.[83] For them, the future being projected is less a matter of choice than necessity.

No doubt the prospects for homeownership will be tough in the years ahead. But it is simply not the case that most millennials do not desire the same things as previous generations, as generational chroniclers Morley Winograd and Mike Hais note in their work. Survey research finds that 84 percent of those aged 18 to 34 who are currently renting say that they intend to buy a home even if they cannot currently afford to do so, and 64 percent said it was "very important" to have an opportunity to own their own home.[84] A *Better Homes and Gardens* survey found that three in four viewed homeownership as "a key indicator of success."[85]

And where do millennials see their dream house? Manhattanite Leigh Gallagher, author of *The End of the Suburbs*, asserts with certitude that "millennials hate the suburbs" and prefer more eco-friendly, singleton-dominated urban environments.[86] Yet according to research at Frank Magid and Associates, 43 percent of millennials describe the suburbs as their "ideal place to live," compared to just 31 percent of older generations. Even though big cities are often preferred among college graduates in their 20s, only 17 percent of millennials say they want to settle permanently in one.[87]

The question of whether millennials will be forced to abandon the ownership dream, it turns out, has less to do with choice, as purported by some new urbanists, than with economic conditions. They could face that prospect in many ways—instead of living like their parents, they could adopt the austere lifestyle of their grandparents—but this more likely reflects their economic circumstances than downwardly mobile aspirations.[88]

None of this suggests, as some social conservatives might hope, that the Ozzie and Harriet family is about to make a major comeback. For one thing, millennials will likely get hitched and have children later than previous generations; their marriages will probably also be less traditional in how they operate, suggest Hais and Winograd.[89]

At the same time, if they get their chance, millennials will not recreate their families or their communities entirely in their parents' images. They may, for example, be more willing to customize their residences for their own unique needs or for greater energy efficiency, and they may place greater emphasis on "technology capabilities" than on a larger kitchen or more traditional suburban accoutrements.[90]

The key question, then, is not whether millennials wish to abandon ambition, but whether conditions that allow for upward mobility for the next generation can be restored.

If not, the next generation faces the prospect of becoming the first in American history to experience constant, pervasive downward mobility. This will impact not just this generation but whole industries, notably homebuilding and the manufacturing of household goods, and this impact will extend to the entire economy. A strong market for single-family homes, driven by new households, remains one of the best guarantors of long-term economic growth; Moody Analytics estimates that a single-family home generates roughly twice as many jobs as an apartment. Persistent slowness in new home demand and a decline in new households may seem a boon to some in the Clerisy and on Wall Street, but for the overall economy the lack of new demand reduces growth for a host of products and services, many of which employ the middle and working classes.[91]

Some urban theorists, greens, real estate speculators, and financiers may regard this downward trend as a net positive, but it is hard to see a pleasant result from an entire generation facing downward mobility. This is not the future most millennials want, or will embrace as they get older. Whatever party or policy agenda can find ways to restore their prospects may ultimately win the support of this troubled, but still far from hopeless, generation.

CHAPTER SEVEN

Renewing Aspiration

In the media and academia, as well as across broad ideological lines, America's pundits foresee generally dismal, downwardly mobile futures for the country's middle and working class. In contrast to previous generations, who generally did far better than their predecessors, the current generations, outside the very rich, do indeed find themselves locked in a struggle to carve out the kind of economic opportunities and access to property that had become accepted norms for Americans throughout the past century.

This deep-seated social change raises a profound dilemma for business. Either the private sector must find a way to boost economic opportunity, or political pressure seems likely to implement fiscal, regulatory, or tax policies that will order redistribution from above. It is doubtful that the majority of Americans will continue to support an economic system that seems to benefit only a relative few. More dire still, as one journalist asks, if America today suffers the kind of inequality that ravaged pre-revolutionary France, "are the bread riots finally coming?"[1]

The class divides stem not only from the concentration of wealth and power but also from the persistence of weak economic growth. By 2020, according to the Economic Policy Institute, almost 30 percent of American workers are expected to hold low-wage jobs—defined as earnings at or below the poverty line—to support a family of four. Due to the combination of high debt and low wages, some projections suggest millennials may have to work until their early 70s.[2]

These prospects make understandable the efforts being touted by neo-populist groups on the left and the right to employ political pressure to assure a decent quality of life. This has sparked the rise of ideologically robust liberals, like New York Mayor Bill de Blasio, as well as initiatives in a series of smaller liberal cities, such as Seattle, to push measures that mandate higher wages and benefits for workers. In most cases, these are the very places, often quite wealthy in aggregate, where the middle class has generally shrunk, while public employee unions, academics, and other members of the Clerisy have gained the preponderance of political power.[3]

The same sense of limited opportunity also explains the popularity of libertarian and Tea Party activism on the right. Instead of state intervention to correct inherent flaws in capitalism, frustrated members of the middle and working class have been attracted to the idea that removing barriers to economic growth will increase social mobility more effectively than redistribution by political fiat. Yet economic arguments that could generate more widespread support have been married with increasingly unpopular, often backward-looking social agendas that have allowed them to be portrayed by the Clerisy as a fringe movement.

Consequently, the new progressive politics of inequality have become the primary themes of the nation's political leaders and the Clerisy. Oddly enough, much of the thinking behind this new focus is drawn primarily from European models, even as Europe's dismal prospects have inspired the lowest levels of political support in several decades.[4] In his influential book *Capital in the Twenty-First Century*, French economist Thomas Piketty argues powerfully that the only way to confront increasing inequality and prevent deeper social fracturing is to expand the "social state" that forcibly redistributes wealth. In his mind, economic growth, traditionally a prime source of social uplift, is little more than an "illusory" solution. Rather than stoke growth to create opportunity, Piketty looks to governmental action to enforce greater equality. Financed by taxes on wealth, the "social state" would not only curb the rich but also provide the Clerisy with even more power to administer and direct its expansion.

Piketty's acolytes, like the liberal journalist Dean Baker, rightfully favor attempts to curb crony capitalist finance. Yet, characteristically of the Clerisy, he largely ignores the new tech and media Oligarchs, who arguably represent the most heavily concentrated, powerful, and politically ascendant business interests in the world. A wealth tax that ignored such enormous concentrations of economic and political power, even if they shrewdly support "progressive" political movements, would have limited effect even if such a measure could be implemented on a national or global scale.[5]

There is little reason to think that redistribution by the state, which would certainly help some, would improve material conditions for much of the middle class, and it might end up expanding the permanent underclass of technologically obsolete and/or economically superfluous dependents. The fifty-year war on poverty in the United States, for example, initially helped reduce the percentage of the poor, but, due in part to a weaker economy, it has achieved few gains since the 1960s. Some significant progress in poverty reduction, at least among those working, have come when both the economy and the job market expands, as occurred during both the Reagan and Clinton eras. Clearly, as these two generally successful presidents recognized, the best antidote to poverty remains a robust job market.

Yet even this progress has not helped the "poorest of the poor," many of whom are marginally connected to the workplace. Indeed, since 1980 the percentage of people living in "deep poverty"—those living 50 percent below the official poverty line—has expanded dramatically.[6] Despite $750 billion spent annually on welfare programs, up 30 percent since 2008, a record 46 million Americans were in poverty in 2012.[7] It is possible that, as Franklin Roosevelt warned, a system of unearned payments, no matter how well intended, can serve as "a narcotic, a subtle destroyer of the human spirit,"[8] and reduce incentives for the recipients to better their lives.

Particularly revealing have been the generally meager gains made by ethnic minorities. Despite the benefits of government programs such as affirmative action, African Americans have not expanded their share of the middle class in recent decades.[9] Indeed, racial and ethnic economic disparities are growing. The black unemployment rate remains more than double the white jobless rate and reaches forty percent among youths.[10]

Similarly, Hispanics, the nation's largest minority, have also done poorly in recent years and, according to Pew, now suffer a 28 percent poverty rate in the nation, the highest of all ethnic groups and well over two and half times that of whites. Latino poverty rates have soared toward historic highs after dropping significantly between 1990 and 2007. More distressing still, child poverty among Latinos has risen to record highs, increasing from 28 percent in 2007 to 35 percent in 2010. Overall six million Latino children, many of them the offspring of recent immigrants, live in poverty, and they now represent a larger population of poor kids than either whites or African Americans.[11]

The activist welfare-based philosophy, or Piketty's ever expanding "social state," following the European model, would likely include not only historically poor populations but also part-time workers, perpetual students, and service employees living hand to mouth, who can make ends meet largely only if taxpayers underwrite their housing, transportation, and other necessities.[12] This trend toward an expansive welfare regime could be bolstered by falling rates of labor participation, which have dropped to the lowest levels in at least twenty-five years and show no signs of an immediate turnaround.[13]

The European experience also provides little support for the benefits of redistribution given the persistently high rates of unemployment, particularly among the young, across most of the EU. Indeed much of the continent's youth is widely described as "the lost generation."[14] Pervasive inequality and limited social mobility have been well documented in larger European countries, such as France, which has among the world's most evolved welfare states.[15] This is even true in Scandinavia, often held up as the ultimate exemplar of egalitarianism. It is true that the Nordic countries have much to recommend themselves—including aspects of their political economy, like their skilled worker training programs[16]— but these policies have not prevented the emergence of rapidly growing inequality there. Indeed, over the past fifteen years, the gap between the wealthy and other classes has increased in Sweden four times more rapidly than in the United States. This pattern was widely felt across the high-income world. A 2008 BBC poll found that two-thirds of people in the OECD countries felt that "the economic developments of the last few years" had not been shared fairly. This is even more true of fast-rising developing countries such as China, India, and Mexico, and it increasingly shapes political discourse in these countries.[17]

To be sure, "progressive," or even ostensibly socialist, approaches can be said to have ameliorated the worst impact on the lower-income people in many countries. But under left-wing government—such as the Socialists in France, New Labour in Britain, and most recently the Obama Administration in the United States—the class chasms have increased markedly. This pattern also occurred in these countries during more conservative rule. In the absence of a focus on how to grow economies more rapidly and broadly, both predominant political philosophies increasingly fall short.[18]

Why the American Dream Is Not Dead

Maintaining the prospect of upward mobility is central to the very idea of America. For generations, the surplus working-class populations of Scandinavia, like those of Latin American and other nations, have flocked to North America or Australia in search of opportunities unavailable in their home countries. In contrast, there remain few places for America's aspirational classes to go. And critically, the United States and other historically aspirational nations consist of an amalgam of highly skilled and lower skilled classes with widely varying ethnic and national backgrounds. The signature economic reality of this country is risk and opportunity. America is simply not well suited, even in the best of conditions, to become a small, tidy, steady-state welfare society, a giant Norway.[19]

But is the die already cast, so that even the idea of restoring wide prosperity and property ownership now seems absurd? Much of conventional opinion on the right generally embraces the idea of a "new normal" and certainly has little appetite, perhaps outside the early Tea Party, to confront either the old oligarchy or even the new one. Most Republicans, particularly in the Senate, embraced the bailout of the large financial institutions, the very essence of the crony capitalism that favors large, established, and connected institutions over smaller ones.[20]

But such negativity and defeatism is not necessary, given the basic strengths of the U.S. economy. The American economy may not possess the "almost limitless resiliency" claimed by Kiplinger during the mid-80s Reagan-era boom, but its capacity for renewal is still much greater than is widely believed.[21] The notion that America faces a negative trajectory has been commonplace since the time of the Depression. Similar thoughts dominated the last long-standing period of economic stagnation, the 1970s, when income, innovation, and economic growth all slowed. The relative decline of America—compared to Europe or

Asia—has been predicted not only by left-leaning academics but also by prominent, well-connected economists and even such moguls as Bill Gates and Warren Buffett.[22]

These predictions have turned out to be wildly off base. Despite the rise, first, of Europe after World War II, then of Japan in the late 1970s, followed by the rest of East Asia and now China, the United States has maintained its share of the world's GDP at roughly 20 percent since the 1970s. By 2013, according to a United Nations survey, the United States and China were among the only major countries with expanding industrial production. Whole industries—notably technology—thought to be lost to Japanese and other Asian competitors have recentralized in the United States. In 1990, six of the world's top ten semiconductor companies were Japanese. But, contradicting the claims of inevitable Japanese technological hegemony, by 2011, five U.S. chip companies dominated the top ten while only two Japanese companies, Toshiba and Renesas, were on it. And their combined revenue in 2012 was less than half that of world leader Intel's $49.7 billion.[23]

Rather than a permanent condition of slow growth, the United States could be on the cusp of another period of broad-based expansion, spurred in part by its rapidly growing natural gas and oil production.[24] The current energy and industrial boom, notes Joe Kaeser, the president of Siemens, "is a once-in-a-lifetime moment." Cheap and abundant natural gas is luring investment from manufacturers from Europe and Asia, who must depend on often insecure and more expensive sources of energy.[25] Others are investing heavily in farmland and other real estate, evidence not of America's decline but of a reprise of the patterns of investment that led to the country's great expansion in the nineteenth century.[26]

How Capitalism Reinvents Itself

In many ways, then, the future debate is less about America's capacity for perpetual renewal—what Japanese scholar Fuji Kamiya once called *sokojikara*, or a latent power to overcome seemingly insurmountable obstacles—than about whether this inherent renewal can occur under the emerging class order.[27] The most fundamental challenge facing the United States is the growing disenfranchisement of the middle and working classes from the benefits of economic activity. This is evidenced by declining incomes or, as has been most striking in recent years, the unprecedented propensity to simply quit the labor force. Briefly put, the current capitalist system tends to favor and encourage transactions among investors and asset inflation, rather than broad-based growth that rewards people adequately for their labor. "For the past 10, 20, 30 years, capital has moved away from labor and toward corporations and investors," notes PIMCO founder Bill Gross. "I'm not sure capitalism can thrive in a system in which... [labor] has a declining interest, in terms of percentage of the pie. Then ultimately the pie itself can't grow, because consumption can't be supported."[28]

Fortunately, the capitalist system, particularly one under democratic control, allows for the possibility of reform. An example is Great Britain, the homeland of the industrial revolution. In response to mass poverty and serious public health challenges during the nineteenth century, social reform movements—usually led by the clergy and a rising professional class—organized to address the most obvious defects caused by economic change. Reform legislation, such as the Municipal Corporations Act in 1835 and the first Public Health Act by Parliament in 1848, brought more efficient administration to the sprawling, chaotic cities. Reformers established parks and washhouses for the poor. New sanitary measures and improvements in medicine lowered urban rates of mortality. Crime, once rampant, dropped dramatically.[29]

It may be one of the great ironies of history that at the very time that Karl Marx was composing *Das Kapital* in the library at the British Museum, life was beginning to improve for the British working class. Rather than having "exhausted its resources" and precipitated all-out class war, inequality, so evident in mid-nineteenth-century Britain, was beginning to narrow through natural economic forces and the growing power of working-class organizations.[30] The working-class revolution in Britain, which Friedrich Engels insisted "must come," never did.[31]

Indeed by mid-century, even ordinary Britons were beginning to enjoy the benefits of mechanization. Spurred by the growth of trade unions, wages, particularly for skilled workers, began to rise consistently.[32] Working-class consumers, who in the past could hardly have hoped to afford them, were able to purchase such items as stockings or dining utensils. Once unthinkable, social mobility became more common, as skilled tradespeople and other industrial laborers ascended into the middle class; elite universities admitted their children; a handful became great lords without proper titles, and some, by marriage or through influence, acquired noble status.[33]

Similar patterns can be seen in the United States, albeit somewhat later in time. The first progressives, for example, did not seek to undermine capitalism as such, but rather to restrain the rise of industrial oligarchies so reminiscent of the present era. Many feared the economy had taken, as the Beards put it, "an alarming turn," concentrating wealth, corrupting politics, and widening societal divides. Woodrow Wilson warned of the outsized influence of "combined capitalists," who had manipulated the nation's political and legal structures. Fear of being overwhelmed by oligarchs informed much of the emerging policy agenda—including assaults on "trusts"—enacted or advocated by the progressive movement. Yet progressives generally also saw themselves as protecting capitalism from both capitalists and those who wished to create a more socialistic system.[34]

Similarly, the Depression, brought on by what Keynes called "a crisis of abundance," was addressed more by conscious measures, over the next few decades, to spur mass demand than by relying on redistribution. In ways far more wide-ranging than the earlier reform era, the New Deal, and then the Second World War against the Axis powers, expanded government support for public works, education, and housing. It also encouraged dispersed property ownership. The government, having won a global war and then engaged in a cold war against the Soviet Union, greatly expanded its economic role, including in critical areas of research and development.[35] But this state expansion was generally aimed at increasing economic opportunity—for example, by developing technologies that could stimulate new industrial sectors, promote the growth of new firms, and create new wealth—rather than simply transferring income from one group to another.

Whatever criticism can be made of mid-century America, during this period the nation transformed what had been a strongly unequal country into one where the blessings of prosperity were more broadly shared and the opportunity for improvement extended far more widely than in previous generations. In the 1950s the bottom 90 percent held two-thirds of the wealth. Today they barely can claim half.[36]

Overcoming the Era of Limits

The shifting attitude toward economic growth, particularly among the Clerisy, today makes a similar improvement more problematic. Whatever their politics, America's mid-century leaders believed in economic growth as the best way to improve the conditions of the middle and working classes. Even many conservationists of this era did not oppose growth with the religious vehemence of today's environmental groups. As historian David Nye notes, their goals were to "restore" nature from abuses by private enterprise while allowing the continued expansion of industry dependent on resources.[37]

In more recent times, however, American progressivism has moved toward a feudalistic worldview that favors what Adam Smith called "a stationary state," which he said is necessarily characterized by "declining melancholy" among the bulk of the populace. This is most notable in the development of the ecology movement after World War II. As early as 1970, noted author James Ridgeway, ecologists were arguing "in radical, indeed revolutionary, terms for re-organization of society, development of a new political economy which would eliminate ruinous competition," with the goal of administering society so people "can better accommodate themselves to the planet."[38]

The 1972 report *The Limits to Growth*, predicting persistent and deepening shortages of raw materials starting as early as the 1980s, marks the most evident shift toward an anti-growth orientation in progressive politics.[39] Protecting the environment was no longer a matter of improving technology or industrial methods to minimize physical impacts associated with growth; instead, the very operation of the economy was the evil that must be restrained. "The discovery that the earth's ecology will no longer sustain an indefinite expansion of productive forces," suggested Christopher Lasch in 1991, "deals the final blow to the belief in progress."[40]

To a remarkable extent, however, *The Limits to Growth* proved to be not prophetic but anachronistic. Like the predictions of mass starvation die-offs made in Paul Ehrlich's *The Population Bomb*, the vast majority of the report's predictions, as the environmental author Bjørn Lonborg has noted, have proved to be "spectacularly wrong."[41]

Yet being wrong seems not to have altered the widespread conviction that economic growth constitutes more of a threat than a benefit to society. The traditional focus on enhancing social mobility and opportunity as core progressive values has been supplanted by a stronger emphasis on limiting impacts on the environment, even at the expense of broad social uplift. This trend, of course, is now most evident among climate change activists. The *Guardian*'s George Monbiot perhaps put it best, suggesting that the era of economic growth needs to come to an inevitable denouement; that "the age of heroism" will be followed by the decline of the "expanders" and the rise of the "restrainers."

Similarly influential figures such as John Holdren, President Obama's Science Advisor, have explicitly argued that "de-development," rather than growth, must be the nation's economic priority.[42] But decades of efforts to restrain economic activity, often for laudable objectives, have imposed enormous costs on the working class, particularly in Europe and North America. Tragically, these costs will have little effect on certain of the Clerisy's goals, such as carbon emission reductions, as long as China, India, Russia, and other countries continue to be unwilling or unable to similarly constrain their own economic growth and consumption.[43]

In this regard, as architect and author Austin Williams notes, sustainability "is an insidiously dangerous concept, masquerading as progress." It poses an agenda that restricts industry, housing, and incomes in a manner that severely undermines social aspiration. Indeed, Williams argues that the Clerisy's attitude toward growth seeks to impose "a poverty of ambition" on most of the less fortunate by constraining economic activity and progress. These are the very things that have been the drivers of unprecedented social achievement in the West, as well as, more recently, in East Asia.

In this sense, he notes, "the ideology of sustainability is unsustainable" and likely to further worsen class relations.[44] A huge shift to renewable fuels, for example, could quadruple the cost of energy, forcing a large percentage of the population into "fuel poverty." Loss of jobs in trucking and manufacturing would hit blue-collar workers and neighborhoods hardest, according to most studies. How this jibes with meeting the high welfare and retirement costs with an urban population increasingly dominated by immigrants, their offspring, and poor children seems problematic at least.[45]

To "save the planet," the Clerisy and most of their tech Oligarch allies seek to limit consumption by eliminating cheaper energy sources in favor of expensive, highly subsidized renewables, or the chance to profit from various mitigation matters. This strategy works well for all partners of the new ruling synergy, although not for the majority. Tech Oligarchs can invest in renewables with the guarantee of public subsidy;[46] the trustifarians promote subsidies and renewable use through their foundations and feel personally vindicated for their efforts; the media Clerisy can celebrate the enlightening shift toward sustainable power; academics receive grants and churn out studies in support; while the lawyers and the upper bureaucracy achieve ever greater job security to administer the entire program. Some of these measures may indeed prove necessary, but the role of special interests, and the implications for class, need to be seriously factored into how policies can be implemented without stunting social mobility or threatening democracy itself.

This confluence of private interest, public power, and the Clerisy— something that alarmed progressives in the Gilded Age—is particularly notable in the valley of the Oligarchs. Valley firms have also been prominent in backing efforts by green activists, such as Bill McKibben, that have relentlessly sought to revoke the "social license" of big oil, as occurred with tobacco companies and with firms that did business in apartheid South Africa. Ironically, besides Valley sources, McKibben's 350.org, dedicated to undermining fossil fuels, is also supported by the Rockefeller Brothers Fund and the Rockefeller Family Fund, the name perhaps most intimately linked to the rise of big oil.[47] Backing for measures to tax oil firms in order to help fund green energy ventures have, not surprisingly, enlisted strong support from firms such as Google and from venture capitalists, all of whom have made heavy investments in alternative energy.[48]

For many in the Clerisy, state expansion to restrain consumption and production in the name of sustainability is an overwhelming ambition. Perhaps nowhere is there greater dissonance between the populace and the leaders of the new class order than in perceptions of the desirability of economic growth and widespread social opportunity. When asked what mattered more to them, most Americans put a greater emphasis on economic growth than on redistribution, noted a 2014 study conducted by a the Global Strategy Group, a Democratic consulting firm. Polls of popular opinion in the United States and the United Kingdom find key ecological concerns such as climate change well down on the list, behind such issues as the economy, immigration, crime, unemployment, and even the state of morality. What Americans wanted most, noted one leading political commentator, was "an economic boom."[49]

The Growth Imperative

Despite the widespread suspicion of growth among the Clerisy, an expanding economy remains the best way to stave off the emergence of a neo-feudal order. Humans have a demonstrated power, as Marx noted, "in possessing the gift of invention" that allows the species to "alter his own nature and its needs." It is in large part technological adjustments that have made the predictions of Ehrlich, Holdren, and others so moot.[50]

Only growth allows for the possibility of greater uplift for the middle and working class without the imposition of politically infeasible and, more significantly, almost certainly ineffective widespread redistribution policies. Growth, noted development economist W. Arthur Lewis, not only increases wealth but "increases the range of human choice."[51] People are more likely to take risks and innovate in a growth economy than in one characterized by slow growth and ever growing regulation. Growing countries then can choose to use their surplus to clean the environment, as has occurred in much of the high-income world, in places as diverse as South Korea, Singapore, the United States, Germany, and Scandinavia. The recent shift toward greater concern over pollution in China reflects as well that country's rapid move toward economic prosperity.[52]

But sparking beneficial economic growth requires a shift in priorities, and thus presents a challenge to the new class order. It is not enough merely to place blame on "the top one percent" or "elites." Instead we must look for ways to shift the benefits of growth away from the current hegemons, notably in the very narrow finance and high-tech sectors, and toward those involved in broad array of productive enterprise.

This shift will require a reordering of economic priorities. Over the past half century, financial service firms have doubled their share of the economy. Often they have regarded productive industries—notably in energy or manufacturing—as hampering short-term financial gains, and they have repeatedly led companies to strip their industrial assets, typically moving them overseas.

The "financialization" of the economy, notes one scholar, at least in part explains why companies have tended to be slow to reinvest their profits in new products and innovations, preferring instead to engage in mergers or "stock buybacks" that raise share prices but do little for the overall economy of the middle orders. Instead, notes economist William Lazonick, they "greatly exacerbate the problem of the eroding middle class as U.S. business corporations neglect the need to invest for the future." The fact that tax laws also encouraged companies to maintain much of their funds overseas, roughly $1.4 trillion in 2011, he adds, further discouraged vital new investment in the domestic economy.[53]

The political regime under both parties, however, has tended to favor major financial institutions over grassroots businesses. The financial industry bailout, as ProPublica's frequently updated map of financial bailout recipients reveals, constituted a massive transfer of funds from taxpayers in the heartland, the suburbs, and the exurbs to the major urban enclaves, particularly around the "money centers" of New York City, Chicago, and San Francisco. Populists as well tend to be outraged that middle-class taxpayers have been transformed into unwitting underwriters of over $20 billion in bonuses paid out in 2013 by Wall Street.[54]

The lower rate on investment capital—and the much higher marginal tax rate paid by the Yeomanry on income, compared with stock-compensated Oligarchs—further widened the social gulf.[55] The share of taxes paid by the top twenty percent of earners, which includes much of the successful Yeomanry, has grown from 65 percent to 90 percent, but the wealthiest 400 individuals in the United States, with gross income over $200 million, paid an effective tax rate well below even those in the top one percent, which includes many small business owners and professionals. Essentially the tax system penalizes the Yeomanry but rewards the Oligarchs.[56]

In the past, the capital gains tax system was justified as spurring economic and income growth by creating incentives for investment. But the recent recovery has ushered in a massive stock boom characterized by relatively low investment in plant and equipment, as well as meager job growth, particularly for full-time work. In this, both political parties are to blame. Republican fealty to the interests of the wealthy has been long-standing, but now much of the backing for "progressive" causes comes from the very people—Wall Street traders, venture capitalists, and tech executives—who benefit most from the federal bailouts, cheap money, low interest rates, and increasingly anachronistic low capital gains tax rates.[57]

Prescriptions for Growth

Promoting broad-based economic growth—as opposed to simply boosting the incomes of investors and top corporate executives—would not only offer opportunities to America's middle and working classes, but it is also essential to maintaining the expanded state that both parties have nurtured over past decades. If it remains true that the country can expect to expand by no more than 1.5 to 2.5 percent in good years, then, as economist Bret Swanson argues, we can anticipate larger deficits—and higher taxes—for the foreseeable future. Faster growth allows for slower growth in deficits, Swanson argues, and with some modest spending cuts, could even serve to bring debt levels back to historic averages.[58] But without growth, this is not possible, even with austerity measures or ever higher taxes.

We also need growth to make the economy work for the broad majority of Americans. Public priorities need to change. Government spending must be shifted from lavish pensions and benefits for public workers—something that Wall Street itself thrives on by investing in public pension assets—to more productive spending.[59] These include investments in basic infrastructure, an area where America has been lagging its major competitors.[60]

Critically, infrastructure spending, unlike the bailouts of major banks or the Federal Reserve's bond buying, helps the middle class. Research by the Council of Economic Advisors suggests that nearly 90 percent of the jobs created by increased infrastructure spending are middle-class jobs, those between the 25th and 75th percentile in the national distribution of wages. Finally, infrastructure spending of this kind is usually approved of by a public that daily copes with the increasing consequences of underinvestment—terrible roadways, poor communications systems, inadequate water storage and delivery systems, and limited energy transmission reliability.[61]

The other pressing opportunity, besides physical infrastructure, lies in education and training. This directly impacts businesses, which often complain of insufficiently trained workers, and also provides a pathway to the middle class for Americans from poorer backgrounds. Investment in adult education will be particularly key, providing workers with a chance to gain new skills as the economy evolves.[62] Programs focused on skill training and improving high school graduation rates have proved to have a significant long-term return on investment.[63]

The Blue-Collar Opportunity

It is commonplace among the Clerisy and many within the tech Oligarchy to downplay the future of America's tangible industries. They envision a future dominated almost exclusively by tech, media, and financial firms.[64] They foresee far fewer good blue-collar jobs and a widening service class. They also envision growth in educational and medical services, which do not pay as well as manufacturing or construction. These industries may not enjoy robust growth given their dependence on loans and government support.[65]

Yet this view of economic trends may be more backward-looking than future-oriented, as is commonly believed.[66] Indeed, since 2010, jobs have expanded in largely private sector areas such as energy, manufacturing, logistics, and, with the return of the housing market in some areas, construction.[67] In this respect, millennials may have finally caught a break. The workforce in many fields is rapidly aging, and the demand for new, updated skills, particularly using computers, has soared, leaving manufacturers desperate for necessary workers.[68] A recent Boston Consulting Group (BCG) study notes that there is already a shortfall of some 100,000 skilled manufacturing positions in the United States. By 2020, according to BCG and the Bureau of Labor Statistics, the nation could face a shortfall of around 875,000 machinists, welders, industrial machinery operators, and other highly skilled manufacturing professionals.[69]

Businesspeople almost everywhere decry such shortages, but they rarely lament a mounting shortage of postmodernist comparative literature scholars or art historians. Indeed, on a 2014 trip to Houston, in many ways the country's most economically dynamic city, developers and energy firms widely complained that they were constrained not by lack of demand but by lack of skilled labor. In some cases, companies are not only beginning to invest in community colleges but also looking to recruit high school students into these professions.[70]

The resurgence of a blue-collar industry and the shift to skills training represents a critical opportunity to expand the ranks of the middle class.[71] The University of Washington's Richard Morrill has found that areas with large concentrations of manufacturing—including largely non-union southern plants—and other higher-wage blue-collar jobs have significantly lower levels of income inequality than areas that rely primarily on service, finance, and tech industries.[72]

Dispersion and the Fate of the Middle Class

America's ability to recover its sense of opportunity requires the creation of new homes and businesses, including on the periphery of our metropolitan regions.[73] This will provide opportunities for middle- and working-class families both in terms of work and a better standard of living. It would also build on the progress made over the last century in improving living space and homeownership for ever expanding parts of the population, something once seen as a progressive value but increasingly opposed by large sections of the Clerisy.[74]

In the attempts to rein in suburbs and single-family houses, the Clerisy is battling the long-held interests of the Yeomanry. For the most part the middle orders can be expected to resist the mania for "cramming" or "pack and stack" housing that has become the supreme principle of urban planning and which is widely favored among architects, who frequently define the urban future as one dominated by an ever denser, high-rise-oriented future. "Building high density," notes Brookings scholar Robert Lang, is the "most important" tactic in the drive to "compact development" and "slow sprawl."[75]

But this attempt at ordering American life likely will be resisted. Notwithstanding every effort to produce a contrary result, most people continue to move to both smaller cities and suburbs. Americans are being urged to concentrate, but, for the most part, they continue to seek out places—suburbs and more affordable cities—where they can pay reasonable rents or own their own homes.[76] The Clerisy may be proclaiming a return to the large cities and the "death" of suburbs, but for many if not most Americans, the preferred future is very much more like that created in the second half of the last century.[77]

Will Technology Enhance Concentration?

In the decades following the Second World War, there was a general consensus that technology would concentrate power in the hands of those who could manage, plan, and foresee future needs. But this belief was largely based on a world built around mainframe computers and rigid ways of organizing work. The ensuing wave of technology—from the personal computer and the Internet to the smartphone and social media—could have a very different effect, allowing for greater dispersion of information and power.

Overall, technology has no inherent values. The key issue now is not whether we need "more" technology but how the implementation of sophisticated new tools impacts society, most particularly in terms of an ever greater concentration of wealth and power. As Manuel Castells noted, technology can enhance the power of the state by becoming an instrument of greater invasion of privacy by both government and private corporations.[78]

Increasingly it is clear that the consolidation of tech in a handful of firms does very little for the economy, outside of those who benefit from selling ad space. The overall economic impacts, notes tech entrepreneur Jigar Shah, have been minimal, particularly in comparison with such innovations as electricity, affordable automobiles, and plane travel. These, he suggests, created hosts of industries and opportunities for working- and middle-class people in ways that social media, for example, has not.[79]

Equally critical, the fact that these industries are increasingly dominated by a handful of firms—Amazon, Apple, Google, Facebook—tends to benefit an ever smaller group of people with unprecedented access to the information of the vast majority. As Jaron Lanier points out, the leading digital companies tend to view people as "small elements in a bigger information machine." He suggests that the modern oligopolies are excused in part by the promise of a future blessed, at least for an influential few, by "high-tech abundance"—what he describes as "the price of heaven."[80]

What is needed instead is a notion that the Internet and core information age technologies be treated as something like a highway—paid for by taxpayers and constructed by government—that should be kept as open as possible to newcomers. Cyberspace today offers an expansive opportunity, much as the vast physical expanse of North America did for previous generations; the promise of a land stake was the great difference between America and other societies in prior centuries.[81]

Is ever greater technological consolidation inevitable? It is possible that as these firms move further from their entrepreneurial roots, many take on what anthropologist David Graeber describes as "a timid, bureaucratic spirit" that responds to the needs of investors and focuses on preserving already established business lines. Many observers, from Adam Smith and Karl Marx to Joseph Schumpeter, agree that monopoly creation, rent seeking, and price fixing are the natural instincts of the monied classes rather than risk taking, hard work, and free enterprise.[82] Over time, this yearning for oligarchy could also threaten a host of other large firms, in media and finance in particular, which have been subject to what one analyst calls the "super-sizing" of big business. The top one-hundred firms on the *Fortune* 500 list have revenues, in adjusted dollars, eight times those during the supposed big-business heyday of the 1960s.[83]

Yet this process of concentration could be reversed—particularly if smaller and newer firms are not hampered in their growth—by, among other things, restraints against oligarchic control. As Japan discovered in the past two decades, or as the United States witnessed in the recent sharp decline of the big three American automakers, corporate concentration tends to slow innovation. In the personal computer boom of the 1980s, scores of companies competed across a broad array of tech sectors, resulting in a rapid evolution of technology. In contrast, it is not easy to argue that today's deeply entrenched Google search engine or Microsoft software code is markedly better, from the average consumer point of view, than three or even five years ago.[84]

More importantly, concentrated industry removes the incentive and opportunity for productive entrepreneurship. Would we be better off with, say, a garage-bound Steve Jobs, using digital tools, developing the software for robotics, than with trusting our innovation to managers in corporate structures that answer primarily to the demands of Wall Street analysts? Having our future in space, transportation, media, or healthcare depend on the profitability and strategies of a handful of companies, and a small, often closely knit group of investors, does not seem to be the best strategy to maintain and deepen our technological lead, much less our political culture.

The 1099 Economy: The Rise of a New Yeomanry?

There are promising signs that many in the Yeomanry are seeking to establish something of a digital version of the rural homestead. Encompassing people writing apps, doing technical consulting, and working in the information sector, the numbers of self-employed tech workers have surged between 2005 and 2010. The percentage of such employees in information sectors grew 15 percent during this period.[85]

Tech is not the only area where the 1099 economy is expanding. According to the U.S. Census Bureau, there were 21.4 million self-employed Americans in 2008, and recent data from EMSI suggests that the figures might be even higher. Tracking workers who are not covered by unemployment insurance, EMSI researchers suggest that more than 40 million Americans operate in the 1099 economy. This represents about one-fifth of the total U.S. workforce, more than twice the percentage seen in 1970.[86]

This rise is partially reflective of hard times, and many of the self-employed earn only modest livings in fields such as childcare and construction. However, the shift to self-employment is likely to accelerate in the future, and into higher-paying professions, for reasons including the ubiquity of the Internet and the reluctance of large firms—often seeking to hollow out their ranks—to hire full-time employees with benefits. Greater regulation of small- and medium-sized businesses could also encourage entrepreneurs to opt for sole proprietorships as a way to evade an ever more intrusive state apparatus.

Urban analyst Bill Fulton, who has looked into this issue, concludes that we may be seeing a fundamental change in how the economy operates. "Even though there may not be jobs in the conventional sense, there is still work," Fulton notes. "That's the whole idea of the 1099 economy. It's just a different way of organizing the economy."[87]

This growth is occurring not only in Silicon Valley or New York but also in cities like Phoenix that were hard hit by the Great Recession, but which have since bounced back. In fact, Phoenix's ranks of the self-employed grew far faster than that seen in such "creative" hotbeds as New York, Los Angeles, San Francisco, and Boston. Some of this may be

part of the same phenomenon seen earlier in migration, as more mid-
dle- and working-class people seek opportunities in less expensive and
regulated areas.

Ultimately the emergence of the 1099 economy suggests the prospects for a revived Yeomanry. Like the nineteenth-century farmstead or
artisanal shop, this economy could shift much of employment back to
the home. In 2009, 1.7 million more employees worked at home than in
2000; the share of employees working at home rose in every major metropolitan area (over 1,000,000 population), with an average increase of
38 percent. In the past decade, the rate of increase in the work-at-home
market share exceeded that of transit in 49 of the 52 major metropolitan areas. Indeed, despite all the talk of increased mass transit usage, the
percentage of Americans working at home has grown 1.5 times faster
over the past decade; there are now more telecommuters than people
who take mass transit to work in 38 out of the 52 U.S. metropolitan
areas.[88]

This emergence of the "electronic cottage," to borrow Alvin Toffler's
phrase, reflects the potential for democratization in the information
age. It also represents an enormous environmental bonus, as it greatly
reduces both energy use and commute times. Indeed, a study by Global
Workplace Analytics finds increased telecommuting could reduce carbon emissions by over 51 million metric tons a year—the equivalent
of taking all of greater New York's commuters off the road. Additional
carbon footprint savings will come from reduced office energy consumption, roadway repairs, urban heating, office construction, business
travel, and paper usage (as electronic documents replace paper). Traf-
fic jams idle away almost 3 billion gallons of gas a year and account for
26 million extra tons of greenhouse gases.[89]

The rapid shift toward home-based business may also enhance the
prospects of the Yeoman class in coming decades. Once again this shift
suggests a growing fundamental conflict between the future largely
embraced by the Clerisy—who favor dense central cities employing
workers who take transit from apartments to offices in central cities—
and what is commonly sought by the Yeomanry. Trying to recenter
metropolitan economies in their downtowns seems a bit of a stretch in all
but a handful cities. In reality, even as some downtowns have recovered,
they have done so less as workplaces than as residential areas for a small

but growing population. We can see these trends as part of the emergence of what may be called "peak office." We simply use offices less than in the past. Back in the mid-1980s, according to the commercial real-estate research firm CoStar, upwards of 200 million square feet of office space was built annually; in 2013, despite the recovery, the country added barely 30 million square feet, according to Reis, Inc.[90]

The growing dispersion of work represents a new chance to spread opportunity and property ownership. Gaining greater control over one's economic assets represents a fundamental value of a market-based system. In contrast to a more concentrated economy, a nation of dispersed communities, self-employed people, and homeowners promises not only greater equality but better prospects for broad economic growth.[91]

Restoring grassroots entrepreneurship is critical to the future of capitalism. To maintain its legitimacy, noted historian Fernand Braudel, a capitalist society must thrive at "its very roots," which is at the local and small-scale basis. This reality was recognized by, among others, Vladimir Lenin, founder of the Soviet state:

> Small-scale commercial production is, every moment of every day, giving birth *spontaneously* to capitalism and the bourgeoisie. . . . Wherever there is small business and freedom of trade, capitalism appears.[92]

The Culture War Worth Having

America's unique culture rests on the twin pillars of widespread dispersion of property and a pattern of voluntary collaboration. In their varied and scattered communities, Tocqueville noted, Americans reveled in "associations," which often performed many services that, even in nineteenth-century Europe, were provided by the state or the state church.[93] This sense of self-reliance marked a key dividing line between the independent spirit of America and the feudal model, where social order, as Johan Huizinga noted, was "venerable and lasting" as well as "ordained by God."[94]

In contemporary America, the attempt by the Clerisy and their allies to provide a central dominating ideology, and to expand the regulatory scope of government, threatens this sense of autonomy and self-help. It turns to government, particularly on the federal level, to take the role of families, churches, and local organizations. This attempt reflects a more important cultural conflict than the misguided efforts by social conservatives to ban gay marriage or the attempts to establish Christianity as a state religion.[95]

The real issue revolves around the future of the American family. The family has long been marked for extinction among political radicals, and its demise is also now widely celebrated by both progressive pundits and some business interests. In his provocative 2012 book *Going Solo*, Eric Klinenberg points out that the percentage of Americans living alone has skyrocketed from nine percent of all households in 1950 to roughly 28 percent today. In Scandinavia, the percentage of single households is even greater: 40 to 45 percent. Klinenberg traces this to, among other things, greater wealth, the growth of welfare states, the women's movement, and the rise of what sociologist Émile Durkheim called "the cult of the individual."[96]

This shift is particularly true in parts of the country that have become exceedingly expensive for the kinds of housing favored by most families.[97] Yet far from the liberating force seen by some, the decline of the family unit, and of marriage, has greatly exacerbated class divisions. Broken families are among the leading causes of downward mobility; more than 20 percent of single-parent families live in long-term poverty compared to only 2 percent of two-parent families with children. According to research by Penn State demographer Molly Martin, fully 40 percent of the increase in income inequality can be traced to a decayed family structure.[98]

Other elements of social community—notably religious institutions—have, like the family, served critically as supports for upward mobility. Church affiliation, if not in free fall, is clearly on the downward trend, particularly among the working class and the young, although interest in spiritual values does not seem to be waning. Secularism, singleness, and childlessness have gained particular social cache for over a generation, especially among the well-educated. Contemporary social thinking, as epitomized by "creative class" theorist Richard Florida, essentially links "advanced" society to the absence of religious values. Indeed, the current fashions in urbanism not only disdain religiosity but often give remarkably short shrift to issues involving families.[99]

The question is not whether there should be a debate or, if you will, a "war" over culture, but on what terms this struggle should be waged.

History does not move backwards, and trying to inspire the next generations to live or think like their parents or grandparents simply lacks any serious appeal and is profoundly ahistorical. There is truth to the Democratic claim that conservative Republicans suffer a "modernity deficit" that could assure them permanent minority status.[100]

Sadly, neither of the rising political tendencies—what might be seen as Clerical liberalism and its libertarian counterpoint—addresses such fundamental social deficits. The Clerisy tends to supplant the family with the state and informal arrangements among individuals. Economically focused libertarianism, rapidly becoming the intellectual foundation of modern conservatism, is almost psychologically incapable of addressing such social issues. "The libertarian priority is meeting market needs," observed one commentator. Other issues are secondary, or they are seen as curable simply through market mechanisms.[101]

Markets are wonderful things, but what if, as they evolve, they can also tilt against families and communities? When everything boils down to what Marx called "the cash nexus" or simple individual "empowerment," then having children, or committing to marriage, becomes far less palatable. It's easy for well-heeled tech entrepreneurs or inheritors of vast wealth to speak about principles of classical liberalism, but if free markets fail to serve society's needs, then popular support for competitive capitalism will necessarily fade. In order to restore, and strengthen, the moral foundation upon which capitalism relies, there remains a need for changes that encourage self-sufficiency in the tax system, through reforming education and expanding those parts of the economy most likely to drive middle- and working-class opportunities.

Standing Up to the New Class Order

"We can have democracy in this country, or we can have great wealth concentrated in the hands of a few," Supreme Court Justice Louis Brandeis once said, "but we can't have both."[102] This notion is not so much anti-capitalist, or even anti-market, as it is against the concentration of power and wealth in few hands, the very possibilities that worried founders Jefferson and Madison.

Increasingly, American politics resembles not so much a rising democracy as an emerging plutocracy, with dueling groups of billionaires right and left determining most political choices. The wealthy have always played an outsized role in our politics, but today, emboldened by Supreme Court rulings, professional electoral consultancies, and weakened controls on campaign contributions, Oligarchs are dominating the electoral map in ways not seen since at least the abuses of the Nixon years.

This can be seen in the emergence of conservative Oligarchs like the energy billionaire Koch brothers and the heirs to the Walmart fortune, who have become a major focus for progressive concerns and a standard talking point for Democrats like Senate Majority Leader Harry Reid.[103] Yet although wealthy conservatives remain a powerful force, much the same reliance on the Oligarchs can be found increasingly in the Democratic Party. In fact, an examination of campaign contributions reveals that the majority of America's wealthiest households seem more inclined to what is considered the left. Among the .01 percent, who increasingly dominate political giving, the largest contributions, besides the conservative Club for Growth, backed by Republican Oligarchs, went to left-leaning groups such as Emily's List, Act Blue, and Moveon.org. Liberal groups accounted for eight of the top ten ideological causes of the ultra-rich; seven of the ten congressional candidates most dependent on their money were Democrats.[104]

The rise of Oligarchic politics in both parties threatens the very viability of the democratic system. It allows specific interests—developers, Wall Street, Silicon Valley, renewable or fossil fuels producers—enormous range to make or break candidates. As the powerful battle, the middle classes increasingly become spectators. This battle of the Oligarchs increasingly resembles the decadent phase at the end of Greek democracy or the late Roman Republic. The nation's founders were well aware of that history and drew their inspiration not from imperial models but those of earlier republics, not only in the classical world but in Enlightenment Europe.[105]

As in the initial progressive era, which produced Brandeis, Americans today are alarmed, and rightfully so, by this concentration of wealth and power. Nearly sixty percent, for example, favor some steps to increase the distribution of wealth, almost twice as many who felt the current system was "fair."[106] Sentiments in this direction are even stronger among millennials, with some surveys suggesting that the majority are even sympathetic to socialism.[107]

Yet, there are signs that many millennials, and most Americans, may not favor the traditional "top-down" approach to income distribution advocated by some progressives. Their approval of Congress, the White House, and other key government institutions has eroded, according to a recent Harvard Institute of Politics study. Young people, notes polling director John Della Volpe, have experienced "an erosion of trust in the individuals and institutions that make government work." This is reflected by increasing alienation not only from the Republicans, who remain enormously unpopular, but increasingly from President Obama and the Democrats as well.[108]

According to generational chronicler and long-time Democratic activist Morley Winograd, this alienation stems in part from millennials' experience with government, which often seems clunky and ineffective. "Millennials," he notes, "have come to expect the speed and responsiveness from any organization they interact with that today's high tech makes possible." Experiences from the NSA scandal to long lines at the DMV to the botched website rollout for Obamacare, he suggests, cause "millennials to be suspicious of, if not downright hostile to, government bureaucracies."[109]

Ultimately, most Americans, not only millennials, express concern about the evolving class structure, but they remain skeptical about the government's ability to do much about it. Less than one in five Americans trusts the federal government. Concern over inequality is widespread, but barely two in five see strong federal action as a reasonable way to address it. There may be a groundswell for the social democratic goals of the New Deal, but it does not likely extend to the reimposition of highly centralized policy prescriptions.[110] This suggests that perhaps we need to develop a new focus that is neither reflexively hostile (as some Tea Partiers appear) to government per se nor simply interested in expanding the list of self-interested political clients. The key to future effective government lies not so much in its radical downsizing but in dispersing power to the local level, something that fits into both the mentality of the new generation and the decentralist traditions that have animated our history.

This notion works against the current drive to consolidate power at the national level.[111] The tendency of administrations to rule through executive orders or regulatory agencies has been growing, particularly during the Obama years, stimulated in part by the exigencies of the Great Recession and then the loss of the House in 2010. Although these steps have been widely endorsed by liberal activists, thoughtful people on the left, such as Yale's Jacob Hacker, understand that such abuses of power could threaten civil liberties and liberal reforms, particularly if there were a change of party in the White House.[112]

Ultimately, the middle classes cannot thrive if power is concentrated in a few hands. The more influence accrues to Washington, the more power to those who can best play "the game" there.[113] The larger the government, generally speaking, the less influence exercised by individuals not connected with the power elites. Despite claims to the contrary, attempts to consolidate cities or expand regional government also frequently end up with higher costs rather than more dispersed arrangements.[114]

In the twenty-first century, with our ubiquity of information, local governments now have access to the kind of expertise that previously required large bureaucracies. There are many areas—water, air quality, arterial road infrastructure—that require cooperation along regional lines. Of course, there are times, as in the case of slavery or racial discrimination, or basic protections for food safety or water and air quality, that the intervention of the federal government has been necessary. But for the most part, the best approach, whenever possible, is to allow localities to control their own fate. It is a decentralized, bottom-up system that, for the most part, has worked for America.

Can the Middle Class Challenge the Oligarchs?

The prospects for standing up to the new class order may not be as daunting as many assume. In the Middle Ages, it took nearly a millennium for such dissent to mount a serious challenge. The numerous peasant rebellions that occurred in Europe, China, and elsewhere lacked the intellectual firepower to build a coherent resistance to the ruling order. Change occurred only with the onset of capitalism and the expansion of literacy. In contrast, today's dissenters are both literate and empowered by information technology. This gives them new weapons to challenge the Clerisy and their allies.

To build resistance against oligarchy and central control requires a new understanding of class dynamics. The nature of the new order—

notably the rise of the Clerisy and the tech Oligarchs—tends to shift the nature of the conflict in ways that defy much of what we have traditionally believed. In many cases, as shown above, the "left" frequently, albeit not purposely, defends entrenched privilege and wealth of a certain kind, and opposes those things, such as single-family houses or industrial jobs, traditionally associated with upward mobility.

What is necessary, then, is the development of a new politics that starts, first and foremost, with the question of how to both reduce inequality and boost opportunity. This will be opposed by certain influential actors in both political parties. As Elizabeth Warren has noted, the priorities of both the Bush and the Obama administrations after the financial crisis were not to help the millions damaged by the Great Recession. "The government's most important job," she remarks, "was to provide a soft landing for the tender fannies of the banks."[115]

Warren's observation reflects the influence exercised by the Oligarchs in both parties. A recent Mercatus Center report confirms this: politically connected banks received larger bailouts from the Federal Reserve during the financial crisis than those financial institutions that spent less or nothing on lobbying and contributions to political campaigns. Another study by two University of Michigan economists found a strong correlation between receiving TARP assistance and a company's degree of connectedness to members of congressional finance committees.[116]

Right now most of the easily identified opposition to the new class order comes from the fringes. The Tea Party, for example, had its origins in opposition to the bank bailouts that followed the financial crisis. This, not surprisingly, has made some large bank executives as wary of this right-wing movement as they were of Occupy Wall Street.[117] And they should be. Opposition to ever closer relations between powerful business interests and government is now widely felt, with the vast majority feeling that government contracts go to the connected, while less than one-third believe that the country operates under a free-market system.[118]

Of course, the right and left may offer different solutions to the new class conflict, but the first step is for people on both sides to recognize the current drift toward a society that offers dismal prospects for the middle and working classes. This trajectory breaks with the historic experience that, for all its obvious flaws, has made America the great-est success story of modern times. Instead of accepting decline, and ever less social mobility, we must forge a future that also offers the chance for the fulfillment of aspirations. We need to provide the next generation with something other than just memories of a former American dream. We should offer them a full chance to experience it for themselves.

Notes

Chapter One: The New Class Order

1. Charles and Mary Beard, *The Rise of American Civilization* (New York: Macmillan, 1930), p. 395.

2. Irving Kristol, "Income Inequality Without Class Conflict," *Wall Street Journal*, December 18, 1997.

3. Pew Charitable Trusts, "Pursuing the American Dream: Economic Mobility Across Generations," July 2012, p. 17; David Wessel, "As Rich-Poor Gap Widens in the U.S., Class Mobility Stalls," *Wall Street Journal*, May 13, 2005; David Wessel, "Fed Chief Warns of Widening Inequality," *Wall Street Journal*, February 7, 2007; Jason DeParle, "Harder for Americans to Rise From Lower Rungs," *New York Times*, January 4, 2012.

4. Pew Research Social & Demographic Trends, "The Lost Decade of the Middle Class: Fewer, Poorer, Gloomier," report, August 22, 2012, http://www.pewsocial-trends.org/files/2012/08/pew-social-trends-lost-decade-of-the-middle-class.pdf.

5. Associated Press, "The Future's NOT So Bright: Americans Predict a Dark Downward Spiral over the Next Four Decades," *Daily Mail*, January 3, 2014.

6. Thomas Piketty, *Capital in the Twenty-First Century*, trans. Arthur Goldhammer (Cambridge, MA: Harvard UP, 2014), pp. 23–24, 192–96, 321–23, 347.

7. Annie Lowrey, "The Rich Get Richer Through the Recovery," *Economix* (blog), *New York Times*, September 10, 2013, http://economix.blogs.nytimes.com/2013/09/10/the-rich-get-richer-through-the-recovery.

8. A study by the Citizens Housing and Planning Council of New York finds that "[f]rom 1963 to 1993, a period spanning the growth of modern environmental regulation, the *relative* price of shelter increased by 26 percent while the *relative* price of energy decreased by 1 percent, transportation by 11 percent, and all commodities by 18 percent." They note that (1) many of these regulations were clearly necessary, such as asbestos regulations; and (2) while no single environmental policy has a profound effect on costs, cumulatively regulations have a huge cost on housing. See Frank P. Braconi, Citizens Housing and Planning Council of New York, Inc., "Environmental Regulation and Housing Affordability," *Cityscape: A Journal of Policy Development and Research*, vol. 2, no. 3 (September 1996): 82–106.

9. Annie Lowrey, "Even Among the Richest of the Rich, Fortunes Diverge," *New York Times*, February 11, 2014; Piketty, *Capital in the Twenty-First Century*, p. 173; Ryan Dezember, "Blowout Haul for Buyout Tycoons," *Wall Street Journal*, March 3, 2014; Lawrence Mishel and Natalie Sabadish, "CEO Pay and the Top 1%," Economic

Policy Institute Issue, *Issue Brief*, no. 331, May 2, 2012, http://www.epi.org/publication/ib331-ceo-pay-top-1-percent.

10. Simon Johnson, "Banking's 'Toxic Cocktail' Is Too Big to Forget," *Bloomberg News*, January 26, 2011, http://www.bloomberg.com/news/2011-01-27/banking-toxic-cocktail-is-too-big-to-forget-commentary-by-simon-johnson.html.

11. TRAC Reports, "Criminal Prosecutions for Financial Institution Fraud Continue to Fall," November 15, 2011, http://trac.syr.edu/tracreports/crim/267; Jenny Anderson, "Wall Street Winners Get Billion-Dollar Pay Days," *New York Times*, April 16, 2008; Bradley Keoun and Phil Kuntz, "Wall Street Aristocracy Got $1.2 Trillion in Secret Loans," *Bloomberg News*, August 22, 2011, http://www.bloomberg.com/news/2011-08-21/wall-street-aristocracy-got-1-2-trillion-in-fed-s-secret-loans.html; Zachary Roth, "Wall Street Pay Hits New Record," *Yahoo Finance*, February 2, 2011; Edward Wyatt, "S.E.C. Is Avoiding Tough Sanctions for Large Banks," *New York Times*, February 3, 2012; Nelson Schwartz and Louise Story, "Hedge Fund Pay Roars Back," *New York Times*, April 1, 2010; Steven M. Davidoff, "In Stock Market Rebound, a Windfall for Wall Street Executives," *New York Times*, October 2, 2012; Andrew Huszar, "Confessions of a Quantitative Easer," *Wall Street Journal*, November 11, 2013; Tyler Durden [pseud.], "'QE Was A Massive Gift Intended To Boost Wealth,' Fed President Admits," *Zero Hedge* (blog), March 21, 2014, http://www.zerohedge.com/news/2014-03-21/qe-was-massive-gift-intended-boost-wealth-fed-president-admits.

12. Theodore Roosevelt, "The Puritan Spirit and the Regulation of Corporations," in *The Works of Theodore Roosevelt*, ed. Hermann Hagedorn (New York: Charles Scribner's Sons, 1925), 18:99.

13. Associated Press, "Despite Fiscal Cliff Deal, Taxes to Rise for Most Americans," *New York Daily News*, January 2, 2013.

14. Lex Haris, "The Super Rich Are Mad as Hell—and Doing Great," *CNN Money*, January 28, 2014, http://money.cnn.com/2014/01/28/news/economy/super-rich-attack.

15. Nick Sorrentino, "Obama Tilts Playing Field to One Percent," *Detroit News*, October 1, 2013.

16. Tyler Durden [pseud.], "David Stockman Explains the Keynesian State-Wreck Ahead—Sundown In America," *Zero Hedge* (blog), October 5, 2013, http://www.zerohedge.com/news/2013-10-05/david-stockman-explains-keynesian-state-wreck-ahead-sundown-america; Hibah Yousuf, "Obama Admits 95% of Income Gains Gone to Top 1%," *CNN Money*, September 15, 2013, http://money.cnn.com/2013/09/15/news/economy/income-inequality-obama; Alexander Eichler, "Consumption Inequality Keeping Up With Rising Income Inequality: Study," *Huffington Post*, April 10, 2012, http://www.huffingtonpost.com/2012/04/10/consumption-inequality-income_n_1413454.html; Alexander Eichler, "Income Inequality Worse under Obama than George W. Bush," *Huffington Post*, April 11, 2012, http://www.huffingtonpost.com/2012/04/11/income-inequality-obama-bush_n_1419008.html; Richard Fry and Paul Taylor, "A Rise in Wealth for the Wealthy; Declines for the Lower 93%," report, Pew Research Social & Demographic Trends, April 23, 2013, http://www.pewsocialtrends.org/files/2013/04/wealth_recovery_final.pdf.

17. Henry Nash Smith, *Virgin Land: The American West as Symbol and Myth* (Cambridge, MA: Harvard UP, 1950), p. 191; Carole Shammas, "A New Long at Long-Term Trends in Wealth Inequality in the United States," *American Historical Review*, vol. 98, no. 2 (April 1993): 427; C. Wright Mills, *The Power Elite* (New York: Oxford UP, 1956), p. 49.

18. H. G. Wells, *Anticipations of the Reaction of Mechanical and Scientific Progress Upon Human Life and Thought* (Mineola, NY: Dover, 1999), p. 53.

19. Daniel Bell, *The Coming of Post-Industrial Society: A Venture in Social Forecasting* (New York: Basic Books, 1973), pp. 15–29, 213; International Trade Administration, U.S. Department of Commerce, "The State of Manufacturing in the United States," July 2010, http://trade.gov/manufactureamerica/facts/tg_mana_003019.asp.

20. Bell, *The Coming of Post-Industrial Society*, p. 344; International Trade Administration, "The State of Manufacturing in the United States."

21. Alex Morrell, "Billionaires 2014: Record Number of Newcomers Includes Sheryl Sandberg, Jan Koum, Michael Kors," *Forbes*, March 3, 2014, http://www.forbes.com/sites/alexmorrell/2014/03/03/billionaires-2014-record-number-of-newcomers-includes-sheryl-sandberg-jan-koum-michael-kors.

22. "A Wealth of Influence," *Financial Times*, October 8, 2005; "Bloomberg Billionaires: Today's Ranking of the World's Richest People," *Bloomberg*, http://www.bloomberg.com/billionaires/2014-01-02/cya/aaaac.

23. Farhad Manjoo, "Silicon Valley Has an Arrogance Problem," *Wall Street Journal*, November 3, 2013.

24. Chrystia Freeland, "Plutocrats vs. Populists," *New York Times*, November 3, 2013; David Callahan, *Fortunes of Change: The Rise of the Liberal Rich and the Remaking of America* (Hoboken, NJ: Wiley, 2010), p. 290.

25. Max Green, *Epitaph for American Labor: How Union Leaders Lost Touch with America* (Washington, DC: AEI Press, 1996), pp. 14–15; Matthew Josephson, *The Money Lords: The Great Finance Capitalists, 1925–1950* (New York: Weybright and Talley, 1972), p. vii.

26. Lachlan Markay, "The Venture Corporatists," *Federalist*, http://thefederalist.com/2013/10/02/the-venture-corporatists.

27. James Freeman, "How Washington Really Redistributes Income," *Wall Street Journal*, October 21, 2012.

28. *Encyclopaedia Britannica Online*, s.v. "Silicon Valley" (by Michael Aaron Dennis), http://www.britannica.com/EBchecked/topic/544409/Silicon-Valley; Adrian Wooldridge, "The Coming Tech-lash," *Economist*, November 18, 2013.

29. G. William Domhoff, *Fat Cats and Democrats: The Role of the Big Rich in the Party of the Common Man* (Englewood Cliffs, NJ: Prentice Hall, 1972), pp. 16, 35–73.

30. Ferdinand Lundberg, *The Rich and the Super-Rich: A Study in the Power of Money Today* (New York: Bantam, 1968), pp. 105–12; David Shribman, "The Democratic Coalition Is Breaking Up: More Blue-Collar Workers Identify as Republicans," *Pittsburgh Post-Gazette*, January 22, 2012; John Dunbar, "Top 10 Donors Make up a Third of Donations to Super PACs," The Center for Public Integrity, http://www.publicintegrity.org/2012/04/26/8753/top-10-donors-make-third-donations-super-pacs.

31. David Siders, "Jerry Brown Says Poverty, Joblessness Due to California Being 'a Magnet,'" *Sacramento Bee*, November 7, 2013.

32. Edward Morrissey, "A Food-Stamp Recovery Is the New Normal," *Fiscal Times*, April 4, 2013, http://www.thefiscaltimes.com/Columns/2013/04/04/A-Food-Stamp-Recovery-Is-the-New-Normal.

33. Terence P. Jeffrey, "Census on Obama's 1st Term: Real Median Income Down $2,627; People in Poverty Up 6,667,000; Record 46,496,000 Now Poor," *CNSNews.com*, http://cnsnews.com/news/article/terence-p-jeffrey/census-obama-s-1st-term-real-median-income-down-2627-people-poverty; Carmen DeNavas-Walt, Bernadette D. Proctor, and Jessica C. Smith "Income, Poverty, and Health Insurance Coverage in the United States: 2012," Current Population Reports, U.S. Census Bureau, September 2013; Anna Bernasek, "Income Gap Grows Wider (and Faster)," *New York Times*, September 1, 2013.

34. Callahan, *Fortunes of Change*, p. 1; fflambeau, "A List of Goldman Sachs People in the Obama Government: Names Attached to the Giant Squid's Tentacles," *Firedoglake* (blog), May 10, 2010, http://my.firedoglake.com/fflambeau/2010/05/10/renteconomist-jonathan-grubers-ties-to-goldman-sachshamilton-project; Charles Gasparino, "Don't Cry for Wall Street," *New York Post*, February 18, 2014.

35. Arthur Squires, Jr., "Who Are the Despised Rich People?" *Cumberland Times-News*, July 28, 2012; Lee Drutman with Ethan Phelps-Goodman, "The Political One Percent of the One Percent," Sunlight Foundation (blog), December 13, 2011, http://sunlightfoundation.com/blog/2011/12/13/the-political-one-percent-of-the-one-percent.

36. Chrystia Freeland, "The Rise of the New Global Elite," *Atlantic*, January/February 2011; Paul Toscano, "Obama Wins 8 of 10 Wealthiest Counties in U.S.," *CNBC*, November 8, 2012; Callahan, *Fortunes of Change*, pp. 39, 170.

37. Beard and Beard, *The Rise of American Civilization*, pp. 302–3; "The Transcontinental Railroad: The Credit Mobilier Scandal," *American Experience* (PBS), *PBS.com*, http://www.pbs.org/wgbh/americanexperience/features/general-article/tcrr-scandal; "Election Central: The Progressives and Direct Democracy," Constitutional Rights Foundation, http://www.crf-usa.org/election-central/the-progressives.html.

38. Daniel Bell, "The Cultural Contradictions of Capitalism," *Journal of Aesthetic Education*, vol. 6, nos. 1–2, *Special Double Issue: Capitalism, Culture and Education* (January–April, 1972): 36–37.

39. Matthew Continetti, "The Predators' Moll," *Washington Free Beacon*, November 1, 2013, http://freebeacon.com/columns/the-predators-moll.

40. Benjamin M. Friedman, *The Moral Consequences of Economic Growth* (New York: Knopf, 2005), p. 4.

41. Andrew Karter, "Al Gore's Mansion," *FactCheck.org*, June 21, 2009, http://www.factcheck.org/2009/06/al-gores-mansion.

42. Louis Uchitelle, "As Class Struggle Subsides, Less Pie for the Workers," *New York Times*, December 5, 1999.

43. Werner Sombart, "Medieval and Modern Commercial Enterprise," in Frederic C. Lane and Jelle C. Riemersma, eds., *Enterprise and Secular Change: Readings in Economic History* (Homewood, IL: Irwin, 1953), p. 28; Henri Pirenne, *Economic and Social History of Medieval Europe* (New York: Harcourt Brace and World, 1937),

p. 45; Carlo Cipolla, *Before the Industrial Revolution: European Society and Economy, 1000–1700* (London: Metheun, 1976), p. 182.

44. Pew Charitable Trusts, Economic Mobility Project, http://www.pewstates.org/projects/economic-mobility-project-328061.

45. Richard Henderson, "Industry Employment and Output Projections to 2020," *Monthly Labor Review*, vol. 135, no. 1 (January 2012): 65–83.

46. Phillip Longman and Paul S. Hewitt, "After Obamacare," *Washington Monthly*, January/February 2014, p. 39. Dan Mangan, "Medical Bills Are the Biggest Cause of U.S. Bankruptcies: Study," *CNBC.com*, June 25, 2013, http://www.cnbc.com/id/100840148; Christina LaMontagne, "NerdWallet Health finds Medical Bankruptcy Accounts for Majority of Personal Bankruptcies," *NerdWallet*, March 26, 2014, http://www.nerdwallet.com/blog/health/2014/03/26/medical-bankruptcy.

47. Ronald Brownstein, "Eclipsed," *National Journal*, May 28, 2011, http://www.nationaljournal.com/columns/political-connections/white-working-class-americans-see-future-as-gloomy-20110526; Ronald Brownstein, "Meet the New Middle Class: Who They Are, What They Want, and What They Fear," *Atlantic*, April 25, 2013, http://www.theatlantic.com/business/archive/2013/04/meet-the-new-middle-class-who-they-are-what-they-want-and-what-they-fear/275307; Phil Izzo, "Bleak News for Americans' Income," *Wall Street Journal*, October 14, 2011.

48. Rich Morin and Seth Motel, "A Third of Americans Now Say They Are in the Lower Classes," Pew Research Social & Demographic Trends, September 10, 2012, http://www.pewsocialtrends.org/2012/09/10/a-third-of-americans-now-say-they-are-in-the-lower-classes.

49. Brownstein, "Eclipsed."

50. Tyler Cowen, *Average is Over: Powering America Beyond the Age of the Great Stagnation* (New York: Dutton, 2013), pp. 23–24.

51. Ibid., p. 36; D. Robert Worley, "In Defense of Conservative Thought," *Huffington Post*, September 18, 2012, http://www.huffingtonpost.com/d-robert-worley/conservatives-progressives_b_1879200.html.

52. Sustainable Silicon Valley (website), http://www.sustainablesv.org.

53. Marcus Wohlsen, "Silicon Valley's Elite Don't Want to Secede. They Just Want to Stay on Top," *Wired*, December 9, 2013, http://www.wired.com/2013/12/balaji-srinivasan-joins-a16z; Manjoo, "Silicon Valley Has an Arrogance Problem."

54. Christopher Lasch, *The Only and True Heaven: Progress and Its Critics* (New York: Norton, 1991), p. 529.

55. Ray Fisman "The New Artisan Economy," *Slate*, July 16, 2012, http://www.slate.com/articles/business/the_dismal_science/2012/07/unemployment_manufacturing_and_construction_jobs_aren_t_coming_back_americans_need_new_skills_.html; Walter Russell Mead et al., "Is *Downton Abbey* the Future of the U.S. Economy?" *American Interest*, November 9, 2013, http://www.the-american-interest.com/blog/2013/11/09/is-downton-abbey-the-future-of-the-us-economy.

56. Pew Charitable Trusts, "'Pursuing the American Dream," pp. 7–8; Peter Francese, "U.S. Consumer—Like No Other On the Planet," *Advertising Age*, January 2, 2006; Christina Passariello, Rachel Dodes, and Stacy Meichtry, "Luxury Goods Weathering Economic Woes in U.S.," *Wall Street Journal*, July 26, 2008.

57. Nelson D. Schwartz, "The Middle Class Is Steadily Eroding. Just Ask the Business World," *New York Times*, February 3, 2014.

58. David Hirschman, "On the Road to Riches: Those Under 35 With $100K House-hold Income," *AdAge.com*, May 22, 2011, http://adage.com/article/adagestat/ll-rich-35-100k-household-income/227671; Ajay Kapur, Niall Macleod, and Narendra Singh, "Revisiting Plutonomy: The Rich Getting Richer," Citigroup Research, March 5, 2006; Brenda Cronin and Ben Casselman, "Wealthier Households Carry the Spending Load," *Wall Street Journal*, March 4, 2013.

59. Morin and Motel, "A Third of Americans Now Say They Are in the Lower Classes"; Gallup, "Confidence in Institutions," June 1–4, 2013, http://www.gallup.com/poll/1597/confidence-institutions.aspx.

60. Gallup, "Confidence in Institutions"; Rasmussen Reports, "New Low: 17% Say U.S. Government Has Consent of the Governed," August 7, 2011, http://www.rasmussenreports.com/public_content/politics/general_politics/august_2011/new_low_17_say_u_s_government_has_consent_of_the_governed.

61. Pew Research Global Attitudes Project, "The New Sick Man of Europe: The European Union," May 13, 2013, http://www.pewglobal.org/2013/05/13/the-new-sick-man-of-europe-the-european-union; Anna Manchin, "Trust in Government Sinks to New Low in Southern Europe," Gallup World, October 30, 2013, http://www.gallup.com/poll/165647/trust-government-sinks-new-low-southern-europe.aspx; Edelman, *2013 Edelman Trust Barometer*, http://www.edelman.com/insights/intellectual-property/trust-2013.

62. Friedman, *The Moral Consequences of Economic Growth*, pp. 14–15, 59.

63. Amy Wilson, "How Texas Dealers Slammed the Door on Tesla," *Automotive News*, September 9, 2013, http://www.autonews.com/article/20130909/RETAIL07/130909878/how-texas-dealers-slammed-the-door-on-tesla; Stefanie Dazio, "In Va., Tesla Motors Has a Showroom Where It Can't Make Sales," *Washington Post*, June 24, 2013; Andrew C. McCarthy, "Republicans Subsidize Mansions," *National Review Online*, November 26, 2011, http://www.nationalreview.com/articles/284101/republicans-subsidize-mansions-andrew-c-mccarthy.

64. Friedman, *The Moral Consequences of Economic Growth*, p. 349.

65. U.S. Department of Transportation, Research and Innovative Technology Administration, Transportation Implications of Telecommuting, http://ntl.bts.gov/DOCS/telecommute.html; Dan Schawbel, "How Millennials Will Shape the Future of Work," *Pando Daily*, September 3, 2013, http://pando.com/2013/09/03/how-millennials-will-shape-the-future-of-work.

66. Alexis de Tocqueville, *Democracy in America*, vol. 1, trans. Henry Reeve (New York: Bantam, 2002), p. 213.

67. Frederick Jackson Turner, *The Significance of the Frontier in American History* (New York: Frederick Unger, 1973), pp. 57–58.

68. Ibid, pp. 58–59.

Chapter Two: Valley of the Oligarchs

1. eBizMBA.com, "Top 15 Most Popular Social Networking Sites," http://www.ebizmba.com/articles/social-networking-websites.

2. George Packer, "Change the World: Silicon Valley Transfers Its Slogans—and Its Money—to the Realm of Politics," *New Yorker*, May 27, 2013, pp. 44–55.

3.   Tom Simonite, "Five Interesting Things Sean Parker Said Yesterday," *MIT Technology Review* (blog), November 16, 2011, http://www.technologyreview.com/view/426138/five-interesting-things-sean-parker-said-yesterday; Robert McMillan, "Meet the Dancing Otter That Helped Obama Win the Presidency," *Wired*, December 4, 2012, http://www.wired.com/2012/12/the-dancing-otter.

4.   Raymond Hernandez, "Young, Rich and Relocating Yet Again in Hunt for Political Office," *New York Times*, July 11, 2013.

5.   Rebecca MacKinnon, *Consent of the Networked: The Worldwide Struggle for Internet Freedom* (New York: Basic Books, 2013).

6.   John Naughton, "Tech Giants Have Power to Be Political Masters as Well as Our Web Ones," *The Observer*, February 26, 2012; Manuel Castells, *The Information Age: Economy, Society and Culture*, vol. 2 of *The Power of Identity* (Oxford: Blackwell, 1997), p. 359.

7.   Beard and Beard, *The Rise of American Civilization*, p. 385.

8.   Philipp Ager, "The Persistence of de Facto Power: Elites and Economic Development in the U.S. South, 1840–1960," *EHES Working Papers in Economic History*, no. 38 (April 2013), Universitat Pompeu Fabra, Barcelona, Spain; "Leadville & Twin Lakes, Colorado History: The Story of Horace & Baby Doe Tabor," Leadville.com, http://www.leadville.com/history/tabor.htm; "A Brief History of Hearst Corporation," Hearst Communications, Inc., http://www.hearst.com/files/hearst-timeline.pdf; Henry Demarest Lloyd, "The Story of a Great Monopoly," *Atlantic*, March 1881.

9.   Morgan Brennan, "Moscow Leads Cities With Most Billionaires," *Forbes*, May 17, 2011, http://www.forbes.com/2011/05/17/cities-with-most-billionaires.html.

10. Andrew Nusca, "Silicon Valley Venture Capital Investment Drops 22 Percent," *Between the Lines* (blog), *ZDNet*, July 22, 2013, http://www.zdnet.com/silicon-valley-venture-capital-investment-drops-22-percent-7000018373.

11. Noreen Malone, "Popular Culture Has Soured on Silicon Valley's Hotshots," *New Republic*, September 8, 2013, http://www.newrepublic.com/article/114618/when-did-tech-guys-become-bad-guys; Umair Haque, Twitter post, September 2, 2013, 11:20am, http://twitter.com/umairh.

12. Kristen Purcell et al., "Search Engine Use 2012," Pew Research Center's Internet & American Life Project, March 9, 2012, http://www.pewinternet.org/files/old-media/Files/Reports/2012/PIP_Search_Engine_Use_2012.pdf; comScore Inc., "comScore Releases July 2013 U.S. Search Engine Rankings," press release, August 14, 2013, http://www.comscore.com/Insights/Press_Releases/2013/8/comScore_Releases_July_2013_US_Search_Engine_Rankings.

13. Piketty, *Capital in the Twenty-First Century*, pp. 444–45.

14. "Gartner Says Worldwide Mobile Phone Sales Declined 1.7 Percent in 2012," Gartner, Inc., February 13, 2013, http://www.gartner.com/newsroom/id/2335616; Jessica E. Lessin et al., "Apple vs. Google vs. Facebook vs. Amazon," *Wall Street Journal*, December 25, 2012.

15. "Facebook Overview Statistics," Socialbakers, http://www.socialbakers.com/facebook-overview-statistics; "North America Internet Usage Stats, Facebook and Population Statistics," Internet World Stats, http://www.internetworldstats.com/america.htm; "Europe Internet Usage Stats, Facebook Subscribers and Population Statistics," Internet World Stats, http://www.internetworldstats.com/stats4.htm;

"European Union Internet Usage Stats and Population Statistics," Internet World Stats, http://www.internetworldstats.com/stats9.htm.

16. Lessin et al., "Apple vs. Google vs. Facebook vs. Amazon."

17. Christopher Helman, "Slide Show: The World's Biggest Oil Companies," *Forbes*, July 9, 2010, http://www.forbes.com/2010/07/09/worlds-biggest-oil-companies-business-energy-big-oil_slide_2.html.

18. "Exxon Mobil Corporation Common Stock: XOM Major Holders," Yahoo! Finance, http://finance.yahoo.com/q/mh?s=xom+Major+Holders; "General Motors Company: NYSE:GM Quotes & News," Google Finance, https://www.google.com/finance?q=NYSE:GM; "Ford Motor Company: NYSE:F Quotes & News," Google Finance, https://www.google.com/finance?cid=13606.

19. Eric K. Clemons, "'Say It Ain't So, Joe, Again, and Again, and Again...': A Legacy of Continued Bad Behavior at Google," *Huffington Post*, May 16, 2012, http://www.huffingtonpost.com/eric-k-clemons/google-privacy-case_b_1522874.htm.

20. Luisa Kroll and Kerry A. Dolan, eds., "The *Forbes* 400: The Richest People in America," profile no. 3, "Larry Ellison," *Forbes*, http://www.forbes.com/profile/larry-ellison.

21. Kroll and Dolan, "The *Forbes* 400," profile no. 1, "Bill Gates," *Forbes*, http://www.forbes.com/forbes-400/gallery/bill-gates.

22. Romain Dillet, "Zuckerberg Now Owns 29.3 Percent of Facebook's Class a Shares and This Stake Is worth $13.6 Billion," *TechCrunch*, February 15, 2013, http://techcrunch.com/2013/02/15/zuckerberg-now-owns-29-3-percent-of-facebook-representing-18-billion; Kroll and Dolan, "The *Forbes* 400," profile no. 20, "Mark Zuckerberg, *Forbes*, http://www.forbes.com/profile/mark-zuckerberg.

23. David Yanofsky, "All of These Companies Have More Cash Right Now than the U.S. Government," *Quartz*, October 10, 2013, http://qz.com/134093/all-of-these-companies-have-more-cash-right-now-than-the-us-government.

24. Brian Solomon, "The World's Youngest Billionaires: 29 Under 40," *Forbes*, March 4, 2013, http://www.forbes.com/sites/briansolomon/2013/03/04/the-worlds-youngest-billionaires-23-under-40.

25. Alvin Toffler, *Future Shock* (New York: Random House, 1970), p. 186.

26. Associated Press, "Twitter Co-Founder Jack Dorsey Says He Wants to Be NYC Mayor Someday," *New York Daily News*, March 18, 2013.

27. Piketty, *Capital in the Twenty-First Century*, p. 85.

28. Jackie Calmes and Nick Wingfield, "Tech Leaders and Obama Find Shared Problem: Fading Public Trust," *New York Times*, December 18, 2013.

29. Frank Newport, "Americans Rate Computer Industry Best, Federal Gov't Worst," *Gallup Politics*, August 29, 2011, http://www.gallup.com/poll/149216/Americans-Rate-Computer-Industry-Best-Federal-Gov-Worst.aspx.

30. Schuyler Velasco, "Wall Street Protesters Boo CEOs, but Mourn Steve Jobs," *Christian Science Monitor*, October 6, 2011.

31. Steven M. Davidoff, "Outrage Over Wall St. Pay, but Shrugs for Silicon Valley?" *New York Times*, February 19, 2014.

32. Brad Stone, "It's Always Sunny in Silicon Valley," *Bloomberg Businessweek*, December 22, 2011, http://www.businessweek.com/magazine/its-always-sunny-in-silicon-valley-12222011.html.

33. Lasch, *The Only and True Heaven*, p. 519.
34. Susan Adams, "The 25 Companies Where Top Millennials Most Want to Work," *Forbes*, May 9, 2013, http://www.forbes.com/sites/susanadams/2013/05/09/the-25-companies-where-top-millennials-most-want-to-work.
35. Tom Standage, *The Victorian Internet: The Remarkable Story of the Telegraph and the Nineteenth Century's On-line Pioneers* (New York: Walker, 1998), pp. vii–ix, 212–13.
36. David Nye, *America as Second Creation: Technology and Narratives of New Beginnings* (Cambridge, MA: MIT Press, 2004), p. 270.
37. D. N. Chorafas, *The Knowledge Revolution: An Analysis of the International Brain Market* (New York: McGraw-Hill, 1968), p. 53.
38. Waldemar Kaempffert, "Miracles You'll See In The Next Fifty Years," *Popular Mechanics*, February 1950, pp. 112–18, 264–72; Jacques Ellul, *The Technological Society*, trans. John Wilkinson (New York: Vintage, 1967), p. 432.
39. C. Wright Mills, *The Power Elite* (Oxford: Oxford UP, 1956), p. 123; John Kenneth Galbraith, *The New Industrial State* (Boston: Houghton Mifflin, 1971), pp. 12, 61.
40. Dirk Hanson, *The New Alchemists: Silicon Valley and the Microelectronics Revolution* (Boston: Little Brown, 1982).pp. 84, 92–94.
41. Myles D. Crandall, "Lockheed Grew up with Sunnyvale," *Silicon Valley Business Journal*, February 25, 2007.
42. Richard Barbrook and Andy Cameron, "The Californian Ideology," *Science as Culture*, vol. 6, no. 1 (1996): 44–72.
43. Arun Rao, with Piero Scaruffi, *A History of Silicon Valley: The Greatest Creation of Wealth in the History of the Planet*, 2nd ed. (Palo Alto, CA: Omniware Group, 2013).
44. Anna Lee Saxenian, *Regional Advantage: Culture and Competition in Silicon Valley and Route 128* (Cambridge, MA: Harvard UP, 1994).
45. Paul Leinberger and Bruce Tucker, *The New Individualists: The Generation After the Organization Man* (New York: Harper Collins, 1991), pp. 400–1; Saxenian, *Regional Advantage*, pp. 59–60, 77, 107; Daisuke Wakabayashi, "How Japan Lost Its Electronics Crown," *Wall Street Journal*, August 15, 2012.
46. Alvin Toffler, *The Third Wave* (New York: Morrow, 1980), pp. 53, 171, 437.
47. Kevin Kelly, *New Rules for a New Economy: Ten Radical Strategies for a Connected World* (New York: Viking, 1998, pp. 118-119.
48. Geoffrey James, *Business Wisdom of the Electronic Elite* (New York: Random House, 1996), pp. 4–5, 222; Leo Marx, "Information Technology in Historical Perspective," in David Schon, Bish Sanyal, and William Mitchell, *High Technology and Low Income Communities* (Cambridge, MA: MIT Press, 1999), p. 136: Thomas Mahon, *Charged Bodies: People, Power and Paradox in Silicon Valley* (New York: New American Library, 1985), p. 31.
49. Nathan Jurgenson, "Silicon Valley's Anti-Capitalism-Capitalism," *The Society Pages*, May 21, 2013, http://thesocietypages.org/cyborgology/2013/05/21/silicon-valleys-anti-capitalism-capitalism.
50. Bell, *The Coming of Post-Industrial Society*, p. 427.
51. Matthew Sparkes, "Young Users See Facebook as 'Dead and Buried,'" *Telegraph* (UK), December 27, 2013.

52. W. H. Ware, "Future Computer Technology and Its Impact," paper, Rand Corporation, March 1966; David Colker, "Willis Ware Dies at 93; Pioneer Predicted the Rise of the Computer," *Los Angeles Times*, November 29, 2013.

53. Castells, *The Information Age*, pp. 300–1.

54. Jaron Lanier, *Who Owns the Future?* (New York: Simon and Shuster, 2013), p. 1.

55. Todd Woody, "Need to Finance a Big Solar Project? The Bank of Google Can Help," *Quartz*, October 10, 2013, http://qz.com/134099/need-to-finance-a-big-solar-project-the-bank-of-google-can-help; Julia Angwin and Jennifer Valentino-DeVries, "Google's iPhone Tracking," *Wall Street Journal*, February 17, 2012; Clemons, "'Say It Ain't So, Joe, Again'"; Claire Cain Miller, "Google to Pay $17 Million to Settle Privacy Case," *New York Times*, November 19, 2013.

56. Claire Cain Miller, "The Plus in Google Plus? It's Mostly for Google," *New York Times*, February 15, 2014.

57. Brent Butt, Twitter post, December 16, 2013, 1:47 p.m., http://twitter.com/brentbutt/status/412700627152961536; Joshua Rivera, "Can We All Just Admit Google Is An Evil Empire?" *Co.Labs* (blog), *Fast Company*, January 13, 2014, http://www.fastcolabs.com/3024789/can-we-all-just-admit-google-is-an-evil-empire.

58. Clemons, "'Say It Ain't So, Joe, Again'"; Shara Tibken, "Judge: We Can't Rely on What Apple Tells Court in Privacy Suit," CNET, March 8, 2013, http://www.cnet.com/news/judge-we-cant-rely-on-what-apple-tells-court-in-privacy-suit; Rosa Golijan, "Consumer Reports: Facebook Privacy Problems Are on the Rise," *NBCNews.com*, May 3, 2012, http://www.nbcnews.com/tech/tech-news/consumer-reports-facebook-privacy-problems-are-rise-f749990; Vincent Trivett, "Mark Zuckerberg Buys His Privacy for $30 Million While Yours Disappears," *Minyanville*, October 11, 2013, http://www.minyanville.com/sectors/technology/articles/fb-zuberberg-facebook-privacy-Facebook-understandably/10/11/2013/id/52199#ixzz32c6lDG38; Vindu Goel, "Facebook Eases Privacy Rules for Teenagers," *New York Times*, October 17, 2013.

59. Kevin J. O'Brien, "Silicon Valley Companies Lobbying Against Europe's Privacy Proposals," *New York Times*, January 26, 2013; Steven Harmon, "Silicon Valley Companies Quietly Try to Kill Internet Privacy Bill," *San Jose Mercury News*, April 20, 2013.

60. Tom Hamburger and Matea Gold, "Google, Once Disdainful of Lobbying, Now a Master of Washington Influence," *Washington Post*, April 12, 2014.

61. "Top Contributors to Barack Obama," OpenSecrets.org, http://www.opensecrets.org/pres12/contrib.php?id=N00009638&cycle=2012.

62. Bas van den Beld, "Top 15 of Eric Schmidt's Remarkable Quotes," *State of Digital*, October 27, 2010, http://www.stateofdigital.com/top-15-of-eric-schmidts-remarkable-quotes.

63. Karel van Wolferen, *The Enigma of Japanese Power: People and Politics in a Stateless Nation* (New York: Knopf, 1989), pp. 46–47.

64. Greg Bensinger and David Benoit, "Icahn Targets Silicon Valley Directors' Club," *Wall Street Journal*, February 24, 2014.

65. Jessica Guynn, "Silicon Valley Staff-Poaching Suit Is Granted Class-Action Status," *Los Angeles Times*, October 25, 2013; Dean Baker, "Silicon Valley Billionaires Believe in the Free Market, as Long as They Benefit," *Guardian*, February 3, 2014; David Streitfeld, "Engineers Allege Hiring Collusion in Silicon Valley," *New York*

Times, February 28, 2014; Angela Moscaritolo, "Suit Reveals Alleged Silicon Valley Anti-Poaching Scheme," *PCMag*, January 30, 2012, http://www.pcmag.com/article2/0,2817,2399555,00.asp.

66. Wooldridge, "The Coming Tech-lash"; PricewaterhouseCoopers LLP, "PwC's M&A Outlook Reveals Dealmakers' Increasing Focus on Quality Execution in Competitive M&A Market," press release, July 23, 2013, http://www.pwc.com/us/en/press-releases/2013/2013-deals-mid-year-ma-forecast-press-release.jhtml;   Chris Morran, "Google Settles With FTC, Agrees To Change Anticompetitive Business Practices," *Consumerist*, January 3, 2013, http://consumerist.com/2013/01/03/google-settles-with-ftc-agrees-to-change-anticompetitive-business-practices; Alisa Melekhina, "Are Social Media Sites Engaging in Anti-Competitive Conduct?" *RegBlog* (blog), Penn Program on Regulation, http://www.regblog.org/2013/02/14-melekhina-social-media-antitrust.html; Bruce Baer Arnold, "Big Fine for a Broken Promise: Microsoft's Antitrust Breach Puts Tech Firms on Notice," *The Conversation*, March 8, 2013, http://theconversation.com/big-fine-for-a-broken-promise-microsofts-antitrust-breach-puts-tech-firms-on-notice-12683; Jeff Elder, "Silicon Valley Tech Giants Struck Deals on Hiring, Say Documents," *Wall Street Journal*, April 20, 2014.

67. John Markoff, "Google Puts Money on Robots Using Man Behind Android," *New York Times*, December 4, 2013; Eric Mack, "Google Launches Calico to Take on Illness and Aging," *CNET*, September 18, 2013, http://www.cnet.com/news/google-launches-calico-to-take-on-illness-and-aging; John Markoff, "Google Adds to Its Menagerie of Robots," *New York Times*, December 14, 2013; Neal E. Boudette and Daisuke Wakabayashi, "Google, Apple Forge Auto Ties," *All Things Digital*, December 29, 2013, http://allthingsd.com/20131229/google-apple-forge-auto-ties.

68. Robert J. Gordon, "Is U.S. Economic Growth Over? Faltering Innovation Confronts the Six Headwinds," NBER Working Paper, no. 18315 (August 2012), http://www.nber.org/papers/w18315.   •

69. Claire Cain Miller and David Gelles, "After Big Bet, Google to Sell Motorola Unit," *New York Times*, January 30, 2014; Dan Gallagher, "Google Still Feathers Its Nest With Big Bets," *Wall Street Journal*, January 23, 2014; "Google Market Cap (GOOG)," YCharts, http://ycharts.com/companies/GOOG/market_cap.

70. Robert Sorokanich, "Google Just Bought Crazy Walking Robot Maker Boston Dynamics," *Gizmodo*, December 14, 2013, http://gizmodo.com/google-just-bought-crazy-walking-robot-maker-boston-dyn-1483235880; Michael Carney, "Gruber: Nest Can Teach Google to Make Hardware. Google Can Help Nest Go Fast," *PandoDaily*, January 14, 2014, http://pando.com/2014/01/14/gruber-nest-can-teach-google-to-make-hardware-google-can-help-nest-go-fast.

71. Jessi Hempel, "Kleiner Perkins' Trae Vassallo: Another Winner in Google's $3.2 Billion Purchase of Nest," *CNN Money*, January 16, 2014, http://tech.fortune.cnn.com/2014/01/16/kleiner-perkins-trae-vassallo-another-winner-in-googles-3-2-billion-purchase-of-nest; Josh Constine, "Who Gets Rich From Google Buying Nest? Kleiner Returns 20X On $20M, Shasta Nets ~$200M," *TechCrunch*, January 13, 2014, http://techcrunch.com/2014/01/13/nest-investors-strike-it-rich; Dan Gallagher, "Google Still Feathers Its Nest With Big Bets," *Wall Street Journal*, January 23, 2014.

72. Michael Mace, "Google the Conglomerate: After Nest, No Industry is Safe," *MobileOpportunity* (blog), January 16, 2014, http://mobileopportunity.blogspot.com/2014/01/google-conglomerate-after-nest-no.html; "The New GE: Google, Everywhere," *Economist*, January 18, 2014.

73. Sebastian Anthony, "Welcome to the Nation of Googlestan, Please Enjoy Your Stay," *ExtremeTech*, http://www.extremetech.com/extreme/178985-welcome-to-the-nation-of-googlestan-please-enjoy-your-stay.

74. Nigel Walton, "The New Conglomerates and the Ecosystem Advantage," Proceedings of the European Business Research Conference, September 5–6, 2013, Rome, Italy, https://eprints.worc.ac.uk/2378.

75. "Robotics Clusters," *Robocosmist* (blog), http://robocosmist.com/robotics-clusters; Jordan Weissmann, "The Logic of Facebook's Multibillion-Dollar Shopping Spree," *Slate*, March 27, 2014, http://www.slate.com/blogs/moneybox/2014/03/27/facebook_buys_oculus_why_zuckerberg_is_spending_so_many_billions.html.

76. Jeff Foust, Twitter post, October 16, 2013, 8:24am, https://twitter.com/jeff_foust/status/390498497428209664; Jaclyn Trop and Diane Cardwell, "Tesla Plans $5 Billion Battery Factory for Mass-Market Electric Car," *New York Times*, February 27, 2014.

77. Tim Worstall, "Google To Build Its Own Driverless Cars," *Forbes*, August 24, 2013, http://www.forbes.com/sites/timworstall/2013/08/24/google-to-build-its-own-driverless-cars; Jennifer Booton, "Google, Apple Tackle the Next Digital Frontier: Cars," *FOX Business*, January 06, 2014, http://www.foxbusiness.com/technology/2014/01/06/google-apple-tackle-next-digital-frontier-cars; Neal E. Boudette and Daisuke Wakabayashi, "Google, Apple Forge Auto Ties," *Wall Street Journal*, December 29, 2013.

78. Andrew Chaikin, "Is SpaceX Changing the Rocket Equation?" *Air & Space Magazine*, January 2012.

79. Blue Origin (website), http://www.blueorigin.com; Sheraz Sadiq, "Silicon Valley Goes to Space," *KQED Science* (blog), November 18, 2013, http://blogs.kqed.org/science/video/silicon-valley-goes-to-space; Max Luke and Jenna Mukuno, "Boldly Going Where No Greens Have Gone Before," *Wall Street Journal*, January 7, 2014.

80. Reid J. Epstein, "Mark Zuckerberg Immigration Group's Status: Looking for Footing," *Politico*, April 4, 2013, http://www.politico.com/story/2013/04/mark-zuckerberg-immigration-groups-status-stumbling-89652.html.

81. Drew FitzGerald and Spencer E. Ante, "Tech Firms Push to Control Web's Pipes," *All Things Digital*, December 17, 2013, http://allthingsd.com/20131217/tech-firms-push-to-control-webs-pipes; Drew FitzGerald and Daisuke Wakabayashi, "Apple Quietly Builds New Networks," *Wall Street Journal*, February 3, 2014.

82. Jim Edwards, "Google Is Now Bigger than Both the Magazine and Newspaper Industries," *Business Insider*, November 12, 2013, http://www.businessinsider.com/google-is-bigger-than-all-magazines-and-newspapers-combined-2013-11; Avi Dan, "Is The Publicis-Omnicom Merger A Sign Of Strength Or Weakness?" *Forbes*, July 29, 2013, http://www.forbes.com/sites/avidan/2013/07/29/is-the-publicis-omnicom-merger-a-sign-of-strength-or-weakness; Patrick Maines, "Beware of Google's Power," *USA Today*, July 19, 2013; Steven Perlberg and Amol Sharma, "A Middling Outlook for the TV 'Upfronts,'" *Wall Street Journal*, April 10, 2014.

83. Analysis of BLS data by Mark Schill, Praxis Strategy Group.

84. Manjoo, "Silicon Valley Has an Arrogance Problem."
85. Callahan, *Fortunes of Change*, p. 109.
86. Noam Cohen and Quentin Hardy, "Snowden Journalist's New Venture to Be Bankrolled by eBay Founder," *New York Times*, October 17, 2013.
87. Matt Welch, "The Death of Contrarianism," *Reason*, May 2013, http://reason.com/archives/2013/03/25/the-death-of-contrarianism.
88. Ravi Somaiyajan, "Major Expansion Ahead at the *Washington Post*," *New York Times*, January 30, 2014.
89. eBizMBA.com, "Top 15 Most Popular News Websites," http://www.ebizmba.com/articles/news-websites; Jeremy Scott, "Netflix Buys TV Series Rights, Jumps Into Content Creation Game," *ReelSEO.com*, http://www.reelseo.com/mastered-distribution-netflix-produce-content.
90. Pew Research Center for the People & the Press, "Internet Gains on Television as Public's Main News Source," January 4, 2011, http://www.people-press.org/2011/01/04/internet-gains-on-television-as-publics-main-news-source.
91. Jessica Guynn, "Facebook IPO Fuels Bay Area Spending Boom," *Los Angeles Times*, May 17, 2012.
92. "Should Local Government Be Run Like Silicon Valley?" *Governing*, April 2013, http://www.governing.com/topics/technology/gov-local-government-run-like-silicon-valley.html.
93. "Libertarian Island: A Billionaire's Utopia," *The Week*, August 18, 2011; Greg Baumann, "Rich State, Poor State: VC's 'Six Californias' Divides Silicon Valley from Have-Nots," *Silicon Valley Business Journal*, February 4, 2014.
94. Kevin Roose, "The Government Shutdown Has Revealed Silicon Valley's Dysfunction Fetish," *Daily Intelligencer* (blog), *New York*, October 16, 2013, http://nymag.com/daily/intelligencer/2013/10/silicon-valleys-dysfunction-fetish.html.
95. Susanne Posel, "Why Does Silicon Valley Want Elite Floating Cities & 6 Californias?" *Occupy Corporatism*, December 26, 2013, http://www.occupycorporatism.com/silicon-valley-want-elite-floating-cities-6-californias.
96. Jonathan Hughes, *American Economic History* (New York: HarperCollins, 1990), p. 277.
97. Eric Lipton and Somini Sengupta, "Latest Product From Tech Firms: An Immigration Bill," *New York Times*, May 5, 2013.
98. Janine Zacharia, "Silicon Valley Ambition Seen as Antidote to Do-Nothing Washington," *SFGate*, October 21, 2013, http://www.sfgate.com/opinion/article/Silicon-Valley-ambition-seen-as-antidote-to-4907812.php.
99. Lipton and Somini Sengupta, "Latest Product From Tech Firms"; "Lobbying Spending Database: Facebook Inc, 2012," OpenSecrets.org, http://www.opensecrets.org/lobby/clientsum.php?id=D000033563&year=2012; "Lobbying Spending Database: Google Inc, 2012," OpenSecrets.org, http://www.opensecrets.org/lobby/clientsum.php?id=D000022008&year=2012; Zacharia, "Silicon Valley Ambition"; Carla Marinucci, "Bay Area Money Fills Obama Campaign Coffers," *SFGate*, November 3, 2012, http://www.sfgate.com/politics/article/Bay-Area-money-fills-Obama-campaign-coffers-4005151.php; Mic Wright, "Silicon Valley Geeks Vote like Pious Democrats. But They Think and Act like Ruthless Republicans," *Politics and Tech* (blog), *Telegraph* (UK), November 6, 2012, http://blogs.telegraph.co.uk/technology/micwright/100008207/silicon-valley-geeks-vote-like-pious-

democrats-but-they-think-and-act-like-ruthless-republicans; Tom Hamburger and Matea Gold, "Google, Once Disdainful of Lobbying, Now a Master of Washington Influence," *Washington Post*, April 12, 2014.

100. Brian S. Hall, "With Help from Silicon Valley, America to Dominate the 21st Century," *Tech.pinions*, August 12, 2013, http://techpinions.com/help-silicon-valley-america-dominate-21st-century/21550.

101. John B. Judis, "The GOP Plan to Crush Silicon Valley What Will Become of Steve Jobs's Angel?" *New Republic*, August 20, 2013, http://www.newrepublic.com/article/114329/republican-budget-cut-would-crush-silicon-valley; Nate Silver, "In Silicon Valley, Technology Talent Gap Threatens G.O.P. Campaigns," *FiveThirtyEight* (blog), *New York Times*, November 28, 2012, http://fivethirtyeight.blogs.nytimes.com/2012/11/28/in-silicon-valley-technology-talent-gap-threatens-g-o-p-campaigns.

102. Matthew Continetti, "The California Captivity of the Democratic Party," *Washington Free Beacon*, May 31, 2013, http://freebeacon.com/columns/the-california-captivity-of-the-democratic-party.

103. Wendy Kaufman, "Cheap and Reliable Power Nurtures Server Farms," *Morning Edition*, NPR, July 10, 2006, http://www.npr.org/templates/story/story.php?storyId=5545145; Erika Fry, "On America's Plains, a War for Server Farms," *CNN Money*, December 4, 2012, http://tech.fortune.cnn.com/2012/12/04/on-americas-plains-a-war-for-server-farms; Google, "Investments: Google Green," http://www.google.com/green/energy/investments.

104. Patrick Howley, "Google's Schmidt Would Bring Climate Activism to Obama Admin," *Daily Caller*, December 6, 2012, http://dailycaller.com/2012/12/06/googles-schmidt-would-bring-climate-activism-to-obama-admin.

105. Tom Steyer, "The Shady Billionaire with Millions of Reasons to Kill Keystone XL," *Daily Caller*, October 8, 2013, http://dailycaller.com/2013/10/08/tom-steyer-the-shady-billionaire-with-millions-of-reasons-to-kill-keystone-xl; "Keystone Activist Tom Steyer to Sell Stake in Pipeline Company," *Washington Free Beacon*, July 8, 2013, http://freebeacon.com/national-security/keystone-activist-tom-steyer-to-sell-stake-in-pipeline-company.

106. Tom McNichol and Michael V. Copeland, "Lighting Up the $1 Trillion Power Market," *CNN Money*, October 30, 2006, http://money.cnn.com/2006/10/26/magazines/business2/solar_siliconvalley.biz2/index.htm.

107. John Pomfret, "Calif. Ballot Battle Over Big Oil May Be Costliest in U.S. History," *Washington Post*, October 20, 2006; Carol D. Leonnig and Joe Stephens, "Federal Funds Flow to Clean-Energy Firms with Obama Administration Ties," *Washington Post*, February 14, 2012; Allysia Finley, "How Government Is Making Solar Billionaires," *Wall Street Journal*, October 21, 2013; Lachlan Markay, "The Venture Corporatists," *The Federalist*, October 2, 2013, http://thefederalist.com/2013/10/02/the-venture-corporatists.

108. Woody, "Need to Finance a Big Solar Project?"

109. "California Proposition 23, the Suspension of AB 32 (2010)," *Ballotpedia*, http://ballotpedia.org/California_Proposition_23,_the_Suspension_of_AB_32_(2010).

110. F. Scott Fitzgerald, "The Rich Boy," in *The Short Stories of F. Scott Fitzgerald: A New Collection*, ed. Matthew J. Bruccoli (New York: Scribner, 1989), p. 318.

111. Norimitsu Onishi, "Corporate Jet Center Exposes Silicon Valley's Class Divide," *New York Times*, May 3, 2013; Erin Carlyle, "A Look Inside Google Billionaire Eric Schmidt's New $22 Million Hollywood House," *Forbes*, February 13, 2014, http://www.forbes.com/sites/erincarlyle/2014/02/13/a-look-inside-google-billionaire-eric-schmidts-new-22-million-hollywood-house.

112. Connie Guglielmo, "John Doerr's Plan To Reclaim The Venture Capital Throne," *Forbes*, May 7, 2013, http://www.forbes.com/sites/connieguglielmo/2013/05/07/john-doerrs-plan-to-reclaim-the-venture-capital-throne.

113. Google, "Ten Things We Know to Be True," http://www.google.com/about/company/philosophy; Drew Johnson, "Google is Flying High and Polluting the Air with Government-Bought Fuel," *The Blaze*, November 21, 2013, http://www.theblaze.com/contributions/google-flying-high-and-polluting-the-air-with-government-bought-fuel; Mark Maremont, "Google Jet Fleet Loses a Pentagon Fuel Perk," *Wall Street Journal*, September 13, 2013.

114. Ann-Marie Slaughter, "Marissa Mayer's Job Is To Be CEO—Not to Make Life Easier for Working Moms," *Atlantic*, March 4, 2013.

115. Lenny Goldberg and David Kersten, "High-Tech, Low Tax: How the Richest Silicon Valley Corporations Pay Incredibly Low Taxes on Their Land," California Tax Reform Association, March 2012.

116. Jillian Berman, "Bill Gates: I Support Taxing The Rich More Than The Poor," *Huffington Post*, October 31, 2011, http://www.huffingtonpost.com/2011/10/31/bill-gates-says-he-supports-taxing-the-rich_n_1067079.html; Laura Saunders, "How Twitter Insiders Cut Their Taxes," *Wall Street Journal*, October 11, 2013; Zachary R. Mider, "Moguls Rent South Dakota Addresses to Shelter Wealth Forever," *Bloomberg*, December 27, 2013, http://www.bloomberg.com/news/2013-12-27/moguls-rent-south-dakota-addresses-to-dodge-taxes-forever.html.

117. Saunders, "How Twitter Insiders Cut Their Taxes."

118. Zach Epstein, "Facebook Paid No Taxes in 2012," *BGR*, February 18, 2013, http://bgr.com/2013/02/18/facebook-taxes-2012-record-profit-330167.

119. Floyd Norris, "Apple's Move Keeps Profit Out of Reach of Taxes," *New York Times*, May 2, 2013.

120. "Apple's Foreign Cash Hoard Piles Up: $54 Billion and Rapidly Growing," *MacDailyNews*, January 11, 2012, http://macdailynews.com/2012/01/11/apples-foreign-cash-hoard-piles-up-54-billion-and-rapidly-growing; Peter Burrows, "Apple Avoids $9.2 Billion in Taxes With Debt Deal," *Bloomberg*, May 3, 2013, http://www.bloomberg.com/news/2013-05-02/apple-avoids-9-2-billion-in-taxes-with-debt-deal.html.

121. Jennifer Liberto, "Offshore Havens Saved Microsoft $7B in Taxes—Senate Panel," *CNN Money*, September 20, 2012, http://money.cnn.com/2012/09/20/technology/offshore-tax-havens/index.html.

122. Lanier, *Who Owns the Future?* p. 10.

123. Charles Duhigg and David Barboza, "In China, Human Costs Are Built Into an iPad," *New York Times*, January 26, 2012.

124. Ibid.

125. Hamilton Nolan, "Hubris, High Socks, and other Habits of the Most Powerful People in the World," *Gawker*, December 13, 2012, http://gawker.com/5968116/

hubris-high-socks-and-other-habits-of-the-most-powerful-people-in-the-world; Chris Benner, "Win the Lottery or Organize: Traditional and non-Traditional Labor Organizing in Silicon Valley," *Berkeley Planning Journal*, Volume 12, 1997/1998, December 8, 1997; Jack Ewing, "Amazon's Labor Relations Under Scrutiny in Germany," *New York Times*, March 4, 2013; Brad Stone, "Amazon May Get Its First Labor Union in the U.S.," *Bloomberg Businessweek*, December 17, 2013, http://www.businessweek.com/articles/2013-12-17/amazon-may-get-its-first-labor-union-in-the-u-dot-s.

126. Tian Luo and Amar Mann, "Survival and Growth of Silicon Valley High-tech Businesses Born in 2000," *Monthly Labor Review*, September 2011, pp. 16–31.

127. Timothy Noah, "Steve Jobs, Jobs-Creator," *New Republic* (blog), October 6, 2011, http://www.newrepublic.com/blog/timothy-noah/95877/steve-jobs-job-creator.

128. John Markoff, "Silicon Valley Reacts to Economy With a New Approach," *New York Times*, April 21, 2001; Robert D. Hof, "Venture Capital's Liquidators," *Bloomberg Businessweek*, December 03, 2008, http://www.businessweek.com/stories/2008-12-03/venture-capitals-liquidators.

129. Paul Abrahams, "End of Second California Gold Rush Leaves the Valley in Shock," *Financial Times*, May 9, 2001.

130. Robert Marquand, "Fast, Cheap, and in English, India Clerks for the World," *Christian Science Monitor*, April 30, 1999.

131. Economic Policy Institute, "EPI Analysis Finds No Shortage of STEM Workers in the United States," press release, April 24, 2013, http://www.epi.org/press/epi-analysis-finds-shortage-stem-workers; Joshua Wright, "Supply of Tech Workers Greater Than Estimated Demand," *New Geography*, September 1, 2011, http://www.newgeography.com/content/002411-supply-tech-workers-greater-than-estimated-demand.

132. Sarah McBride, "Special Report: Silicon Valley's Dirty Secret—Age Bias," Reuters, November 27, 2012, http://www.reuters.com/article/2012/11/27/us-valley-ageism-idUSBRE8AQ0JK20121127.

133. Andrew S. Ross, "In Silicon Valley, Age Can Be a Curse," *SFGate*, August 20, 2013, http://www.sfgate.com/business/bottomline/article/In-Silicon-Valley-age-can-be-a-curse-4742365.php.

134. Charlotte Allen, "Silicon Chasm: The Class Divide on America's Cutting Edge," *Weekly Standard*, December 2, 2013; Vivek Wadhwa, "Silicon Valley's Dark Secret: It's All About Age," *TechCrunch*, August 28, 2010, http://techcrunch.com/2010/08/28/silicon-valley%E2%80%99s-dark-secret-it%E2%80%99s-all-about-age.

135. Mickey Kaus, "Zuckerberg Buys Beltway Fakery," *Daily Caller*, April 25, 2013, http://dailycaller.com/2013/04/25/facebook-founder-buys-beltway-fakery.

136. Enrico Moretti, "Where the Good Jobs Are—and Why," *Wall Street Journal*, September 17, 2013.

137. Chris Benner, "Win the Lottery or Organize: Traditional and non-Traditional Labor Organizing in Silicon Valley," *Berkeley Planning Journal*, vol. 12 (1998): 50–71.

138. Martha Mendoza, "Silicon Valley Poverty Is Often Ignored By The Tech Hub's Elite," *Huffington Post*, March 10, 2013, http://www.huffingtonpost.com/2013/03/10/silicon-valley-poverty_n_2849285.html; Keith Matheny, "Techies Can Appear Slow to Embrace Philanthropy," *USA Today*, June 18, 2012; "Why Is Silicon Valley's

Philanthropy Sluggish?" *Nonprofit Quarterly*, June 20, 2012, https://www.nonprofitquarterly.org/philanthropy/20534-why-is-silicon-valleys-philanthropy-sluggish.html.

139. Economic Modeling Specialists Intl., http://www.economicmodeling.com; Amar Mann and Tony Nunes, "After the Dot.com Bubble: Silicon Valley Employment and Wages in 2001 and 2008," regional report, United States Department of Labor, Bureau of Labor Statistics, August 2009.

140. Jim Russell, "Rust Belt of Silicon Valley: San Jose Is Dying," *Pacific Standard*, September 10, 2013, http://www.psmag.com/navigation/business-economics/burgh-disapora/rust-belt-silicon-valley-san-jose-dying-66044.

141. Leslie Parks, interview by the author.

142. Scott Sterling, "Is Silicon Valley's Legendary Office Culture a Business Liability?" *Digital Trends*, December 5, 2012, http://www.digitaltrends.com/opinion/is-silicon-valleys-legendary-office-culture-a-business-liability; Matt Richtel, "Housecleaning, Then Dinner? Silicon Valley Perks Come Home," *New York Times*, October 20, 2012; James B. Stewart, "Looking for a Lesson in Google's Perks," *New York Times*, March 16, 2013.

143. Laurie Segall and Erica Fink, "Silicon Valley's Other Entrepreneurs: Sex Workers," *CNN Money*, April 15, 2013, http://money.cnn.com/2013/04/15/technology/silicon-valley-sex-workers/index.html.

144. Julianne Pepitone, "Silicon Valley Fights to Keep Its Diversity Data Secret," *CNN Money*, November 9, 2011, http://money.cnn.com/2011/11/09/technology/diversity_silicon_valley/index.htm; Mike Cassidy, "Facebook, Google and Other Hypocrites Need to Lean in to Some Honesty about Lack of Diversity in Hiring," *Silicon Beat* (blog), *San Jose Mercury News*, March 20, 2013, http://www.siliconbeat.com/2013/03/20/facebook-google-and-other-hypocrites-need-to-lean-in-to-some-honesty-about-lack-of-diversity-in-hiring.

145. Mike Swift, "Blacks, Latinos and Women Lose Ground at Silicon Valley Tech Companies," *San Jose Mercury News*, February 13, 2010.

146. Silicon Valley Index, http://www.siliconvalleyindex.org.

147. Esther Yu-Hsi Lee and Aviva Shen, "Class Divide Widens Between Low-Wage And High-Wage Workers In Silicon Valley," *ThinkProgress*, October 16, 2013, http://thinkprogress.org/immigration/2013/10/16/2779601/wage-immigrants-silicon-valley.

148. Jake Blumgart, "How Google and Silicon Valley Screw Their Non-Elite Workers," *AlterNet*, June 8, 2013, http://www.alternet.org/labor/how-google-and-silicon-valley-screw-their-non-elite-workers.

149. Silicon Valley Index, http://www.siliconvalleyindex.org; Robert Johnson, "Welcome to 'the Jungle': The Largest Homeless Camp In Mainland USA Is Right In The Heart Of Silicon Valley," *Business Insider*, September 7, 2013, http://www.businessinsider.com/the-jungle-largest-homeless-camp-in-us-2013-8.

150. George Avalos, "Silicon Valley Job Growth Has Reached Dot-Com Boom Levels, Report Says," *San Jose Mercury News*, February 7, 2013.

151. Rory Carroll, "How Wealth of Silicon Valley's Tech Elite Created a World Apart," *Observer* (UK), May 25, 2013; Avalos, "Silicon Valley Job Growth"; Caille Millner, "Why We're Invisible to Google Bus Riders," *San Francisco Chronicle*, April 26, 2013; Joseph Malchow, "Those Nonsensical 'Google Bus' Attacks," *Wall Street Journal*,

March 10, 2014; Vauhini Vara, "Tech Firms Log On to San Francisco's Mayoral Race," *Wall Street Journal*, November 7, 2011; Yoona Ha, "Twitter, Other Tech Companies Get S.F. Tax Breaks but Show Little Progress Hiring in Neighborhood," *San Francisco Public Press*, November 11, 2013, http://sfpublicpress.org/news/2013-11/twitter-other-tech-companies-get-sf-tax-breaks-but-show-little-progress-hiring-in-neighborhood.

152. Jason Henry, "Backlash by the Bay: Tech Riches Alter a City," *New York Times*, November 24, 2013; Emily Badger, "Where Even the Middle Class Can't Afford to Live Any More," *CityLab* (blog), *Atlantic*, October 10, 2013, http://www.citylab.com/housing/2013/10/where-even-middle-class-cant-afford-live-any-more/7194; Geoffrey A. Fowler, "Moore's Rules for Giving It Away," *Wall Street Journal*, September 19, 2012.

Chapter Three: The New Clerisy

1. Bell, *The Coming of Post-Industrial Society*, pp. 15, 33, 43, 391.
2. The National Archives (UK), "Domesday Book: The Church," http://www.nationalarchives.gov.uk/domesday/world-of-domesday/church.htm; Thomas P. Oakley, "Religion and the Middle Ages" (New York: Missionary Society of St. Paul The Apostle, 1939), reproduced at CatholicCulture.org, http://www.catholicculture.org/culture/library/view.cfm?recnum=523; Georges Lefebvre, *The Coming of the French Revolution*, trans. R. R. Palmer (Princeton, NJ: Princeton UP, 1947), p. 7.
3. Ben Knights, *The Idea of the Clerisy in the Nineteenth Century* (Cambridge: Cambridge UP, 2010).
4. Suzy Khimm, "The Right's Latest Weapon: Think-Tank Lobbying Muscle," *Wonkblog* (blog), *Washington Post*, January 24, 2013, http://www.washingtonpost.com/blogs/wonkblog/wp/2013/01/24/the-rights-latest-weapon-think-tank-lobbying-muscle.
5. Callahan, *Fortunes of Change*, pp. 239–43.
6. Walter Russell Mead et al., "Putin Smashes Washington's Cocoon," *American Interest*, March 1, 2014, http://www.the-american-interest.com/blog/2014/03/01/putin-smashes-washingtons-cocoon.
7. NAICS analysis by Gary Girod.
8. NAICS analysis by Gary Girod; United States Census Bureau, "About School Enrollment," http://www.census.gov/hhes/school/about/index.html.
9. Malia Wollan and Elizabeth A. Harris, "Occupy Wall Street Protesters Shifting to College Campuses," *New York Times*, November 14, 2011; Saki Knafo, "Occupy Wall Street Spreads To Colleges With Protests Against Student Debt," *Huffington Post*, http://www.huffingtonpost.com/2012/03/01/occupy-wall-street_n_1314948.html.
10. Toffler, *Future Shock*, p. 474.
11. Richard E. Redding, "Scientific Groupthink and Gay Parenting," *The American*, December 18, 2013, http://www.american.com/archive/2013/december/scientific-groupthink-and-gay-parenting.
12. "Actress Out of San Francisco Production after Endorsing Tea Party Candidate," *CBS San Francisco*, January 18, 2014, http://sanfrancisco.cbslocal.com/2014/01/18/actress-out-of-san-francisco-production-after-endorsing-tea-party-candidate.

13. Neil Gross and Solon Simmons, "How Religious are America's College and University Professors?" Essay Forum on the Religious Engagements of American Undergraduates, Social Science Research Council, February 6, 2007, http://religion.ssrc.org/reforum/Gross_Simmons.pdf; Amy Harmon, "A Lonely Quest for Facts on Genetically Modified Crops," *New York Times*, January 4, 2014.

14. Stefan Collini, Donald Winch, and John Burrow, *That Noble Science of Politics: A Study in Nineteenth-Century Intellectual History* (Cambridge: Cambridge UP, 1983), p. 150.

15. William Gibson, *The Church of England: 1688 to 1832: Unity and Accord* (New York: Routledge, 2000), p. 5.

16. Arno Mayer, *The Persistence of the Old Regime: Europe to the Great War* (New York: Pantheon, 1981), pp. 8–9; Peter Burke, *Venice and Amsterdam: A Study of Seventeenth-Century Elites* (Cambridge, MA: Polity Press, 1994), p. 15.

17. Max Weber, *The Protestant Ethic and the Spirit of Capitalism*, trans. Talcott Parsons (New York: Scribner, 1958), p. 158; James Henry Thornwell, "A Southern Christian View of Slavery," December 4, 1861, in *The Annals of America* (Chicago: Encyclopedia Britannica, 1968–87), 5:298–303, reproduced at TeachingAmericanHistory. org, http://teachingamericanhistory.org/library/document/a-southern-christian-view-of-slavery.

18. Henri de Saint Simon, *Social Organization and the Science of Man*, trans. Felix Markham (New York: Harper and Row, 1952), pp. 14–15, 46–47, 68.

19. Wells, *Anticipations of the Reaction*, pp. 154–58.

20. Samuel Hays, *The Response to Industrialism: 1885-1914* (Chicago: Univ. of Chicago Press, 1957, pp. 72, 93; Beard and Beard, *The Rise of American Civilization*, p. 419.

21. Hugh McLeod, *Class and Religion in the Late Victorian City* (Hamden, CO: Archon Books, 1974), pp. 232–35; Lasch, *The Only and True Heaven*, p. 58; Tocqueville, *Democracy in America*, p. 643.

22. Bell, *The Coming of Post-Industrial Society*, p. 87; Toffler, *Future Shock*, p. 119.

23. David Dayen, "National Poverty Rate Approaching Pre-Great Society Highs," Firedoglake, July 23, 2012, http://news.firedoglake.com/2012/07/23/national-poverty-rate-approaching-pre-great-society-highs.

24. Martin Earnshaw, "Communities on the Couch," in Dave Clements et al., eds., *The Future of Community: Reports of a Death Greatly Exaggerated* (London: Pluto Press, 2008), pp. 148–49.

25. Michael Lind, *Land of Promise: An Economic History of the United States* (New York: HarperCollins, 2012), pp. 400–2; Harrington, *Toward a Democratic Left: A Radical Program for a New Majority* (New York: Macmillan, 1968), pp. 77–100.

26. Charles Murray, *Losing Ground: American Social Policy 1950–1980* (New York: Basic Books,1984), pp. 14, 25.

27. Harrington, *Towards a Democratic Left*.

28. Galbraith, *The New Industrial State*, pp. 32–33, 288–89; Bell, *The Coming of Post-Industrial Society*, p. 41.

29. Callahan, *Fortunes of Change*, p. 13; Kathy Robertson, "Obamacare Means Big Business for Lawyers," *Sacramento Business Journal*, February 15, 2013; Elizabeth Lesly Stevens, "Will Law School Students Have Jobs after They Graduate?" *Washington Post*, October 31, 2012.

30. Chris Moody, "Washington, D.C. Area Now the Richest in the Nation," *Yahoo News*, October 19, 2011, http://news.yahoo.com/blogs/ticket/washington-d-c-area-now-richest-nation-191806412.html; Chris Edwards, "Overpaid Federal Workers," *Downsizing the Federal Government* (Cato Institute), August 2013, http://www.downsizinggovernment.org/overpaid-federal-workers; Charles Lane, "Federal Washington Cashes in on Connections," *Washington Post*, January 6, 2014.

31. OpenSecrets.org, "Lobbying Database," http://www.opensecrets.org/lobby; OpenSecrets.org, "Non-Profit Institutions," http://www.opensecrets.org/lobby/indusclient.php?id=W02.

32. Mike Patton, "The Growth Of Government: 1980 To 2012," *Forbes*, January 24, 2013, http://www.forbes.com/sites/mikepatton/2013/01/24/the-growth-of-the-federal-government-1980-to-2012; Green, *Epitaph for American Labor*, pp. 38–44; Steven Greenhut, *Plunder!: How Public Employees Unions Are Raiding Treasuries, Controlling Our Lives and Bankrupting the Nation* (Santa Ana, CA: Forum Press, 2009), pp. 3–11; Steven Greenhouse, "Labor Unions Claim Credit for Obama's Victory," *The Caucus* (blog), *New York Times*, November 7, 2012, http://thecaucus.blogs.nytimes.com/2012/11/07/labor-unions-claim-credit-for-obamas-victory; Roper Center, "Demographics of How Groups Voted 2012," http://www.roper-center.uconn.edu/elections/how_groups_voted/voted_12.html; OpenSecrets.org, "Heavy Hitters: Top All-Time Donors, 1989–2014," http://www.opensecrets.org/orgs/list.php.

33. Chip Mellor, "An Intelligible Principle To Restrain Unelected Government Officials," *Forbes*, May 16, 2011, http://www.forbes.com/2011/05/16/regulation-constitution-washington.html.

34. Herman Kahn, *The Coming Boom: Economic, Political, and Social* (New York: Simon and Shuster, 1982), pp. 188–89; Andrew Becker and G. W. Schulz, "Local Cops Ready for War With Homeland Security-Funded Military Weapons," *Daily Beast*, December 21, 2011, http://www.thedailybeast.com/articles/2011/12/20/local-cops-ready-for-war-with-homeland-security-funded-military-weapons.html; Shaun Waterman, "Drones over U.S. Get OK by Congress," *Washington Times*, February 7, 2012; "GHEI: ATF's Latest Gun Grab" (editorial), *Washington Times*, September 6, 2012; John Diedrich and Raquel Rutledge, "ATF Uses Rogue Tactics in Storefront Stings across Nation," *Journal Sentinel* (Milwaukee), December 7, 2013; Joe Smyth, "The BLM's Corrupt Coal Leasing Program: Billions in Subsidies to Peabody, Gigatons of Carbon Pollution for the Rest of Us," *ClimateProgress*, http://thinkprogress.org/climate/2012/06/22/504322/the-blms-corrupt-coal-leasing-program-billions-in-subsidies-to-peabody-gigatons-of-carbon-pollution-for-the-rest-of-us; Steven F. Hayward, "Bureaucracy In America Now Goes All The Way Down," *Forbes*, January 20, 2014, http://www.forbes.com/sites/stevenhayward/2014/01/20/bureaucracy-in-america-now-goes-all-the-way-down; Jaime Fuller, "Everything You Need to Know about the Long Fight between Cliven Bundy and the Federal Government," *The Fix* (blog), *Washington Post*, http://www.washingtonpost.com/blogs/the-fix/wp/2014/04/15/everything-you-need-to-know-about-the-long-fight-between-cliven-bundy-and-the-federal-government.

35. Peter Orszag, "Too Much of a Good Thing," *New Republic*, September 14, 2011, http://www.newrepublic.com/article/politics/magazine/94940/peter-orszag-

democracy; Thomas L. Friedman, "Our One-Party Democracy," *New York Times*, September 8, 2009.

36. Arnold Toynbee, *The Study of History* (Oxford: Oxford UP, 1957), p. 376.

37. Norman Birnbaum, The Crisis of Industrial Society (New York: Oxford UP, 1969), p. 13; Hays, *The Response to Industrialism*, p. 25; Pew Research Religion & Public Life Project, "'Nones' on the Rise: One-in-Five Adults Have No Religious Affiliation," October 9, 2012, http://www.pewforum.org/files/2012/10/NonesOn-TheRise-full.pdf.

38. Kerry A. Dolan and Luisa Kroll, eds., "The World's Billionaires," *Forbes*, http://www.forbes.com/billionaires.

39. Lili Ladaga, "Journalism, the New Politics," *Yahoo News*, August 31, 2009; Michael Cieply, "A Movie Mogul Rising," *New York Times*, January 15, 2013; Julie Bort, "Larry Ellison's 27-Year-Old Daughter Is Responsible For Two More Hollywood Hits," *Business Insider*, January 13, 2014, http://www.businessinsider.com/megan-ellison-has-2-more-hollywood-hits-2014-1.

40. Daniel Bell, "The Cultural Contradictions of Capitalism," *Journal of Aesthetic Education*, vol. 6, nos. 1–2 (January–April 1972): 11–38; Brett Zongker, "Arts Funding Is Supporting a Wealthy, White Audience: Report," *Huffington Post*, October 10, 2011, http://www.huffingtonpost.com/2011/10/10/arts-funding-report_n_1003065.html.

41. Thomas Frank, *The Conquest of Cool: Business Culture, Counterculture, and the Rise of Hip Consumerism* (Chicago: Univ. of Chicago Press, 1997), pp. 230–32.

42. Michael M'Gonigle and Justine Starke, *Planet U: Sustaining the World, Reinventing the University* (Gabriola Island, BC: New Society Publishers, 2006), pp. 3–40; Harrington, *Toward a Democratic Left*, pp. 88–89.

43. James Taylor, "Global Warming Activist Michael Mann Wages War on Government Transparency," *Forbes*, August 9, 2013, http://www.forbes.com/sites/jamestaylor/2013/08/09/global-warming-activist-michael-mann-wages-war-on-government-transparency; Carl Elliott, "The Deadly Corruption of Clinical Trials," *Mother Jones*, September/October 2010; John Fauber, "UW Group Ends Drug Firm Funds," *Journal Sentinel* (Milwaukee), April 20, 2011.

44. Derek Hanson, *The New Alchemists: Silicon Valley and the Microelectronics Revolution* (Boston: Little, Brown, 1982), pp. 86–87, 102.

45. Tyler Kingkade, "9 Reasons Why Being an Adjunct Faculty Member Is Terrible," *Huffington Post*, November 11, 2013, http://www.huffingtonpost.com/2013/11/11/adjunct-faculty_n_4255139.html.

46. Jeffrey J. Williams, "The Great Stratification," *Chronicle of Higher Education*, December 2, 2013; Richard K. Vedder, "Cut Off Harvard to Save America," *Bloomberg View*, February 20, 2014, http://www.bloombergview.com/articles/2014-02-19/cut-off-harvard-to-save-america.

47. Pew Charitable Trusts, "Pursuing the American Dream," p. 17; David Wessel, "As Rich-Poor Gap Widens in the U.S., Class Mobility Stalls," *Wall Street Journal*, May 13, 2005; David Wessel, "Fed Chief Warns of Widening Inequality," *Wall Street Journal*, Feb. 7, 2007.

48. Jeffrey Snider, "An Economy Wrecked By Ivy League Ph.Ds," *Real Clear Markets*, December 20, 2013, http://www.realclearmarkets.com/articles/2013/12/20/

an_economy_wrecked_by_ivy_league_phds_100807.html; Marian Wang, "Public Universities Ramp Up Aid for the Wealthy, Leaving the Poor Behind," *ProPublica*, September 11, 2013, http://www.propublica.org/article/how-state-schools-ramp-up-aid-for-the-wealthy-leaving-the-poor-behind; Richard Vedder and Christopher Denhart, "How the College Bubble Will Pop," *Wall Street Journal*, January 8, 2014.

49. Beard and Beard, *The Rise of American Civilization*, p. 415.

50. Ronald Bailey, "Ugly Climate Models," *Reason*, January 2014; Met Office (UK), "The Recent Pause in Warming," July 2013, http://www.metoffice.gov.uk/research/news/recent-pause-in-warming.

51. "A Sensitive Matter," *Economist*, March 30, 2013.

52. Sohrab Ahmari, "How Free Speech Died on Campus," *Wall Street Journal*, November 16, 2002; Charles Krauthammer, "The Myth of 'Settled Science,'" *Washington Post*, February 20, 2014.

53. M'Gonigle and Starke, *Planet U*, p. 202; Bell, *The Coming of Post-Industrial Society*, p. 404; James Ridgeway, *The Politics of Ecology* (New York: Dutton, 1970), p. 195; Yoel Inbar and Joris Lammers, "Political Diversity in Social and Personality Psychology," *Perspectives on Psychological Science*, vol. 7, no. 5 (September 2012): 496–503; John Tierney, "The Left-Leaning Tower," *New York Times*, July 22, 2011.

54. Pew Research Religion & Public Life Project, "Lobbying for the Faithful: Religious Advocacy Groups in Washington, D.C.," May 15, 2012, http://www.pewforum.org/2011/11/21/lobbying-for-the-faithful-exec.

55. Laura Byrne, "96 Percent of Ivy League Presidential Donations Were for Obama," *Daily Caller*, http://dailycaller.com/2012/11/29/96-percent-of-ivy-league-presidential-donations-were-for-obama; Scott Jaschik, "Moving Further to the Left," *Inside Higher Ed*, October 24, 2012, http://www.insidehighered.com/news/2012/10/24/survey-finds-professors-already-liberal-have-moved-further-left.

56. Brian Resnick and Brian McGill, "More Top Obama Officials Have Graduate Degrees from Oxford than Any Public University in the United States," *National Journal*, July 19, 2013, http://www.nationaljournal.com/decision-makers/more-top-obama-officials-have-graduate-degrees-from-oxford-than-any-public-university-in-the-united-states-20130719.

57. M'Gonigle and Stark, *Planet U*, pp. 204-211; Austin Williams, *Enemies of Progress: The Dangers of Sustainability* (Exeter: Societas, 2008), pp. 73–81.

58. Pew Research Center for the People & the Press, "Press Widely Criticized, But Trusted More than Other Information Sources," September 22, 2011, http://www.people-press.org/2011/09/22/press-widely-criticized-but-trusted-more-than-other-institutions.

59. Erik Wemple, "America*: Media Still 'Too Liberal,'" Erik Wemple's blog, *Washington Post*, September 19, 2013, http://www.washingtonpost.com/blogs/erik-wemple/wp/2013/09/19/america-media-still-too-liberal; Meg Sullivan, "Media Bias Is Real, Finds UCLA Political Scientist," UCLA Newsroom, press release, http://newsroom.ucla.edu/releases/Media-Bias-Is-Real-Finds-UCLA-6664.

60. Lars Willnat and David H. Weaver, *The American Journalist in the Digital Age: Key Findings* (Bloomington, IN: School of Journalism, Indiana University, 2014), http://news.indiana.edu/releases/iu/2014/05/2013-american-journalist-key-findings.pdf.

61. Josh Rogin, "Another Journalist Joins the Obama Administration," *Daily Beast*, October 21, 2013, http://www.thedailybeast.com/articles/2013/10/21/another-journalist-joins-the-obama-administration.html; Matthew Continetti, "The Caste," *Washington Free Beacon*, June 7, 2013, http://freebeacon.com/columns/the-caste; Matthew Continetti, "All In the Family," *Washington Free Beacon*, June 14, 2013, http://freebeacon.com/columns/all-in-the-family-3.

62. Patrick Caddell, "Mainstream Media Is Threatening Our Country's Future," *Fox News*, September 29, 2012, http://www.foxnews.com/opinion/2012/09/29/mainstream-media-threatening-our-country-future.

63. Matthew Continetti, "Dirty Pool," *Washington Free Beacon*, December 6, 2013, http://freebeacon.com/politics/dirty-pool.

64. Emily Guskin, Tom Rosenstiel, and Paul Moore, "Network News: Durability & Decline," *The State of the News Media 2011*, Pew Research Center's Project for Excellence in Journalism, http://stateofthemedia.org/2011/network-essay.

65. "The New Establishment 2013: The 25 Powers That Be," *Vanity Fair*, November 2013, http://www.vanityfair.com/business/2013/11/new-establishment-powers-that-be.

66. Arthur S. Brisbane, "Success and Risk as The Times Transforms," *New York Times*, August 25, 2012.

67. Devin Dwyer, "Anna Wintour on Obama Short List for U.S. Ambassador," *Political Punch* (blog), *ABC News*, December 4, 2012, http://abcnews.go.com/blogs/politics/2012/12/anna-wintour-reportedly-on-obama-short-list-for-us-ambassador; Ishmael Reed, "The President of Cool," *New York Times*, December 19, 2013.

68. Nathan Allen, "Reddit's Science Forum Banned Climate Deniers. Why Don't All Newspapers Do the Same?" *Huffington Post*, December 17, 2013, http://www.huffingtonpost.com/nathan-allen/reddits-science-forum-ban_b_4455825.html; Robert C. Illig, "Al Gore, Oprah, and Silicon Valley: Bringing Main Street and Corporate America into the Environmental Movement," *Journal of Environmental Law and Litigation*, vol. 23 (Spring 2008): 223–39; J. Scott Armstrong, "*Los Angeles Times* Endorses Censorship with Ban on Letters from Climate Skeptics," *Fox News*, October 18, 2013, http://www.foxnews.com/opinion/2013/10/18/los-angeles-times-endorses-censorship-with-ban-on-letters-from-climate-skeptics; Brendan O'Neill, "Reddit Has Banned Climate Change Deniers, and Ripped Its Own Reputation to Shreds," *Telegraph* (UK), December 18, 2013, http://blogs.telegraph.co.uk/news/brendanoneill2/100250918/reddit-has-banned-climate-change-deniers-and-ripped-its-own-reputation-to-shreds; Julia A. Seymour, "Networks Do 92 Climate Change Stories; Fail to Mention 'Lull' in Warming All 92 Times," Media Research Center, Business and Media Institute, June 25, 2013, http://www.mrc.org/bias-numbers/networks-do-92-climate-change-stories-fail-mention-lull-warming-all-92-times.

69. The MetLife Mature Market Institute, "The MetLife Study of Inheritance and Wealth Transfer to Baby Boomers," December 2010, http://www.metlife.com/assets/cao/mmi/publications/studies/2010/mmi-inheritance-wealth-transfer-baby-boomers.pdf; Robert Frank, "The 1% Captures Most Growth From Recovery," *Wall Street Journal*, March 6, 2012; Callahan, *Fortunes of Change*, p. 257; Ryan Mac, "The World's Youngest Billionaires 2014: 31 Under 40," *Forbes*, March 3, 2014, http://www.forbes.com/sites/ryanmac/2014/03/03/the-worlds-youngest-billionaires-

2014-31-under-40; Alex Morrell, "Billionaires 2014: Record Number of Newcomers Includes Sheryl Sandberg, Jan Koum, Michael Kors," *Forbes*, March 3, 2014, http://www.forbes.com/sites/alexmorrell/2014/03/03/billionaires-2014-record-number-of-newcomers-includes-sheryl-sandberg-jan-koum-michael-kors.

70. John J. Havens and Paul G. Schervish, "Why the $41 Trillion Wealth Transfer Estimate Is Still Valid: A Review of Challenges and Comments," *Journal of Gift Planning*, vol. 7, no. 1 (January 2003): 11–15, 47–50.

71. Bell, *The Coming of Post-Industrial Society*, pp. 146–47.

72. Lester M. Salamon, S. Wojichiech Sokolowski, and Stephanie L. Geller, "Holding the Fort: Non-Profit Employment During an Age of Turmoil," The Johns Hopkins Non-Profit Data Project, Bulletin 39, 2010; Bureau of Labor Statistics.

73. Urban Institute, "Research Area: Nonprofit Sector," http://www.urban.org/non-profits/more.cfm.

74. Johns Hopkins University Center for Civil Society Studies, Nonprofit Economic Data Project, "Nonprofits Show Job Growth through Decade of Turmoil, but Lose Market Share," January 19, 2012, http://ccss.jhu.edu/new-report-nonprofits-show-job-growth-through-decade-of-turmoil-but-lose-market-share.

75. Andrew Carnegie, *The Gospel of Wealth and Other Timely Essays* (New York: The Century Co., 1901); Adam Meyerson, "When Philanthropy Goes Wrong," *Wall Street Journal*, March 9, 2012.

76. Heather Mac Donald, "The Billions of Dollars That Made Things Worse," *City Journal*, Autumn 1996; Lannik Law, LLC, "Trust-Fund Progressives: A New Breed of Young, Wealthy Inheritors," press release, April 19, 2013; Paul Sullivan, "Among Young Inheritors, an Urge to Redistribute," *New York Times*, March 26, 2013.

77. Fredreka Schouten, "'Dark Money' of Non-Profit Political Groups Targeted," *USA Today*, June 11, 2013; Matea Gold, "Seeking to Harness Obama's Campaign Resources for a Second Term," *Los Angeles Times*, January 17, 2013; Liz Bartolomeo, "The Political Spending of 501(c)(4) Nonprofits in the 2012 Election," Sunlight Foundation, May 21, 2013, http://sunlightfoundation.com/blog/2013/05/21/the-political-spending-of-501c4-nonprofits-in-the-2012-election; Adrian Chen, "Mark Zuckerberg's Self-Serving Immigration Crusade," *Gawker*, April 30, 2013, http://gawker.com/mark-zuckerbergs-self-serving-immigration-crusade-484912430; Chrystia Freeland, "Plutocrats vs. Populists," *New York Times*, November 3, 2013; Guy Sorman, "The Philanthropic Spectacle," *City Journal*, Autumn 2013; OpenSecrets.org, "Non-profits, Foundations & Philanthropists," http://www.opensecrets.org/industries/indus.php?ind=W02.

78. Dolan and Kroll, "The World's Billionaires," profile no. 64, "Laurene Powell Jobs & Family," *Forbes*, http://www.forbes.com/profile/laurene-powell-jobs; Jessica E. Lessin and Miriam Jordan, "Laurene Powell Jobs Goes Public to Promote Dream Act," *Wall Street Journal*, May 16, 2013.

79. Charles M. Blow, "Dinosaurs and Denial," *New York Times*, December 8, 2012; Bell, *The Coming of Post-Industrial Society*, p. 308.

80. Bjørn Lomborg, "The Limits of Panic," *Slate*, June 26, 2013, http://www.slate.com/articles/business/project_syndicate/2013/06/climate_panic_ecological_collapse_is_not_upon_us_and_we_haven_t_run_out.html; Jeff Jacoby, "Majority Rules on Climate Science?" *Boston Globe*, December 4, 2013; Paul Ehrlich, *The Population Bomb* (New York: Ballantine Books, 1968), pp. 15–44, 66–67, 136–37.

81. Bell, *The Coming of Post-Industrial Society*, pp. 168–69, 380, 387.
82. Frank Furedi, "Elevating Environmentalism over 'Less Worthy' Lifestyles," *Spiked*, November 9, 2009, http://www.spiked-online.com/newsite/article/7684#. U4GA7C8TFsE.
83. Ray Kurzweil, *The Singularity is Near: When Humans Transcend Biology* (New York: Penguin, 2005), p. 10.
84. Ibid., p. 29.
85. Alex Knapp, "Ray Kurzweil's Predictions For 2009 Were Mostly Inaccurate," *Forbes*, March 20, 2012, http://www.forbes.com/sites/alexknapp/2012/03/20/ray-kurzweils-predictions-for-2009-were-mostly-inaccurate; Robert Jonathan, "Google Exec Ray Kurzweil Takes 150 Vitamin Supplements Every Day," *Inquisitr*, October 20, 2013, http://www.inquisitr.com/1000017/google-exec-ray-kurzweil-takes-150-vitamin-supplements-every-day; Eric Mack, "Google Launches Calico to Take on Illness and Aging," *CNET*, September 18, 2013, http://www.cnet.com/news/google-launches-calico-to-take-on-illness-and-aging; Holman W. Jenkins, Jr., "Will Google's Ray Kurzweil Live Forever?" *Wall Street Journal*, April 12, 2013.
86. John Markoff, "Brainlike Computers, Learning from Experience," *New York Times*, December 29, 2013; Nick Bilton, "Computer-Brain Interfaces Making Big Leaps," *Bits* (blog), *New York Times*, August 4, 2013, http://bits.blogs.nytimes.com/2013/08/04/disruptions-rather-than-time-computers-might-become-panacea-to-hurt.
87. David Gelernter, "The Closing of the Scientific Mind," *Commentary*, January 1, 2014, http://www.commentarymagazine.com/article/the-closing-of-the-scientific-mind.
88. Paul Joseph Watson, "The Dark Side of Ray Kurzweil's Transhumanist Utopia," *Infowars.com*, June 20, 2013, http://www.infowars.com/the-dark-side-of-ray-kurzweils-transhumanist-utopia; Victoria Woollaston, "We'll Be Uploading Our Entire MINDS to Computers by 2045 and Our Bodies Will Be Replaced by Machines within 90 Years, Google Expert Claims," *Daily Mail* (UK), June 19, 2013; Kurzweil, *The Singularity is Near*, p. 469.
89. Bill Joy, "Why the Future Doesn't Need Us," *Wired*, April 2000.

Chapter Four: The Proletarianization of the Middle Class

1. Crystal Galyean, "Levittown: The Imperfect Rise of the American Suburbs," U.S. History Scene, August 13, 2012, http://www.ushistoryscene.com/uncategorized/levittown; James Madison, "Federalist No. 10," in Alexander Hamilton et al., *The Federalist*, ed. Charles R. Kesler and Clinton Rossiter (New York: New American Library, 1999), p. 46; Thomas Jefferson, letter to James Madison, October 28, 1785, in *The Papers of Thomas Jefferson*, ed. Julian P. Boyd et al. (Princeton, NJ: Princeton UP, 1950), 8:681–82.
2. Lasch, *The Only and True Heaven*, p. 204.
3. Stephanie Coontz, *The Way We Never Were: American Families and the Nostalgia Trap* (New York: Basic Books, 1992), p. 24; Piketty, *Capital in the Twenty-First Century*, pp. 29, 61.

4. Alan Zibel and Nick Timiraos, "Homeownership Rate Declines to 15-Year Low," *Wall Street Journal*, April 30, 2012; Conor Dougherty et al., "Home Ownership Falls to 1990s Levels," *Wall Street Journal*, May 4, 2014.

5. Lasch, *The Only and True Heaven*, p. 526.

6. Ruy Teixeira and Alan Abramowitz, "The Decline of the White Working Class and the Rise of a Mass Middle Upper Class," Brookings, working paper, April 2008.

7. Green, *Epitaph for American Labor*, pp. 18–19; William A. Galston, "Behind the Middle-Class Funk," *Wall Street Journal*, August 6, 2013; Jan Diehm and Katy Hall, "Middle Class Jobs, Income Quickly Disappearing," *Huffington Post*, June 6, 2013, http://www.huffingtonpost.com/2013/06/06/middle-class-jobs-income-_n_3386157.html.

8. Analysis of Bureau of Labor Statistics; Derek Thompson, "If Corporate Profits Are at an All-Time High, Why Are Corporate Taxes Near a 60-Year Low?" *Atlantic*, May 23, 2013.

9. Harrison Jacobs, "The Decline of the U.S. Middle Class Is Getting Even Worse," *Business Insider*, October 1, 2013, http://www.businessinsider.com/decline-of-theus-middle-class-2013-10.

10. Gregory Acs, "Downward Mobility from the Middle Class: Waking Up from the American Dream," Pew Economic Mobility Project, September 2011.

11. Joseph Lawler, "Report: Almost Half of U.S. Families Earning below 250 Percent of Poverty Level," *Washington Examiner*, December 4, 2013, http://washingtonexaminer.com/report-almost-half-of-u.s.-families-earning-below-250-percent-of-poverty-level/article/2540155; Merrill Goozner, "Millions Now Stuck in the Rut of Self-Employment," *Fiscal Times*, August 21, 2012, http://www.thefiscaltimes.com/Articles/2012/08/21/Millions-Now-Stuck-in-the-Rut-of-Self-Employment; David J. Lynch, "Americans Say Dream Fading as Income Gap Hurts Chances," *Bloomberg*, December 11, 2013, http://www.bloomberg.com/news/2013-12-11/americans-say-dream-fading-as-income-gap-hurts-chances.html.

12. Ronald Brownstein, "Meet the New Middle Class: Who They Are, What They Want, and What They Fear," *Atlantic*, April 25, 2013; Ronald Brownstein, "Eclipsed," *National Journal*, May 26, 2011, http://www.nationaljournal.com/columns/political-connections/white-working-class-americans-see-future-as-gloomy-20110526.

13. Edward Morrissey, "A Food-Stamp Recovery Is the New Normal," *Fiscal Times*, April 4, 2013, http://www.thefiscaltimes.com/Columns/2013/04/04/A-Food-Stamp-Recovery-Is-the-New-Normal; Josh Mitchell, "Who are the Long-term Unemployed," Urban Institute, July 2013; Arthur Delaney, "Long-Term Unemployed Left Out Of Recovery: Study," *Huffington Post*, December 13, 2012, http://www.huffingtonpost.com/2012/12/13/long-term-unemployed_n_2291767.html; Elizabeth Kneebone and Alan Berube, *Confronting Suburban Poverty in America* (Washington, DC: Brookings Institution Press, 2013).

14. U.S. Census Bureau, "Statistics of U.S. Businesses," http://www.census.gov/econ/susb.

15. Ryan Tracy, "Tally of U.S. Banks Sinks to Record Low," *Wall Street Journal*, December 3, 2013; J. D. Harrison, "United States' New Business Formation Rate Continues Dropping Steadily," *On Small Business* (blog), *Washington Post*, May 2, 2012, http://

www.washingtonpost.com/blogs/on-small-business/post/united-states-new-business-formation-rate-continues-dropping-steadily/2012/05/02/gIQAjKOewT_blog.html.

16. Ian Hathaway and Robert E. Litan, "Declining Business Dynamism in the United States: A Look at States and Metros," Economic Studies at Brookings, May 2014.

17. Elizabeth Williamson, "Outspoken Group Bears Brunt of Canceled Health-Insurance Policies," *Wall Street Journal*, November 1, 2013; Scott Shane, "Why Aren't Banks Lending to Small Business? Ask Bernanke," *The American* (AEI), May 2, 2012, http://www.american.com/archive/2012/may/why-arent-banks-lending-to-small-business-ask-bernanke; U.S. Department of Labor, Bureau of Labor Statistics, "Business Employment Dynamics," http://data.bls.gov/cgi-bin/surveymost?bd.

18. Lymari Morales, "U.S. Business Owners Now Among Least Approving of Obama," Gallup Politics, July 26, 2012, http://www.gallup.com/poll/156206/business-owners-among-least-approving-obama.aspx; Catherine Rampell, "Small Businesses Still Struggle, and That's Impeding a Recovery," *New York Times*, February 13, 2013; Alex Klein, "'Big Business is Doing Fine': Romney's Tellingly Accurate Gaffe," *Daily Beast*, August 24, 2012, http://www.thedailybeast.com/articles/2012/08/24/big-business-is-doing-fine-romney-s-tellingly-accurate-gaffe.html.

19. Elizabeth Williamson, "Outspoken Group Bears Brunt of Canceled Health-Insurance Policies," *Wall Street Journal*, November 1, 2013; Shane, "Why Aren't Banks Lending to Small Business?"; "U.S. House Speaker John Boehner Says New Business Startups Are at the Lowest Levels in 30 Years," *PolitiFact*, March 7, 2012, http://www.politifact.com/ohio/statements/2012/mar/23/john-boehner/us-house-speaker-john-boehner-says-new-business-st; Harrison, "United States' New Business Formation Rate"; Joe McKendrick, "Startups Creating Fewer Jobs than Before: Study," *SmartPlanet*, July 28, 2011, http://www.smartplanet.com/blog/business-brains/startups-creating-fewer-jobs-than-before-study.

20. Nicole V. Crain and W. Mark Crain, "The Impact of Regulatory Costs on Small Firms," Small Business Administration, Office of Advocacy, September 2010; Jeffrey Dorfman, "The Democratic Party Is Now the Party of Big Business," *Real Clear Markets*, December 2, 2013, http://www.realclearmarkets.com/articles/2013/12/02/the_democratic_party_is_now_the_party_of_big_business_100768.html; Romina Boccia, "Smaller Paycheck? Welcome to Obama's Post-Fiscal-Cliff World," *The Foundry*, January 15, 2013, http://blog.heritage.org/2013/01/15/smaller-paycheck-payroll-tax-hike; Ryan Grim, "Finally, A List Of All The Center For American Progress' 2013 Corporate Donors," *Huffington Post*, December 13, 2013, http://www.huffingtonpost.com/2013/12/13/cap-corporate-donors_n_4440134.html; Paul Buchheit, "Average American Families Pays $6K a Year in Big Business Subsidies," *Moyers & Company*, September 24, 2013, http://billmoyers.com/2013/09/24/average-american-family-pays-6k-a-year-in-subsidies-to-big-business; Crain and Crain, "The Impact of Regulatory Costs on Small Firms."

21. Tracy, "Tally of U.S. Banks Sinks to Record Low"; Harrison, "United States' New Business Formation Rate."

22. Noah Smith, "The End of Labor: How to Protect Workers From the Rise of Robots," *Atlantic*, January 14, 2013; Thomas B. Edsall, "Hard Times, for Some," *New York Times*, August 21, 2013.

23. Neil Munro, "Billionaire Steve Case Says Immigrants Will Offset Middle Class Job Losses," *Daily Caller*, December 5, 2013, http://dailycaller.com/2013/12/05/billion-aire-steve-case-says-immigrants-will-offset-middle-class-job-losses.
24. Green, *Epitaph for American Labor*, pp. 18–19.
25. Ian Lovett, "Critics Say California Law Hurts Effort to Add Jobs," *New York Times*, September 4, 2012; David H. Autor and David Dorn, "How Technology Wrecks the Middle Class," *New York Times*, August 24, 2013; William Fulton, "Do Environmental Regulations Hurt the Economy?" *Governing*, March 2010; Zaid Jilani, "Top 'U.S.' Corporations Outsourced More Than 2.4 Million American Jobs Over The Last Decade," *ThinkProgress*, April 19, 2011, http://thinkprogress.org/econ-omy/2011/04/19/159555/us-corporations-outsourced-americans; Brent Kendall, "EPA Emission Rules Face Test at High Court," *Wall Street Journal*, February 18, 2014.
26. Eileen Appelbaum, "Report Gives New Insight in the Decline of the Middle Class," *U.S. News and World Report*, August 25, 2012; Louis Uchitelle, "The Wage That Meant Middle Class," *New York Times*, April 20, 2008; Rick Nauert, "Economic Changes Squeeze Blue-Collar Workers Out of Good Jobs, Family," *PsychCentral*, August 14, 2013, http://psychcentral.com/news/2013/08/14/economic-changes-squeeze-blue-collar-workers-out-of-good-jobs-family/58439.html; Michael Snyder, "If You Are a Blue Collar Worker in America You Are an Endangered Species," *The Economic Collapse* (blog), January 15, 2012, http://theeconomiccollapseblog.com/archives/if-you-are-a-blue-collar-worker-in-america-you-are-an-endangered-species; Howard Gold, "White-Collar Recession, Blue-Collar Depression," *Seeking Alpha*, November 2, 2010, http://seekingalpha.com/article/233960-white-collar-reces-sion-blue-collar-depression; Lasch, *The Only and True Heaven*, p. 484.
27. William A. Galston, "Visions of a Permanent Underclass," *Wall Street Journal*, October 1, 2013.
28. Galston, "Visions of a Permanent Underclass"; Ray Fisman, "The New Arti-san Economy," *Slate*, July 16, 2012, http://www.slate.com/articles/business/the_dismal_science/2012/07/unemployment_manufacturing_and_construction_jobs_aren_t_coming_back_americans_need_new_skills_.
29. Kevin Drum, "Welcome, Robot Overlords. Please Don't Fire Us?" *Mother Jones*, May/June 2013; Fisman, "The New Artisan Economy."
30. Richard Tomkins, "Stuck in the Muddle," *Financial Times,* March 9, 2007.
31. Robert Lopez, *The Birth of Europe* (New York: Evans and Company, 1967), p. 398.
32. Peter Hall, *Cities in Civilization: Culture, Innovation, and Urban Order* (New York: Pantheon, 1998), p. 88.
33. Werner Sombart, "Medieval and Modern Commercial Enterprise," in Frederic C. Lane and Jelle C. Riemersma, eds., *Enterprise and Secular Change: Readings in Eco-nomic History* (New York: Irwin, 1953), p. 28; Henri Pirenne, *Economic and Social History of Medieval Europe* (New York: Harcourt Brace and World, 1937), p. 45; Fernand Braudel, *The Structures of Everyday Life*, trans. Sian Reynolds (Berkeley: Univ. of California, 1992), p. 281.
34. Norman Cantor, *Medieval History: The Life and Death of a Civilization* (New York: Macmillan, 1963), p. 537.
35. Michael Sturmer, *The German Empire: 1870–1918* (New York: Modern Library, 2000), p. 53; Braudel, *The Structures of Everyday Life*, p. 334.

36. Beard and Beard, *The Rise of American Civilization*, pp. 16, 125; Andro Linklater, *Owning the Earth: The Transforming History of Land Ownership* (New York: Bloomsbury, 2013), p. 52.

37. Arnold Toynbee, *The Industrial Revolution* (Boston: Beacon Press, 1956, pp. 33–35; Karl Marx, *Capital: A Critique of Political Economy*, vol. 1, trans. Ben Fowkes (New York: Vintage, 1977), p. 883; Linklater, *Owning the Earth*, pp. 13–15, 17.

38. Jonathan Hughes, *American Economic History* (New York: HarperCollins, 1990), pp. 14–15, 88–89, 92–94: E. J. Hobsbawm, *The Age of Revolution: 1789–1848* (New York: Mentor, 1962), p. 207; Jonathan Israel, *The Dutch Republic: Its Rise, Its Greatness, Its Fall: 1477–1806* (Oxford: Oxford UP, 1995), pp. 113, 330, 999, 1012–13; Linklater, *Owning the Earth*, p. 219.

39. Piketty, *Capital in the Twenty-First Century*, p. 152.

40. Henry Nash Smith, *Virgin Land: The American West as Symbol and Myth* (Cambridge, MA: Harvard UP, 1950), pp. 124–25, 173.

41. "The Homestead Act of 1862," National Archives, http://www.archives.gov/education/lessons/homestead-act.

42. "Household Type, Relationship to Householder, and Home Ownership Rate, for the United States: 1850 to 2010," figure 6-3 of Campbell Gibson, *American Demographic History Chartbook: 1790 to 2010* (website), http://www.demographicchartbook.com/Chartbook/images/figures/fig6-3.pdf; Michael R. Haines, "Homeownership and Housing Demand in Late Nineteenth Century America: Evidence from State Labor Reports," working paper, Colgate University, Hamilton, NY, 2011; "Return of Owners of Land in 1873," UK Genealogy Archives, http://ukga.org/OwnersofLand.html; "Population," selection 3 of "1871 Census: General Report," reproduced at *Vision of Britain Through Time*, http://www.visionofbritain.org.uk/census/SRC_P/3/EW1871GEN; "Homestead Act (1862)," *Our Documents: 100 Milestone Documents from the National Archives*, http://www.ourdocuments.gov/doc.php?flash=true&doc=31.

43. Hughes, *American Economic History*, pp. 14–15, 88–89, 92–94: Hobsbawm, *The Age of Revolution*, p. 207; Israel, *The Dutch Republic*, pp. 113, 330, 999, 1012–13; Linklater, *Owning the Earth*, p. 219.

44. U.S. Census Bureau, "United States Summary: 2010: Population and Housing Unit Counts," September 2012, http://www.census.gov/prod/cen2010/cph-2-1.pdf.

45. Weber, *Economy and Society: An Outline of Interpretive Sociology*, trans. Ephraim Fischoff et al. (New York: Bedminster Press, 1968), 1:137; Marx, *Capital*, p. 365.

46. Linklater, *Owning the Earth*, p. 277; Amy Gluckman, "A Primer on Henry George's 'Single Tax,'" *Dollars & Sense*, March/April 2006.

47. Smith, *Virgin Land*, pp. 190–91; Joshua Rosenbloom and Gregory Stutes, "Reexamining the Distribution of Wealth in 1870," paper, Northwestern University Economic History Seminar, September 2005.

48. Hughes, *American Economic History*, pp. 414, 444; Beard and Beard, *The Rise of American Civilization*, p. 327.

49. Lind, *Land of Promise*, pp. 208–9.

50. Eric John Abrahamson, *Building Home: Howard F. Ahmanson and the Politics of the American Dream* (Berkeley: Univ. of California Press, 2013), pp. 5–11.

51. Robert J. Samuelson, "The Withering of Affluent Society," *Wilson Quarterly* (Summer 2012), pp. 42–47.

52. Thomas Piketty and Emmanual Saez, "The Evolution of Top Incomes: A Historical and International Perspective," American Economics Association, 2006.
53. Abrahamson, *Building Home*, p. 5; Coontz, *The Way We Never Were*, p. 77.
54. Abrahamson, *Building Home*, p. 111; Daniel K. Fetter, "The 20th Century Increase in U.S. Home Ownership: Facts and Hypotheses," in Eugene N. White, Kenneth Snowden, and Price Fishback, *Housing and Mortgage Markets in Historical Perspective* (Chicago: Univ. of Chicago Press, 2014).
55. Justin Pritchard, "Mortgage Crisis Overview: What Caused the Mortgage Crisis?" About.com, http://banking.about.com/od/mortgages/a/mortgagecrisis.htm.
56. Martin J. Weiner, *English Culture and the Decline of the Industrial Spirit* (Cambridge: Cambridge UP, 1981), pp. 93–94.
57. Lean Alfred Santos, "'Happy' but Poor? Measuring Development in Bhutan," *Devex*, December 2, 2013, https://www.devex.com/news/happy-but-poor-measuring-development-in-bhutan-82420; "Happiness Is a Week in Bhutan," *Weekly Standard*, May 6, 2013.
58. "Happiness Is a Week in Bhutan."
59. Georgia McCafferty, "World's Happiest Nations Are…" *CNN*, September 9, 2013, http://edition.cnn.com/2013/09/09/business/earth-institute-world-happiness-rankings; Friedman, *The Moral Consequences of Economic Growth*, p. 88; John Muscat, "The Illusions of Charles Montgomery's Happy City," *New Geography*, January 25, 2014, http://www.newgeography.com/content/004149-the-illusions-charles-montgomerys-happy-city.
60. George Monbiot, "This Is Bigger than Climate Change. It Is a Battle to Redefine Humanity," *Guardian*, December 14, 2009; Dan Bednarz, "Power, Identity and Social Change as We Enter Degrowth," *Health After Oil* (blog), August 12, 2013, http://healthafteroil.wordpress.com/2013/08/12/power-identity-and-social-change-as-we-enter-degrowth.
61. "Renewable Energy Subsidies 6.4 Times Greater than Fossil Fuel Subsidies," Institute for Energy Research, May 31, 2012, http://instituteforenergyresearch.org/analysis/12704.
62. Kenneth P. Green, "Five-Time Father Ted Turner Calls for One-Child Policy," *AEIdeas*, December 7, 2010, http://www.aei-ideas.org/2010/12/five-time-father-ted-turner-calls-for-one-child-policy.
63. *Titanic: The Final Word with James Cameron*, National Geographic video documentary, 2012; Patrick Michaels, "Will the Overselling of Global Warming Lead to a New Scientific Dark Age?" *Forbes*, February 3, 2014, http://www.forbes.com/sites/patrickmichaels/2014/02/03/will-the-overselling-of-global-warming-lead-to-a-new-scientific-dark-age.
64. John Gittelsohn, "U.S. Moves Toward Home 'Rentership Society,' Morgan Stanley Says," *Bloomberg*, July 20, 2011, http://www.bloomberg.com/news/2011-07-20/u-s-moves-to-rentership-society-as-owning-tumbles-morgan-stanley-says.html.
65. Michael A. Fletcher, "Wall Street Betting Billions on Single-Family Homes in Distressed Markets," *Washington Post*, April 21, 2013; Mary Ellen Podmolik, "Wall Street moving in on American Dream," *Chicago Tribune*, December 15, 2013; Campbell/Inside Mortgage Finance, "Investors Continued to Increase Housing Market Presence in November, New HousingPulse Survey Results Reveal," press release, December 23, 2013, http://campbellsurveys.com/housingreport/

press_122313.htm; Nathaniel Popper, "Behind the Rise in House Prices, Wall Street Buyers," *New York Times*, June 3, 2013.

66. Derek Thompson and Jordan Weissmann, "The Cheapest Generation," *Atlantic*, September 2012.

67. Lasch, *The Only and True Heaven*, p. 531.

68. John Aziz, "A Mortgage Is a Terrible Investment," *The Week*, May 1, 2014.

69. Richard Fry and Paul Taylor, "A Rise in Wealth for the Wealthy; Declines for the Lower 93%," Pew Research Social & Demographic Trends, April 23, 2013, http://www.pewsocialtrends.org/2013/04/23/a-rise-in-wealth-for-the-wealthydeclines-for-the-lower-93; Benjamin Ross, "Disaster in the Age of McMansions: America's Dangerous Addiction to Suburban Sprawl," *Salon*, May 4, 2014, http://www.salon.com/2014/05/04/disaster_in_the_age_of_mcmansions_americas_dangerous_addiction_to_suburban_sprawl; Dan McLaughlin, "In Defense of Homeownership (or, Why Food and Housing Are Different)," *Federalist*, May 5, 2014, http://thefederalist.com/2014/05/05/in-defense-of-homeownership-or-why-food-and-housing-are-different; Josh Barro, "Everyone Wants to Be a Homeowner. Why Not a Foodowner?" *New York Times*, May 6, 2014; Joel Kotkin, *Retrofitting the Dream: Housing the 21st Century* (Pinatubo Press, 2013), http://www.newgeography.com/files/Retrofitting-the-Dream-EVersion.pdf.

70. Galston, "Visions of a Permanent Underclass"; Claire Thompson, "Millennial Medium Chill: What the Screwed Generation Can Teach Us about Happiness," *Grist*, April 30, 2013, http://grist.org/living/millennial-medium-chill; Richard Tomkins, "Stuck in the Muddle," *Financial Times*, March 11, 2007.

71. Dave Sackett and Katie Handel, "Key Findings from National Survey of Voters," The Tarrance Group, May 21, 2012, http://www.wilsoncenter.org/sites/default/files/keyfindingsfromsurvey_1.pdf; Eric Jaffe, "The Suburbs Are Dead, Long Live the Suburbs, *CityLab*, August 27, 2013, http://www.citylab.com/housing/2013/08/suburbs-are-dead-long-live-suburbs/6680.

72. Toynbee, *The Industrial Revolution*, pp. 66–67.

73. Andrew Lees, *The City Perceived: Urban Society in European and American Thought, 1820–1940* (New York: Columbia UP, 1985), p. 29.

74. Friedrich Engels, *The Condition of the Working Class in England*, trans. W. O. Henderson and W. H. Chaloner (Stanford, CA: Stanford UP, 1968), pp. 145, 160–66.

75. Lasch, *The Only and True Heaven*, pp. 58–62.

76. Beard and Beard, *The Rise of American Civilization*, pp. 722–27; Weber, *Economy and Society*, 1:375; Hays, *The Response to Industrialism*.

77. "People & Events: Mrs. America: Women's Roles in the 1950s," supplemental online material for "The Pill," an episode of *The American Experience* (PBS), www.pbs.org/wgbh/amex/pill/peopleevents/p_mrs.html; Angelique Jannsens, "Economic Transformation, Women's Work and Family Life," in Kertzer and Barbagli, *Family Life in the Twentieth Century* (New Haven, CT: Yale UP, 2003), pp. 62–67; Coontz, *The Way We Never Were*, p. 24; Allan C. Carlson, "The Family in America: Retrospective and Prospective," *The Family in America* 23, no. 3 (Fall 2009): 1–13.

78. Jannsens, "Economic Transformation, Women's Work and Family Life"; Coontz, *The Way We Never Were*, pp. 24–26; Carlson, "The Family in America."

79. Pew Research Center for the People & the Press, "Growing Support for Gay Marriage: Changed Minds and Changing Demographics," March 20, 2013, http://www.

people-press.org/2013/03/20/growing-support-for-gay-marriage-changed-minds-and-changing-demographics; Charles Murray, *Coming Apart: The State of White America, 1960-2010* (New York: Crown Forum, 2012), pp. 153–55.

80. Kay S. Hymowitz, "The Single-Mom Catastrophe," *Los Angeles Times*, June 3, 2012.
81. Nicholas D. Kristof, "The White Underclass," *New York Times*, February 8, 2012.
82. Pew Research, "'Nones' on the Rise."
83. Acs, "Downward Mobility from the Middle Class."
84. Walter E. Williams, "Increase in White Illegitimacy Takes Issue out of Racial Arena," *Deseret News*, January 9, 1994.
85. Rick Nauert, "Economic Changes Squeeze Blue-Collar Workers Out of Good Jobs, Family," *PsychCentral*, August 14, 2013, http://psychcentral.com/news/2013/08/14/economic-changes-squeeze-blue-collar-workers-out-of-good-jobs-family/58439.html.
86. Public Policy Institute of California, "How Fertility Changes Across Immigrant Generations," *Research Brief* 58 (April 2002); Wendy Wang and Paul Taylor, "For Millennials, Parenthood Trumps Marriage," Pew Research Social & Demographic Trends, March 9, 2011, http://www.pewsocialtrends.org/2011/03/09/for-millennials-parenthood-trumps-marriage.
87. Rachel Grate, "The Life of 'Julia' as a Future Standard for Women," *Ms.* (blog), January 20, 2013, http://msmagazine.com/blog/2013/01/20/the-life-of-julia-as-a-future-standard-for-women.
88. Dylan Matthews, "Poverty in the 50 Years since 'the Other America,' in Five Charts," *Wonkblog* (blog), *Washington Post*, July 11, 2012, http://www.washingtonpost.com/blogs/wonkblog/wp/2012/07/11/poverty-in-the-50-years-since-the-other-america-in-five-charts.
89. Robert Samuelson, "How We Won—and Lost—the War on Poverty," *Real Clear Politics*, January 13, 2014, http://www.realclearpolitics.com/articles/2014/01/13/how_we_won_--_and_lost_--_the_war_on_poverty_121197.html.
90. David Shipler, *The Working Poor: Invisible in America* (New York: Vintage, 2004), pp, 6–7.

Chapter Five: Geography of Inequality

1. *Encyclopædia Britannica Online*, s.v. "Vidal de La Blache, Paul," http://www.britannica.com/EBchecked/topic/627886/Paul-Vidal-de-La-Blache.
2. William Bogart, *Don't Call It Sprawl: Metropolitan Structure in the 21st Century* (Cambridge: Cambridge UP, 2006), p. 10.
3. Samuel H. Williamson and Louis P. Cain, "Measuring Slavery in 2011 Dollars," MeasuringWorth, http://www.measuringworth.com/slavery.php.
4. Smith, *Virgin Land*, pp. 190-191.
5. Joshua Rosenbloon and Gregory Stutes, "Reexamining the Distribution of Wealth in 1870," Northwestern Economic History Seminar, September 2005.
6. Kate Rogers, "Death of the Suburb: Why Americans are Flocking to Cities," *FOX Business*, May 30, 2013, http://www.foxbusiness.com/personal-finance/2013/05/30/death-suburb-why-americans-are-flocking-to-cities.

7. Diane Cardwell, "Mayor Says New York Is Worth the Cost," *New York Times*, January 8, 2003.
8. Joe Coscarelli, "Michael Bloomberg Thinks He's a 'Godsend,'" *Daily Intelligencer* (blog), *New York*, September 20, 2013, http://nymag.com/daily/intelligencer/2013/09/michael-bloomberg-billionaires-are-a-godsend.html.
9. Piketty, *Capital in the Twenty-First Century*, p. 26.
10. Chrystia Freeland, "The Rise of the New Global Elite," *Atlantic*, January/February 2011; Michelle Conlin, "Housing Market Is Terrific, If You Are Rich," *USA Today*, September 21, 2011. Fred Siegel, "It's a Hell of a Town," *Commentary*, May 2009; Laura Battle, "Sales of Two Cities," *Financial Times*, March 18, 2012.
11. Fernand Braudel, *The Perspective of the World*, vol. 3 of *Civilization and Capitalism: 15th–18th Century*, trans. Sian Reynolds (New York: Harper and Rox, 1979), p. 30.
12. Sven Beckert, *The Monied Metropolis: New York City and the Consolidation of the American Bourgeoisie* (Cambridge: Cambridge UP, 2001), p. 7.
13. Peter Hall, *Cities in Civilization* (New York: Pantheon, 1998), p. 7.
14. Marcus Gee, "Cities Seeing a Reversal of the Flight to the Suburbs," *Globe and Mail* (Canada), October 5, 2012.
15. Alan Ehrenhalt, "Cities of the Future May Soon Look Like Those of the Past," *Governing*, April 2012.
16. Joel Kotkin, "The U.S. Cities That Have Profited the Most in the Stock Market and Housing Boom," *Forbes*, March 13, 2014, http://www.forbes.com/sites/joelkotkin/2014/03/13/the-u-s-cities-that-have-profited-the-most-in-the-stock-market-and-housing-boom.
17. Lloyd Alter, "It's Time to Dump the Tired Argument That Density and Height Are Green and Sustainable," *TreeHugger*, January 3, 2014, http://www.treehugger.com/urban-design/its-time-dump-tired-argument-density-and-height-are-green-and-sustainable.html.
18. Simon Kuper, "Priced Out of Paris," *Financial Times Magazine*, June 14, 2013; Sarah Kendzior, "Expensive Cities Are Killing Creativity," *Al Jazeera*, December 17, 2013, http://www.aljazeera.com/indepth/opinion/2013/12/expensive-cities-are-killing-creativity-2013121065856922461.html.
19. Bell, *The Coming of Post-Industrial Society*, p. 344.
20. Sarah Maslin Nir, "The End of Willets Point," *New York Times*, November 24, 2013.
21. Kuper, "Priced Out of Paris"; Kendzior, "Expensive Cities"; Nathaniel Baum-Snow and Ronni Pavan, "Inequality and City Size," *Review of Economics and Statistics*, vol. 95, no. 5 (December 2013): 1535–48; Edward L. Glaeser, Matt Resseger, and Kristina Tobio, "Urban Inequality," working paper, Harvard Kennedy School, Taubman Center for State and Local Government, Cambridge, MA, 2008.
22. Richard Child Hill and June Woo Kim, "Global Cities and Developmental States," *Urban Studies*, vol. 37, no. 12 (2000): 2173; Hilary Potkewitz, "Airline Pilots Detour Around NY," *Crain's New York Business*, October 28, 2007.
23. Sam Roberts, "In Manhattan, Poor Make 2 Cents for Each Dollar to Rich," *New York Times Magazine*, September 4, 2005.
24. According to the American Community Survey (2008–2012), Manhattan's GINI index is 0.599. According to World Bank figures, pre-Mandela South Africa was 59.3 in 1993.

25. McGeehan, "More Earners at Extremes"; Roberts, "Income Data Shows Widening Gap."

26. David W. Chen and Megan Thee-Brenan, "Poll Finds Support for de Blasio, if Not All His Ideas," *New York Times*, October 4, 2013; McGeehan, "More Earners at Extremes"; Roberts, "Income Data Shows Widening Gap."

27. Richard Florida, "The High Inequality of U.S. Metro Areas Compared to Countries," *CityLab*, October 9, 2012, http://www.citylab.com/work/2012/10/high-inequality-us-metro-areas-compared-countries/3079; Alan Berube, "All Cities Are Not Created Unequal," Brookings Institution, February 20, 2014, http://www.brookings.edu/research/papers/2014/02/cities-unequal-berube; George Galster, Jackie Cutsinger, and Jason C. Booza, "Where Did They Go? The Decline of Middle-Income Neighborhoods in Metropolitan America," Brookings Institution, June 2006, http://www.brookings.edu/research/reports/2006/06/poverty-booza.

28. Richard Morrill, "Inequality of the Largest U.S. Metropolitan Areas," *New Geography*, September 11, 2013, http://www.newgeography.com/content/003921-inequality-largest-us-metropolitan-areas.

29. Berube, "All Cities Are Not Created Unequal."

30. Manuel Castells, "The Informational City is a Dual City: Can It Be Reversed," in Donald Schon, Bish Sanyal, and William Mitchell, eds., *High Technology and Low Income Communities: Prospects for the Positive Unse of Advanced Information Technology* (Cambridge, MA: MIT Press, 1999), pp. 30–31.

31. Greg Ip, "The Declining Value of Your College Degree," *Wall Street Journal*, July 17, 2008; Michael Mandel, "What the Income Report Tells Us about College Grads," *Business Week*, September 4, 2007: Steven Greenhouse, "Many Entry-Level Workers Feel Pinch of Rough Market," *New York Times*, September 4, 2006; David G. Blanchflower, "Credit Crisis Creates Lost Generation," *Bloomberg*, January 22, 2009, http://www.bloomberg.com/news/2010-01-22/credit-crisis-creates-lost-generation-david-g-blanchflower.html.

32. Joel Kotkin, "The Cities Where a Paycheck Stretches the Furthest," *New Geography*, July 9, 2012, http://www.newgeography.com/content/002950-the-cities-where-a-paycheck-stretches-the-furthest.

33. Richard Florida, "The Rise of the Creative Class," *Washington Monthly*, May 2002, pp. 15–25.

34. Francis Wilkinson, "Why Are Liberal Cities Bad for Blacks?" *Bloomberg View*, April 9, 2014, http://www.bloombergview.com/articles/2014-04-09/why-are-liberal-cities-bad-for-blacks.

35. Aaron M. Renn, "The White City," *New Geography*, October 18, 2009, http://www.newgeography.com/content/001110-the-white-city; Urban Institute, "How Do the Top 100 Metro Areas Rank on Racial and Ethnic Equity?" report, February 2, 2012, http://www.urban.org/publications/901478.html.

36. Heather Knight, "Families' Exodus Leaves S.F. Whiter, Less Diverse," *SFGate*, June 10, 2013, http://www.sfgate.com/bayarea/article/Families-exodus-leaves-S-F-whiter-less-diverse-3393637.php; Nikole Hannah-Jones, "In Portland's Heart, 2010 Census Shows Diversity Dwindling," *Oregonian*, April 30, 2011; Dick Morrill, "Seattle Is Shedding Diversity; The State's Minority Populations Grow," *Crosscut*, April 29, 2011, http://crosscut.com/2011/04/29/seattle/20804/Seattle-is-shedding-diversity-states-minority-popu.

37. Dean Meminger, "Report Cites Bronx As Poorest Urban County," *NY1* (Time Warner Cable), September 29, 2009, http://www.ny1.com/content/news/106559/report-cites-bronx-as-poorest-urban-county.

38. U.S. Census Bureau, "QuickFacts: Kings County (Brooklyn Borough)," http://quickfacts.census.gov/qfd/states/36/36047.html; Michael Howard Saul, "New York City Leads Jump in Homeless," *Wall Street Journal*, March 4, 2013.

39. Wendell Cox, "Suburban & Urban Core Poverty: 2012: Special Report," *New Geography*, October 23, 2013.

40. Mark J. Stern and Susan C. Seifert, "From Creative Economy to Creative Society," *Creativity & Change* (The Reinvestment Fund and the Social Impact of the Arts Project), January 2008, http://www.trfund.com/wp-content/uploads/2013/06/Economy.pdf; "Jamie Peck on Struggling With the Creative Class," interview, *ScienceWatch*, November 2010, http://archive.sciencewatch.com/dr/fmf/2010/10novfmf/10novfmfPeck; Jamie Peck, "Struggling with the Creative Class," *International Journal of Urban and Regional Research*, vol. 29, no. 4 (December 2005): 740–70.

41. Aaron M. Renn, "Is Urbanism the New Trickle-Down Economics?" *New Geography*, February 7, 2013, http://www.newgeography.com/content/003470-is-urbanism-new-trickle-down-economics; Richard Florida, "More Losers Than Winners in America's New Economic Geography," *CityLab*, January 30, 2013, http://www.citylab.com/work/2013/01/more-losers-winners-americas-new-economic-geography/4465.

42. Joel Kotkin, "The Geography of Aging: Why Millennials Are Headed to the Suburbs," *New Geography*, December 9, 2013, http://www.newgeography.com/content/004084-the-geography-of-aging-why-millennials-are-headed-to-the-suburbs.

43. Alan Mallach, "The Heavy Hand of Demographic Change," *Rooflines*, February 25, 2013, http://www.rooflines.org/3100/the_heavy_hand_of_demographic_change.

44. Matthew Davis, "Controversial Pure Michigan Ad Better than Granholm's 'Cool Cities' Program," *MLive*, January 17, 2013, http://www.mlive.com/politics/index.ssf/2013/01/matthew_davis_controversial_pu.html.

45. Richey Piiparinen, "The Psychology of the Creative Class: Not as Creative as You Think," *Richey Piiparinen* (blog), March 1, 2013, http://richeypiiparinen.wordpress.com/2013/03/01/the-psychology-of-the-creative-class-uniquely-conforming-creatively-monotonizing; Alec MacGillis, "The Ruse of the Creative Class," *American Prospect*, December 18, 2009, http://prospect.org/article/ruse-creative-class-0.

46. Richey Piiparinen, "The Creative Destruction of Creative Class-ification," *New Geography*, September 3, 2012, http://www.newgeography.com/content/003060-the-creative-destruction-creative-class-ification; Alan Mallach, "The Heavy Hand of Demographic Change," *Rooflines*, February 25, 2013, http://www.rooflines.org/3100/the_heavy_hand_of_demographic_change.

47. Dan Alexander, "California Leads All States (and All but 2 Countries) with 111 Billionaires," *Forbes*, March 7, 2014, http://www.forbes.com/sites/danalexander/2014/03/07/california-leads-all-states-and-all-but-2-countries-with-111-billionaires.

48. Kathleen Short, "The Research Supplemental Poverty Measure: 2011," report, U.S. Census Bureau, November 2012, http://www.census.gov/prod/2012pubs/p60-244.

pdf; Michael Gardner, "Is California the Welfare Capital?" *San Diego Union Tribune*, July 28, 2012.

49. Carey McWilliams, *Factories in the Field: The Story of Migratory Farm Labor in California* (Berkeley: Univ. of California Press, 2000), p. 4.

50. Tüzin Baycan and Peter Nijkamp, "A Socio-Economic Impact Analysis of Cultural Diversity: Research Memorandum 2011–12," working paper, Faculty of Economics and Business Administration, Vrije Universiteit, Amsterdam, the Netherlands, 2011, http://dare.ubvu.vu.nl/bitstream/handle/1871/19159/rm%202011-12.pdf; Michael Bernick, "When Jobs Were Plentiful in 1950s California," *Fox&Hounds*, November 4, 2009, http://www.foxandhoundsdaily.com/2009/11/5712-when-jobs-were-plentiful-1950s-california.

51. Peter Henderson, "California Still Leads U.S., including in Inequality," Reuters, May 19, 2011, http://www.reuters.com/article/2011/05/19/us-usa-economy-california-idUSTRE74I88V20110519.

52. Norimitsu Onishi, "Overrun by Crime, Oakland Looks to Make Allies in Community," *New York Times*, March 11, 2013; Vince Veneziani and Antonina Jedrzejczak, "The 20 Most Unemployed Cities In America," *Business Insider*, May 25, 2010, http://www.businessinsider.com/tough-times-meet-americas-cities-with-the-highest-unemployment-rate-2010-5; Victor Davis Hanson, "Liberal Apartheid," *RealClearPolitics*, July 8, 2013, http://www.realclearpolitics.com/articles/2013/07/08/liberal_apartheid_119115.html.

53. Michael Bastasch, "Report: Costly State Energy Policies to Raise California Power Costs by 33 Percent," *Daily Caller*, January 24, 2013, http://dailycaller.com/2013/01/24/report-costly-state-energy-policies-to-raise-california-power-costs-by-33-percent; U.S. Energy Information Administration, "Electric Power Monthly," May 21, 2014, http://www.eia.gov/electricity/monthly/epm_table_grapher.cfm?t=epmt_5_6_a.

54. Elizabeth Campbell and Megan Durisin, "California Farms Going Thirsty as Drought Burns $5 Billion Hole," *Bloomberg*, January 28, 2014, http://www.bloomberg.com/news/2014-01-29/california-farms-going-thirsty-as-drought-burns-5-billion-hole.html; Paul Rogers, "California Drought: Past Dry Periods Have Lasted More than 200 Years, Scientists Say," *San Jose Mercury News*, January 25, 2014; Bettina Boxall, "Severe Drought? California Has Been Here Before," *Los Angeles Times*, February 23, 2014.

55. U.S. Census Bureau, "Educational Attainment by State: 1990 to 2009," table 233 of *Statistical Abstract of the United States: 2012*, p. 153, http://www.census.gov/compendia/statab/2012/tables/12s0233.pdf.

56. Andy Kroll, "California Education's Painful Decline," *Salon*, October 2, 2012, http://www.salon.com/2012/10/02/california_educations_painful_decline; U.S. Department of Labor, Bureau of Labor Statistics, "Local Area Unemployment Statistics: Unemployment Rates for Metropolitan Areas," March 2014, http://www.bls.gov/web/metro/laummtrk.htm; U.S. Census Bureau, "Educational Attainment by State: 1990 to 2009"; Hans Johnson and Ria Sengupta, "Closing the Gap: Meeting California's Need for College Graduates," report, Public Policy Institute of California, April 2009, http://www.ppic.org/content/pubs/report/R_409HJR.pdf.

57. Center for Economic Research and Forecasting, California Lutheran University, "The United States and California Economic Forecast," September 2009, http://www.clucerf.org/forecasts/2009/09; Brad Plumer, "Watch the Growth of U.S. Income Inequality with This Animated Map," *Wonkblog* (blog), *Washington Post*, September 19, 2013, http://www.washingtonpost.com/blogs/wonkblog/wp/2013/09/19/watch-the-growth-of-u-s-income-inequality-with-this-animated-map; Sarah Bohn and Eric Schiff, "The Great Recession and Distribution of Income in California," report, Public Policy Institute of California, December 2011, http://www.ppic.org/content/pubs/report/R_1211SBR.pdf.

58. Wendell Cox, "California Declares War on Suburbia II: The Cost of Radical Densification," *New Geography*, April 18, 2012, http://www.newgeography.com/content/002781-california-declares-war-suburbia-ii-the-cost-radical-densification.

59. Joel Kotkin, "California's Demographic Dilemma," *New Geography*, January 4, 2013, http://www.newgeography.com/content/003398-californias-demographic-dilemma.

60. Ibid.

61. Elizabeth Lee, "Researchers See Trend of People Moving Between Texas, California," *Voice of America*, July 24, 2011, http://www.voanews.com/content/researchers-see-trend-of-people-moving-between-texas-california-126149453/163236.html; Phillip Reese, "Golden State Losing Folks as Old Dust Bowl Beckons," *Sacramento Bee*, June 14, 2009; "Is the Middle Class Dream an Illusion for Californians? What We Can Learn from Domestic and Foreign Migration Patterns," *Dr. Housing Bubble*, December 2, 2012, http://www.doctorhousingbubble.com/middle-class-california-dream-what-is-middle-class-for-california-incomes-real-estate-prices-migration.

62. Janet Viveiros and Maya Brennan, "An Annual Look at the Housing Affordability Challenges of America's Working Households," National Housing Conference and the Center for Housing Policy, May 2013, http://www.nhc.org/media/files/Landscape2013.pdf; Blanca Torres, "Bay Area Housing Prices Jump 43 Percent, but Don't Celebrate," *San Francisco Business Times*, July 8, 2013.

63. Braudel, *The Perspective of the World*, p. 201.

64. Joel Garreau, *The Nine Nations of North America* (Boston: Houghton Mifflin, 1981).

65. Richard Florida, "Foreclosures Still Concentrated in Sunbelt Cities," *Atlantic*, January 28, 2011.

66. Michael Boyajian, "The Death of the American Sunbelt," *Room Eight*, July 19, 2010, http://www.r8ny.com/blog/judgeboyajian/the_death_of_the_american_sunbelt.html; Matthew O'Brien, "Why Is the American Dream Dead in the South?" *Atlantic*, January 26, 2014, http://www.theatlantic.com/business/archive/2014/01/why-is-the-american-dream-dead-in-the-south/283313.

67. Jed Kolko, "Metros Clobbered by the Housing Crisis Are Growing Again," *CityLab*, March 14, 2013, http://www.citylab.com/housing/2013/03/metros-clobbered-housing-crisis-are-growing-again/4991; Joel Kotkin, "Forget What the Pundits Tell You, Coastal Cities Are Old News—It's the Sunbelt That's Booming," *Daily Beast*, March 1, 2014, http://www.thedailybeast.com/articles/2014/03/01/forget-what-the-pundits-tell-you-coastal-cities-are-old-news-it-s-the-sunbelt-that-s-booming.html.

68. Ralph Bivins, "Boom On! Houston Notches More New Home Starts than the Entire State of California," *CultureMap Houston*, April 2, 2014, http://houston.culturemap. com/news/real-estate/04-02-14-boom-on-houston-notches-more-housing-starts-than-the-entire-state-of-california.

69. Joel Kotkin, "The Changing Geography of Asian America: To the South and the Suburbs," *New Geography*, September 13, 2012, http://www. newgeography.com/content/003080-the-changing-geography-asian-amer-ica-to-the-south-and-the-suburbs; Joel Kotkin and Wendell Cox, "Aspirational Cities: U.S. Cities That Offer Both Jobs and Culture Are Mostly Southern and Modest Sized," *New Geography*, July 30, 2013, http://www.newgeography.com/ content/003852-aspirational-cities-us-cities-that-offer-both-jobs-and-culture-are-mostly-southern-and-modest-sized; Joel Kotkin, "Why the Red States Will Profit Most from More U.S. Immigration," *Forbes*, February 22, 2013, http://www.forbes. com/sites/joelkotkin/2013/02/22/why-the-red-states-will-profit-most-from-more-u-s-immigration.

70. Vikki Ortiz Healy, "More Minorities Moving to Suburbs," *Chicago Tribune*, March 2, 2011; Judy Keen, "Blacks' Exodus Reshapes Cities," *USA Today*, May 19, 2011.

71. Robert Bruegmann, *Sprawl: A Compact History* (Chicago: Univ. of Chicago Press, 2005), pp. 111–12, 132.

72. American Community Survey, 2012.

73. Lind, *Land of Promise*, p. 342; Howard Ahmanson, "The Old Regionalism vs. the New Cosmopolitan Hyper-Localism," *American Conservative*, October 7, 2013.

74. Robert Caro, *The Power Broker: Robert Moses and the Fall of New York* (New York: Vintage, 1975), pp. 143–44; Becky Nicolaides, "How Hell Moved From the Cities to the Suburbs," in Kevin M. Kruse and Thomas J. Sugure, *The New Suburban History* (Chicago: Univ. of Chicago Press, 2006), p. 87.

75. Jane Jacobs, *The Death and Life of Great American Cities* (New York: Random House, 1961), p. 357.

76. Nicolaides, "How Hell Moved From the Cities to the Suburbs," pp. 91–97.

77. William Vogt, *Road to Survival* (New York: William Sloane, 1948), p. 284.

78. Michael Janofsky, "Gore Offers Plan to Control Suburban Sprawl," *New York Times*, January 12, 1999.

79. James Howard Kunstler, *The Long Emergency: Surviving the Converging Catastrophes of the 21st Century* (New York: Atlantic Monthly Press, 2005), p. 3.

80. James Howard Kunstler, "The Ghastly Tragedy of the Suburbs," TED2004 Conference, February 2004, http://www.ted.com/talks/james_howard_kunstler_ dissects_suburbia; Leslee Goodman, "The Decline and Fall of the Suburban Empire," interview with James Howard Kunstler, *The Sun* (magazine), October 2009, issue 406.

81. Irvin Dawid, "New Urbanism Examined by Time Magazine, Andrés Duany," *Planetizen*, December 24, 2007, http://www.planetizen.com/node/29063; Brian Stone, "Land Use as Climate Change Mitigation," *Environmental Science and Technology*, November 12, 2009; Ronald D. Utt, "The Oberstar Transportation Plan: A Costly Exercise in Lifestyle Modification," Heritage Foundation Web Memo, November 10, 2009.

82. Peter Calthorpe, "Urbanism in the Age of Climate Change: Urbanism Expanded," *StreetsBlogSF*, February 1, 2011, http://sf.streetsblog.org/2011/02/01/urbanism-in-the-age-of-climate-change-urbanism-expanded.

83. Lindsay Wilson, America's Carbon Cliff: Dissecting the Decline in U.S. Carbon Emissions," report, *Shrink That Footprint*, March 2013, http://shrinkthatfootprint.com/wp-content/uploads/2013/03/Americas-Carbon-Cliff.pdf.

84. Brad Plumer, "Global Carbon Emissions Grew More Slowly in 2012. But Will They Ever Decline?" *Wonkblog* (blog), *Washington Post*, November 1, 2013, http://www.washingtonpost.com/blogs/wonkblog/wp/2013/11/01/global-carbon-emissions-grew-more-slowly-in-2012-will-they-ever-decline; McKinsey & Company, "Reducing U.S. Greenhouse Gas Emissions: How Much at What Cost?" executive report, December 2007, http://www.mckinsey.com/client_service/sustainability/latest_thinking/reducing_us_greenhouse_gas_emissions.

85. U.S. Environmental Protection Agency, "Regulatory Impact Analysis: Final Rule-making for 2017-2025 Light-Duty Vehicle Greenhouse Gas Emission Standards and Corporate Average Fuel Economy Standards," August 2012, http://www.epa.gov/otaq/climate/documents/420r12016.pdf; U.S. Environmental Protection Agency, "Final Rulemaking to Establish Light-Duty Vehicle Greenhouse Gas Emission Standards and Corporate Average Fuel Economy Standards Regulatory Impact Analysis," April 2010, http://www.epa.gov/otaq/climate/regulations/420r10009.pdf.

86. TerraPass, http://www.terrapass.com.

87. McKinsey & Company, "Reducing U.S. Greenhouse Gas Emissions," p. ix. This report was cosponsored by Environmental Defense Fund, the Natural Resources Defense Council (NRDC), Shell, National Grid, DTE Energy and Honeywell, pp. xii, 80.

88. Lara Farrar, "Is America's suburban dream collapsing into a nightmare?," *CNN*, June 21, 2008; Richard Morrill, "The Geography of Class in Greater Seattle," *New Geography*, June 16, 2009, http://www.newgeography.com/content/00857-the-geography-class-greater-seattle; interview with author.

89. Pew Research Social & Demographic Trends, "Suburbs Not Most Popular, But Suburbanites Most Content," February 26, 2009, http://www.pewsocialtrends.org/2009/02/26/suburbs-not-most-popular-but-suburbanites-most-content;   Jan K. Brueckner and Ann G. Largey, "Social Interaction and Urban Sprawl," October 2006; Ed Braddy, "Smart Growth and the New Newspeak," *New Geography*, April 4, 2012, http://www.newgeography.com/content/002740-smart-growth-and-the-new-newspeak; Brookings Institution Metropolitan Policy Program, "State of Metropolitan America: On the Front Lines of Demographic Trans-formation," report, 2010, http://www.brookings.edu/~/media/Files/Programs/Metro/state_of_metro_america/metro_america_report.pdf; Elizabeth Kneebone and Jane Williams, "New Census Data Underscore Metro Poverty's Persistence in 2012," Brookings, September 19, 2013, http://www.brookings.edu/research/reports/2013/09/19-census-data-poverty-kneebone-williams.

90. Jeffry Gardner, "Misguided Aim: 'Smart Growth' Proponents Target Not Develop-ers but Families Who Can't Afford Fancy Digs," *Albuquerque Tribune*, July 23, 2004; Wendell Cox, "California Declares War on Suburbia," *Wall Street Journal*, April 9, 2012.

91. Turner, *The Significance of the Frontier*, pp. 53–54.
92. Molly Young, "Joblessness in Oregon, County by County," *OregonLive*, http://www.oregonlive.com/money/index.ssf/2013/03/joblessness_in_oregon_county_b.html; Eric Mortenson, "Official: Rural Oregon's Economy 'Dire,' but Not Hopeless," *Wallowa.com*, January 24, 2014, http://wallowa.com/free/official-rural-oregon-s-economy-dire-but-not-hopeless/article_07124602-8557-11e3-8762-001a4bcf887a.html.
93. Young, "Joblessness in Oregon, County by County"; Mortenson, "Official: Rural Oregon's Economy 'Dire,' but Not Hopeless."
94. John Morgan, "MarketWatch: A U.S. Manufacturing Revival Is Taking Root. Really," *MoneyNews*, November 4, 2013, http://www.moneynews.com/Economy/Reeves-manufacturing-jobs-economy/2013/11/04/id/534632.
95. Associated Press, "Colorado Panel OKs New Oil, Gas Drilling Emissions Rules," *Greeley Tribune*, http://www.greeleytribune.com/news/10334679-113/rules-colorado-gas-oil.
96. Diana Furchtgott-Roth and Andrew Gray, "The Economic Effects of Hydrofracturing on Local Economies: A Comparison of New York and Pennsylvania," *Growth and Prosperity Report*, no. 1, May 2013, http://www.manhattan-institute.org/html/gpr_01.htm.
97. Fred Siegel, "The Poverty of Environmentalism," *Society*, vol. 51, no. 3 (June 2014): 258–61.
98. Karl Sharro, "Density or Sprawl," in Dave Clements et al., *The Future of Community*, pp. 68–77.
99. Witold Rybczynski, "Behind the Façade," *Architect*, November 2013.
100. Bruce Nussbaum, "Al Gore's Carbon Footprint Is Big," *Bloomberg Businessweek*, February 27, 2007, http://www.businessweek.com/innovate/NussbaumOnDesign/archives/2007/02/gores_carbon_fo.html; David Zahniser, "Do As We Say, Not As We Do," *LA Weekly*, May 30, 2007.
101. Karrie Jacobs, "It's a Small World," *Metropolis Magazine*, April 2013; Susan Johnston, "Micro Apartments Offer Small Slice of City Living," *U.S. News and World Report*, November 15, 2013; Carolyn Said, "Micro-Apartment Developments on Rise in S.F.," *SFGate*, November 11, 2013, http://www.sfgate.com/business/article/Micro-apartment-developments-on-rise-in-S-F-4951775.php; Roger Vincent, "$50-Million Complex of Micro Apartments Finished in Santa Monica," *Los Angeles Times*, July 4, 2013; Matt Johnson, "Micro Apartments? Not in Our Neighborhood, Hollywood Residents Say," *KATU News*, November 20, 2013, http://www.katu.com/news/local/Micro-apartments-Not-in-our-neighborhood-232744831.html.
102. Vinnie Mancuso, "Micro-Apartments Could Be Hazardous to Your Mental Health," *New York Observer*, December 20, 2013.
103. National Multifamily Housing Council, "Quick Facts: Resident Demographics," http://www.nmhc.org/Content.aspx?id=4708#characteristic_of_apartment_households.
104. Charlotte Allen, "Silicon Chasm," *Weekly Standard*, December 2, 2013; California Association of Realtors, "January Home Sales and Price Report," February 19, 2014, http://www.car.org/newsstand/newsreleases/2014releases/jan2014sales.

105. Analysis of census data by Wendell Cox at the *Demographia* website, http://www.demographia.com.

106. David Leonhardt, "In Climbing Income Ladder, Location Matters," *New York Times*, July 22, 2013.

107. The study measured upward mobility compared to the economic status of parents. However, the age at which upward mobility (30 years old) was measured was suggested to be too early for reliable prediction. See: Wendell Cox, "Distortions and Reality about Income Mobility," *New Geography*, August 7, 2013, http://www.newgeography.com/content/003868-distortions-and-reality-about-income-mobility.

108. Ibid.

109. Richard Morrill, "The Emerging Geography of Inequality," *New Geography*, September 4, 2013, http://www.newgeography.com/content/003912-the-emerging-geography-inequality.

110. David King, "Sprawl and Economic Mobility: A Comment," *Getting from Here to There* (blog), July 29, 2013, http://davidaking.blogspot.com/2013/07/sprawl-and-economic-mobility-comment.html.

111. Jim Russell, "Richard Florida Explains Why Density Doesn't Impact Innovation," *Pacific Standard*, January 11, 2014, http://www.psmag.com/navigation/business-economics/richard-florida-explains-density-doesnt-impact-innovation-72679; Wendell Cox, "Density is Not the Issue: The Urban Scaling Research," *New Geography*, July 30, 2012, http://www.newgeography.com/content/002987-density-not-issue-the-urban-scaling-research; Bruce Katz, "Big Idea 2014: Goodbye Silicon Valley, Hello Silicon Cities," Brookings Institution, December 30, 2013, http://www.brookings.edu/research/opinions/2013/12/30-silicon-cities-katz.

112. Gypsy Taub, "The Naked Truth about San Francisco's Nudity Ban," *Guardian*, November 23, 2012.

113. Kotkin, "The Geography of Aging"; Joel Kotkin, "Where Working-Age Americans Are Moving," *New Geography*, December 19, 2013, http://www.newgeography.com/content/004100-where-working-age-americans-are-moving.

114. Gavin W. Jones, "Recent Fertility Trends, Policy Responses and Fertility Prospects in Low Fertility Countries of East and Southeast Asia," paper, UN Expert Group Meeting on Recent and Future Trends in Fertility, November 30, 2009, http://www.un.org/esa/population/meetings/EGM-Fertility2009/P05_Jones.pdf.

115. Stanley Kurtz, "Regionalism: Obama's Quiet Anti-Suburban Revolution," *The Corner* (blog), *National Review*, July 30, 2013, http://www.nationalreview.com/corner/354734/regionalism-obamas-quiet-anti-suburban-revolution-stanley-kurtz.

116. David Siders, "Jerry Brown Says Poverty, Joblessness Due to California Being 'a Magnet,'" *Capitol Alert* (blog), *Sacramento Bee*, November 7, 2013, http://blogs.sacbee.com/capitolalertlatest/2013/11/jerry-brown-calls-poverty-flip-side-of-californias-incredible-attractivenes.html.

117. Nicole Belson Goluboff, "Washington Opens The Virtual Office Door," *New Geography*, December 28, 2010, http://www.newgeography.com/content/001923-washington-opens-the-virtual-office-door; Wendell Cox, "Reducing Vehicle Miles Traveled Produces Meager Greenhouse Gas Emission Reduction Returns," *New Geography*, August 6, 2009, http://www.newgeography.com/content/00950-reducing-vehicle-miles-traveled-produces-meager-greenhouse-gas-emission-reduction-retu.

118. Andy Kiersz, "Americans are Still Moving to the Suburbs," *Business Insider*, February 12, 2014, http://www.businessinsider.com/census-american-migration-data-2014-2.

Chapter Six: A Screwed Generation?

1. Josh Sanburn, "Millennials: The Next Greatest Generation?" *Time*, May 9, 2013; Jonah Goldberg, "Obama Deserves Share of Blame for Millennial Cynicism," *Townhall.com*, March 14, 2014, http://townhall.com/columnists/jonahgoldberg/2014/03/14/obama-deserves-share-of-blame-for-millennial-cynicism-n1808714.
2. Richard Fry, D'Vera Cohn, Gretchen Livingston, and Paul Taylor, "The Rising Age Gap in Economic Well-Being," Pew Research Social & Demographic Trends, November 7, 2011, http://www.pewsocialtrends.org/2011/11/07/the-rising-age-gap-in-economic-well-being.
3. Penny Starr, "Average Teen Unemployment Rate in D.C. is 50.1%, Analysis Shows," *CNSNews.com*, August 12, 2011, http://cnsnews.com/news/article/average-teen-unemployment-rate-dc-501-analysis-shows-0; Andrew Sum et al., "The Plummeting Labor Market Fortunes of Teens and Young Adults," report, Brookings Institution Metropolitan Policy Program, March 2014, http://www.brookings.edu/~/media/Research/Files/Reports/2014/03/14%20youth%20workforce/Youth_Workforce_Report_FINAL.pdf.
4. Pew Research Center, "Millennials: A Portrait of Generation Next," report, February 2010, http://www.pewsocialtrends.org/files/2010/10/millennials-confident-connected-open-to-change.pdf.
5. Kimberly Palmer, "Even Grandparents Agree: Life is Harder Today," *Alpha Consumer* (blog), *U.S. News and World Report*, March 15, 2012, http://money.usnews.com/money/blogs/alpha-consumer/2012/03/15/even-grandparents-agree-life-is-harder-today; James R. Hagerty, "Young Adults See Their Pay Decline," *Wall Street Journal*, March 9, 2012; Richard Fry, "A Rising Share of Young Adults Live in Their Parents' Home," Pew Research Social & Demographic Trends, August 1, 2013, http://www.pewsocialtrends.org/2013/08/01/a-rising-share-of-young-adults-live-in-their-parents-home; Aaron M. Renn, "The Decline of Work," *Urbanophile*, February 23, 2014, http://www.urbanophile.com/2014/02/23/the-decline-of-work.
6. Fry et al., "The Rising Age Gap in Economic Well-Being."
7. Mike Shedlock, "The Fed's Serial Bubble Machine at Work: How Millennials Are Being Buried Financially," *David Stockman's Contra Corner*, April 4, 2014, http://davidstockmanscontracorner.com/the-feds-serial-bubble-machine-at-work-how-millennials-are-being-buried-financially.
8. Jennifer Benz et al., "Working Longer: Older Americans Attitudes' on Work and Retirement," report, Associated Press-NORC Center for Public Affairs Research, October 2013, http://www.apnorc.org/PDFs/Working%20Longer/AP-NORC%20Center_Working%20Longer%20Report-FINAL.pdf.
9. Melanie Hicken, "Many Middle-Class Americans Plan to Work until They Die," *CNN Money*, October 23, 2013, http://money.cnn.com/2013/10/23/retirement/middle-class-retirement.

10. Catherine Rampell, "More Young Americans Out of High School Are Also Out of Work," *New York Times*, June 6, 2012.
11. Spencer Jakab, "Help Wanted: A Better Jobs Gauge for the Fed," *Wall Street Journal*, February 6, 2014; Bureau of Labor Statistics, U.S. Department of Labor, "Labor Force Participation Projected to Fall for People under Age 55 and Rise for Older Age Groups," January 6, 2014, http://www.bls.gov/opub/ted/2014/ted_20140106. htm.
12. Eurostat, http://epp.eurostat.ec.europa.eu; Liz Alerman, "Young and Educated in Europe, but Desperate for Jobs," *New York Times*, November 16, 2013.
13. Neil Howe, "'Dear Graduating Class of 2012: You Are So Not Special,'" *The Saeculum Decoded*, June 20, 2012, http://blog.lifecourse.com/2012/06/dear-graduating-class-of-2012-you-are-so-not-special.
14. U.S. National Debt Clock, http://www.usdebtclock.org.
15. Walter Russell Mead, "Time to Occupy State Pensions?" *American Interest*, June 25, 2012, http://www.the-american-interest.com/wrm/2012/06/25/time-to-occupy-the-pension-funds.
16. U.S. National Debt Clock; Bruno Waterfield, "Germany to Impose Tax on the Young to Help the Old," *Telegraph* (UK), April 4, 2012; Mariko Kato, "Experts Say Japan Must Change How It Is Handling Its Birthrate," *Japan Times*, January 5, 2010; Yuka Hayashi, John Murphy, and Daisuke Wakabayashi, "As Factories Vanish, Japan Seeks to Fashion a New Economy," *Wall Street Journal*, April 14, 2009; Yuka Hayashi, "Japan Lifts Sales Tax to Tackle Debt," *Wall Street Journal*, August 11, 2012.
17. Sheryl Nance-Nash, "Why Congress Needs to Hurry Up and Decide What to Do With Student Loans," *Forbes*, June 25, 2012, http://www.forbes.com/sites/sherylnancenash/2012/06/25/why-congress-needs-to-hurry-up-and-decide-what-to-do-with-student-loans; Chris Denhart, "How the $1.2 Trillion College Debt Crisis Is Crippling Students, Parents and the Economy," *Forbes*, August 7, 2013, http://www.forbes.com/sites/specialfeatures/2013/08/07/how-the-college-debt-is-crippling-students-parents-and-the-economy.
18. John Uebersax, "College Tuition Inflation," *Satyagraha*, July 14, 2009, http://satyagraha.wordpress.com/2009/07/14/college-tuition-hyperinflation; "Tutorial: The Real Cost of Higher Education," Savingforcollege.com, http://www.savingforcollege.com/tutorial101/the_real_cost_of_higher_education.php; Phil Oliff, Vincent Palacios, Ingrid Johnson, and Michael Leachman, "Recent Deep State Higher Education Cuts May Harm Students and the Economy for Years to Come," report, Center on Budget and Policy Priorities, March 19, 2013, http://www.cbpp.org/cms/?fa=view&id=3927.
19. Pew Research Social & Demographic Trends, "The Rising Cost of Not Going to College," report, February 11, 2014, http://www.pewsocialtrends.org/files/2014/02/SDT-higher-ed-FINAL-02-11-2014.pdf.
20. Lizzie Guerra, interview with researcher Gary Girod.
21. Samantha Melamed, "In Tough Times, Grads Become Overqualified Nannies," *Pittsburgh Post-Gazette*, May 4, 2014; Charley Stone, Carl Van Horn, and Cliff Zukin, "Chasing the American Dream: Recent College Graduates and the Great Recession," report, The John J. Heldrich Center for Workforce Development, Rutgers University, May 2012, http://www.heldrich.rutgers.edu/sites/default/files/

content/Chasing_American_Dream_Report.pdf; Lee Lawrence, "Bachelor's Degree: Has It Lost Its Edge and Its Value?" *Christian Science Monitor*, June 17, 2012.

22. Adam Cohen, "Just How Bad Off Are Law School Graduates?" *Time*, March 11, 2013; Peter Lattman, "Mass Layoffs at a Top-Flight Law Firm," *New York Times*, June 24, 2013.

23. Sharon Jayson, "Who's Feeling Stressed? Young Adults, New Survey Shows," *USA Today*, February 7, 2013; Higher Education Research Institute, "Incoming College Students Rate Emotional Health at Record Low, Annual Survey Finds," press release, January 26, 2011, http://heri.ucla.edu/pr-display.php?prQry=55.

24. Bonnie Kavoussi, "Half Of Recent College Graduates Lack Full-Time Job, Study Says," *Huffington Post*, May 10, 2012, http://www.huffingtonpost.com/2012/05/10/college-graduates-full-time-jobs-study_n_1496827.html.

25. Cohen, "Just How Bad Off Are Law School Graduates?"; Richard Vedder et al., "From Wall Street to Wal-Mart: Why College Graduates Are Not Getting Good Jobs," policy paper, Center for College Affordability and Productivity, December 16, 2010, http://www.centerforcollegeaffordability.org/uploads/From_Wall_Street_to_Wal-Mart.pdf; Friedman, *The Moral Consequences of Economic Growth*, pp. 6–7; Emily Beller and Michael Hout, "Intergenerational Social Mobility: The United States in Comparative Perspective," *The Future of Children*, vol. 16, no. 2 (Fall 2006): 19–36. See table 4 in Beller and Hout's study: From 1930–1939, 49 percent of American men were upwardly mobile, 25 percent downwardly mobile, and 26 percent immobile. Due to the lessening of poverty after the depression, this decreased with every successive generation, but even between 1970–1979 more American men were upwardly mobile than stagnant or heading downward.

26. Richard Vedder, "The College-Graduate Glut: Evidence From Labor Markets," *Innovations* (blog), *Chronicle of Higher Education*, July 11, 2012, http://chronicle.com/blogs/innovations/the-college-graduate-glut-evidence-from-labor-markets/32997.

27. Miya Tokumitsu, "In the Name of Love," *Slate*, January 16, 2014, http://www.slate.com/articles/technology/technology/2014/01/do_what_you_love_love_what_you_do_an_omnipresent_mantra_that_s_bad_for_work.html.

28. Samantha Stainburn, "Following the Money: Calculating the Net Worth of a College Degree," *New York Times*, August 2, 2013.

29. The White House, "Remarks by the President on Opportunity for All and Skills for America's Workers," press release, January 30, 2014, http://www.whitehouse.gov/the-press-office/2014/01/30/remarks-president-opportunity-all-and-skills-americas-workers.

30. Michael Stratford, "Progressive Push on Debt," *Inside Higher Ed*, March 7, 2014, http://www.insidehighered.com/news/2014/03/07/progressive-groups-launch-new-campaign-tackle-student-debt-college-affordability.

31. U.S. Department of Education, "Default Rates Continue to Rise for Federal Student Loans," press release, September 30, 2013, http://www.ed.gov/news/press-releases/default-rates-continue-rise-federal-student-loans.

32. Associated Press, "$1 Trillion Student Loan Debt Widens U.S. Wealth Gap," *CNBC*, March 27, 2014, http://www.cnbc.com/id/101531304.

33. Clare Ansberry, "As Job Market Mends, Dropouts Fall Behind," *Wall Street Journal*, February 21, 2012; Jaison R. Abel, Richard Deitz, and Yaqin Su, "Are Recent

College Graduates Finding Good Jobs?" *Current Issues in Economics and Finance*, vol. 20, no. 1 (2014), http://www.newyorkfed.org/research/current_issues/ci20-1. pdf; Tami Luhby, "Recent College Grads Face 36% 'Mal-Employment' Rate," *CNN Money*, June 25, 2013, http://money.cnn.com/2013/06/25/news/economy/malemployment-rate.

34. Justin Sullivan, "Temp Jobs Become a Permanent Way of Life for Some," *NBC News*, August 2, 2012, http://economywatch.nbcnews.com/_news/2012/08/02/13070977-temp-jobs-become-a-permanent-way-of-life-for-some; Bureau of Labor Statistics, U.S. Department of Labor, "College Enrollment and Work Activity of 2013 High School Graduates," press release, April 22, 2014, http://www.bls.gov/news.release/hsgec.nr0.htm.

35. Walter Russell Mead, "American Tinderbox," *American Interest*, August 7, 2011, http://www.the-american-interest.com/wrm/2011/08/07/american-tinderbox.

36. Xandra Clark, "Low-Wage Jobs Drive Silicon Valley Employment Growth, Forcing More Workers into Long Commutes," *Peninsula Press*, August 28, 2012, http://peninsulapress.com/2012/08/28/low-wage-jobs-drive-silicon-valley-employment-growth-forcing-more-workers-into-long-commutes; Sullivan, "Temp Jobs Become a Permanent Way of Life."

37. Pew Research Social & Demographic Trends, "Millennials in Adulthood: Detached from Institutions, Networked with Friends," report, March 7, 2014, http://www.pewsocialtrends.org/files/2014/03/2014-03-07_generations-report-version-for-web.pdf; Carl Van Horn et al., "Left Out. Forgotten? Recent High School Graduates and the Great Recession," John J. Heldrich Center for Workforce Development, Rutgers University, June 2012, http://www.heldrich.rutgers.edu/sites/default/files/content/Left_Out_Forgotten_Work_Trends_June_2012.pdf.

38. Frederick Engels, *The Origin of the Family, Property and the State*, trans. Evelyn Reed (New York: Pathfinder, 1972), pp. 160–61, 206–7; Albert Hourani, *A History of the Arab Peoples* (New York: Warner Books, 1991), p. 105; Numa Denis Fustgel de Coulanges, *The Ancient City: A Study on the Religion, Laws, and Institutions of Greece and Rome* (Baltimore: John Hopkins UP, 1980), pp. 77–85.

39. Ibn Khaldun, *The Muqaddimah*, trans. Franz Rosenthal (Princeton, NJ: Princeton UP, 1967), pp. 119, 124–27; 2005 Iranian policy labeled (translation by Ali Modarres) "The Goals and Objectives for Formation of Families, Their Stability, and Growth," the following objectives were listed: realization of Islamic view on the importance and position of families and the function of families in Islamic system. There are seven items under this policy, all relating to the importance of family.

40. William Theodore de Bary, Wing-Tsit Chan, and Burton Watson, eds., *The Sources of Chinese Tradition* (New York: Columbia UP, 1960), pp. 4–5, 28.

41. Charles Hucker, *China's Imperial Past: An Introduction to Chinese History and Culture* (Stanford, CA: Stanford UP, 1975), pp. 10, 33, 57, 84.

42. Phillippe Aries, *Centuries of Childhood: A Social History of Family Life*, trans. Robert Baldick (New York: Vintage, 1962), p. 128; Steven Ozment, *Ancestors: The Loving Family in Old Europe* (Cambridge, MA: Harvard UP, 2001), p. 54; Katherine Lynch, *Individuals, Families and Communities in Europe 1200–1800* (Cambridge: Cambridge UP, 2003), pp. 44–46, 69.

43. Avner Greif, "Family Structure, Institutions, and Growth: The Origin and Implications of Western Corporations," *AEA Papers and Proceedings*, vol. 96, no. 2 (May 2006): 308–12.

44. Aries, *Centuries of Childhood*, p. 133.

45. Simon Schama, *The Embarrassment of Riches: An Interpretation of Dutch Culture in the Golden Age* (New York: Vintage, 1987), p. 481.

46. Nathan Rosenberg and L. E. Birdzell, Jr., *How the West Grew Rich: The Economic Transformation of the Industrial World* (New York: Basic Books, 1986), pp. 113–14; F. R. H. Du Boulay, *An Age of Ambition: English Society in the Late Middle Ages* (London: St. Paul's Press, 1970), p. 126.

47. Tocqueville, *Democracy in America*, pp. 718–27.

48. Irwin Yellowitz, "Child Labor," *History Channel* (website), http://www.history.com/topics/child-labor.

49. Herbert S. Klein, "The Changing American Family," *Hoover Digest*, no. 3 (2004): 177–81.

50. Maria Cancian and Deborah Reed, "Family Structure, Childbearing, and Parental Employment: Implications for the Level and Trend in Poverty," in Maria Cancian and Sheldon Danziger, eds., *Changing Poverty, Changing Policies* (New York: Russell Sage Foundation, 2009), pp. 92–121.

51. Eric Klinenberg, *Going Solo: The Extraordinary Rise and Surprising Appeal of Living Alone* (New York: Penguin, 2012), p. 14.

52. Kate Bolick, "All the Single Ladies," *Atlantic*, November 2011.

53. "UF Study: Men More Traditional than Women about Marriage, Children," press release, University of Florida, October 24, 2007, http://news.ufl.edu/2007/10/24/childlessness-2.

54. Tanya Koropeckyj-Cox and Gretchen Pendell, "The Gender Gap in Attitudes about Childlessness in the United States," *Journal of Marriage and Family*, vol. 69, no. 4 (2007): 899–915; "UF Study: Men More Traditional than Women."

55. Pew Research, "Millennials in Adulthood"; "Living at Home Generation: A Modern Day Feudalism Awaits Young Americans as the Prospect of Homeownership Falls out of Grasp," *Dr. Housing Bubble*, January 27, 2014, http://www.doctorhousingbubble.com/living-at-home-generation-young-renters-young-american-home-buyers; Kopin Tan, "Leaving the Nest, Finally," *Barron's*, January 18, 2014.

56. U.S. Census bureau data, analysis by Wendell Cox.

57. Daniel Gross, "Renting Prosperity," *Wall Street Journal*, May 4, 2012.

58. Richard Florida, "Why the U.S. Needs to Fall Out of Love With Homeownership," *CityLab*, September 17, 2013, http://www.citylab.com/housing/2013/09/why-us-needs-fall-out-love-homeownership/6517; Emily Badger, "Where Even the Middle Class Can't Afford to Live Any More," *CityLab*, October 10, 2013, http://www.citylab.com/housing/2013/10/where-even-middle-class-cant-afford-live-any-more/7194.

59. John Gittelsohn, "U.S. Moves Toward Home 'Rentership Society,' Morgan Stanley Says," *Bloomberg News*, July 20, 2011, http://www.bloomberg.com/news/2011-07-20/u-s-moves-to-rentership-society-as-owning-tumbles-morgan-stanley-says.html.

60. Aaron M. Renn, "Beware of the Aristocrats: Architects and the Elite by a Texas Architect," *Urbanophile*, April 8, 2014, http://www.urbanophile.com/2014/04/08/beware-of-the-aristocrats-architects-and-the-elite-by-a-texas-architect.

61. Mike Shedlock, "The Fed's Serial Bubble Machine at Work: How Millennials Are Being Buried Financially," *David Stockman's Contra Corner*, April 4, 2014, davidstockmanscontracorner.com/the-feds-serial-bubble-machine-at-work-how-millennials-are-being-buried-financially; "The Baby Boomers Forgot about Their Kids: Do We Have Any Housing Bulls in Their 20s and 30s, the Traditional Age of First Time Buyers in High Priced Areas?" *Dr. Housing Bubble*, march 14, 2014, http://www.doctorhousingbubble.com/baby-boomer-home-ownership-rates-young-buyers-first-time-buyers.

62. William Briat, "The 'Vanishing' First-Time Home Buyer; What It Means for the Housing Market," *Trefis*, February 3, 2014, http://www.trefis.com/stock/bzh/articles/224772/the-vanishing-first-time-home-buyer-what-it-means-for-the-housing-market/2014-02-03.

63. Ronda Kaysen, "The Truly Affordable New York Apartment," *New York Times*, February 2, 2014; Emily Badger, "Is It Time to Bring Back the Boarding House?" *CityLab*, July 18, 2013, http://www.citylab.com/housing/2013/07/it-time-bring-back-boarding-house/6236.

64. Scott Neuman, "Generation Rent: Slamming Door Of Homeownership," *NPR*, June 7, 2012, http://www.npr.org/2012/06/07/154504195/generation-rent-slamming-door-of-homeownership.

65. Centers for Disease Control and Prevention, "National Marriage and Divorce Rate Trends," http://www.cdc.gov/nchs/nvss/marriage_divorce_tables.htm; Carol Morello and Ted Mellnik, "Whites' Deaths Outnumber Births for First Time," *Washington Post*, June 13, 2013.

66. David E. Bloom et al., "Population Aging: Facts, Challenges, and Responses," working paper, Program on the Global Demography of Aging, Harvard University, May 2011, http://www.hsph.harvard.edu/pgda/WorkingPapers/2011/PGDA_WP_71.pdf; Paul Mackun and Steven Wilson, "Population Distribution and Change: 2000 to 2010," 2010 Census Briefs, U.S. Census Bureau, March 2011, http://www.census.gov/prod/cen2010/briefs/c2010br-01.pdf; Christina Finn, "Financial Pressures and Lack of Affordable Housing Linked to Low Fertility Rates," *TheJournal.ie* (Ireland), December 18, 2013, http://www.thejournal.ie/financial-pressures-and-lack-of-affordable-housing-linked-to-low-fertility-rates-1226760-Dec2013.

67. Gretchen Livingston and D'Vera Cohn, "Birth Rates Hit Record Low for Those under 25, Still on the Rise for Those 40+," Pew Research Center, July 3, 2013, http://www.pewresearch.org/fact-tank/2013/07/03/birth-rates-hit-record-low-for-those-under-25-still-on-the-rise-for-those-40.

68. Wolfgang Lutz, Vegard Skirbekk, and Maria Rita Testa, "The Low Fertility Trap Hypothesis: Forces That May Lead to Further Postponement and Fewer Births in Europe," *Vienna Yearbook of Population Research* (2006): 167–92.

69. "Birth Rate in the United States in 2010, by Family Income," *Statista*, http://www.statista.com/statistics/241530/birth-rate-by-family-income-in-the-us.

70. James Freeman, "How Washington Really Redistributes Income," *Wall Street Journal*, October 21, 2012.

71. William H. Gross, "Towards the Paranormal," PIMCO, January 2012, http://latam.pimco.com/EN/insights/pages/towards-the-paranormal-jan-2012.aspx.

72. Robert Samuelson, "The Clash of Generations," *RealClearPolitics*, December 9, 2013, http://www.realclearpolitics.com/articles/2013/12/09/the_clash_of_generations_120891.html; Robert J. Samuelson, "The Withering of the Affluent Society," *Wilson Quarterly*, vol. 36, no. 3 (Summer 2012): 42–47.

73. Brian O'Connell, "Meet America's New Poverty Class: The Millennials," *MainStreet. com*, May 18, 2012, http://www.mainstreet.com/article/career/students/gen-y/meet-america-s-new-poverty-class-millennials.

74. Tamara Draut, "The Millennial Squeeze," *American Prospect*, May 30, 2013, http://prospect.org/article/millennial-squeeze.

75. Claire Thompson, "Millennial Medium Chill: What the Screwed Generation Can Teach Us about Happiness," *Grist*, April 30, 2013, http://grist.org/living/millennial-medium-chill.

76. Thompson and Weissmann, "The Cheapest Generation."

77. Thompson, "Millennial Medium Chill."

78. Edward Morgan, "Sex (or Not) and the Japanese Single," *New Geography*, August 14, 2012, http://www.newgeography.com/content/003019-sex-or-not-and-japanese-single.

79. Andrew Miller, "Increasing Number of Japanese Men Opt for Bachelorhood," *Japan Today*, January 19, 2013, http://www.japantoday.com/category/lifestyle/view/increasing-number-of-japanese-men-opting-for-bachelorhood.

80. Abigail Haworth, "Why Have Young People in Japan Stopped Having Sex?" *Observer*, October 19, 2013; Martin Fackler, "Japan Goes From Dynamic to Disheartened," *New York Times*, October 16, 2010; Steven Simonitch, "Young Japanese Women Becoming Less Interested in Sex, Survey Says," *Japan Today*, August 12, 2012, http://www.japantoday.com/category/national/view/young-japanese-women-becoming-less-interested-in-sex-survey-says; Morgan, "Sex (or Not) and the Japanese Single."

81. Eamonn Fingleton, "The Myth of Japan's Failure," *New York Times*, January 6, 2012; Frank Bruni, "America the Shrunken," *New York Times*, May 4, 2014.

82. Ansuya Harjani, "Adult Diapers Will Soon Outsell Baby Nappies in Japan," *CNBC*, September 3, 2013, http://www.cnbc.com/id/101003141; UN Population Prospects, 2010.

83. Mary Beth Sammons, "What Millennials Want: Homes, Kids and Lots of Cash, Study Shows," *ParentDish*, December 20, 2010, http://www.parentdish.com/2010/12/20/what-millennials-want-a-house-a-kid-and-lots-of-cash.

84. "Study Finds 84 Percent of Renters Intend on Buying a Home," *National Mortgage Professional Magazine*, May 21, 2012, http://nationalmortgageprofessional.com/news29699/study-finds-84-percent-renters-intend-buying-home; Wendell Cox, "84% of 18-to-34-Year-Olds Want To Own Homes," *New Geography*, May 22, 2012, http://www.newgeography.com/content/002859-84-18-34-year-olds-want-to-own-homes.

85. Better Homes and Gardens Real Estate, "Better Homes and Gardens Real Estate Survey Shows New 'Kids' On the Block Willing to Work Hard to Make Home as Unique as They Are," news release, March 12, 2013, http://www.bhgrealestate.com/Views/MediaCenter/News.aspx?id=3058.

86. Leigh Gallagher, *The End of the Suburbs* (New York: Portfolio/Penguin, 2013), p. 20.

87. Morley Winograd and Michael D. Hais, "The Millennial Metropolis," *New Geography*, April 19, 2010, http://www.newgeography.com/content/001511-the-millennial-metropolis.

88. Pew Research Center for the People and the Press, "A Pro-Government, Socially Liberal Generation: Democrats' Edge among Millennials Slips," news release, February 18, 2010, http://www.pewresearch.org/files/old-assets/pdf/1497.pdf; Joel Kotkin and Ali Modarres, "The Childless City," *City Journal*, Summer 2013.

89. Winograd and Hais, "The Millennial Metropolis."

90. Better Homes and Gardens Real Estate, "Survey Shows New 'Kids' On the Block."

91. Tan, "Leaving the Nest, Finally"; Neil Irwin, "Why the Housing Market Is Still Stalling the Economy," *New York Times*, April 27, 2014.

Chapter Seven: Renewing Aspiration

1. Jonathan D. Ostry, Andrew Berg, and Charalambos G. Tsangarides, "Redistribution, Inequality, and Growth," International Monetary Fund, Staff Discussion Note, February 2014, http://www.imf.org/external/pubs/ft/sdn/2014/sdn1402.pdf; James Traub, "Let Them Eat Apple Pie," *Foreign Policy*, April 11, 2014.

2. Joseph Egoian, "73 Will Be The Retirement Norm For Millennials," *Nerdwallet*, October 23, 2013, http://www.nerdwallet.com/blog/investing/2013/73-retirement-norm-millennials; Tami Luhby, "Low-Paying Jobs Are Here to Stay," *CNN Money*, August 2, 2012, http://money.cnn.com/2012/08/02/news/economy/low-pay-jobs/index.htm.

3. Harold Meyerson, "The Revolt of the Cities," *American Prospect*, April 2014, http://prospect.org/article/revolt-cities; John Nichols, "Could a Socialist Actually Win Seattle's City Council Race? Yes," *Nation*, November 13, 2013; Chris Smith, "De Blasio's Budget Proves He's Doubling Down on Being a Lefty Crusader," *Daily Intelligencer* (blog), *New York*, May 9, 2014, http://nymag.com/daily/intelligencer/2014/05/mayors-budget-moves-ahead-progressive-vision.html.

4. Pew Research Global Attitudes Project, "The New Sick Man of Europe: The European Union," report, May 13, 2013, http://www.pewglobal.org/2013/05/13/the-new-sick-man-of-europe-the-european-union; Edelman, *2013 Edelman Trust Barometer*.

5. Richard Morrill, "Inequality of the Largest U.S. Metropolitan Areas," *New Geography*, September 11, 2013, http://www.newgeography.com/content/003921-inequality-largest-us-metropolitan-areas; Piketty, *Capital in the Twenty-First Century*, pp. 93–95, 471; Dean Baker, "Economic Policy in a Post-Piketty World," *Huffington Post*, April 22, 2014, http://www.huffingtonpost.com/dean-baker/economic-policy-in-a-post_b_5187840.html; John B. Judis, "Coming Soon: The United States of Comcast Comcast Time-Warner Merger Will Create Orwellian Monopoly," *New Republic*, February 13, 2014; Paul Buchheit, "Average American Families Pays $6K a Year in Big Business Subsidies," *Moyers & Company*, September 24, 2013, http://billmoyers.com/2013/09/24/average-american-family-pays-6k-a-year-in-subsidies-to-big-business.

6. Annie Lowrey, "50 Years Later, War on Poverty Is a Mixed Bag," *New York Times*, January 4, 2014; Neil Shah, "U.S. Poverty Rate Stabilizes—For Some," *Wall Street Journal*, October 11, 2013.

7. Keith Hall and Charles Blahous, "Jobs: The Best Way to Fight Poverty," *The Hill*, April 30, 2014, http://thehill.com/blogs/congress-blog/economy-budget/204579-jobs-not-handouts-fight-poverty.
8. William Niskasen, "Welfare and the Culture of Poverty," *Cato Journal*, 1996.
9. Acs, "Downward Mobility from the Middle Class."
10. Tami Luhby, "Worsening Wealth Inequality by Race," *CNN Money*, June 21, 2012, http://money.cnn.com/2012/06/21/news/economy/wealth-gap-race/index.htm; Michael A. Fletcher, "Fifty Years after March on Washington, Economic Gap between Blacks, Whites Persists," *Washington Post*, August 27, 2013; Pew Research Social & Demographic Trends, "King's Dream Remains an Elusive Goal; Many Americans See Racial Disparities," report, August 22, 2013, http://www.pewsocialtrends.org/2013/08/22/kings-dream-remains-an-elusive-goal-many-americans-see-racial-disparities; Walter Williams, "Why Is Black Unemployment So High?" *RealClearPolitics*, April 10, 2013, http://www.realclear-politics.com/2013/04/10/why_is_black_unemployment_so_high_305475.html.
11. Dylan Matthews, "Poverty in the 50 Years since 'the Other America,' in Five Charts," *Wonkblog* (blog), *Washington Post*, July 11, 2012, http://www.washingtonpost.com/blogs/wonkblog/wp/2012/07/11/poverty-in-the-50-years-since-the-other-america-in-five-charts; Mark Hugo Lopez and Gabriel Velasco, "Childhood Poverty Among Hispanics Sets Record, Leads Nation," Pew Research Hispanic Trends Project, September 28, 2011, http://www.pewhispanic.org/2011/09/28/childhood-poverty-among-hispanics-sets-record-leads-nation.
12. Robert Samuelson, "How We Won—and Lost—the War on Poverty," *RealClear-Politics*, January 13, 2014, http://www.realclearpolitics.com/articles/2014/01/13/how_we_won_—_and_lost_—_the_war_on_poverty_121197.html.
13. Glenn Hubbard, "The Unemployment Puzzle: Where Have All the Workers Gone?" *Wall Street Journal*, April 4, 2014.
14. Eurostat, "Euro Area Unemployment Rate at 12.0%," news release, January 31, 2014, http://epp.eurostat.ec.europa.eu/cache/ITY_PUBLIC/3-31012014-AP/EN/3-31012014-AP-EN.PDF; Eurostat, "Labour Force Survey Overview 2012," http://epp.eurostat.ec.europa.eu/statistics_explained/index.php/Labour_force_survey_overview_2012; Max Tholl, "Home Is Where the Hardship Is," *European*, May 7, 2014, http://www.theeuropean-magazine.com/max-tholl—2/8433-europes-lost-generation.
15. "The Evolution of Income Inequality in France," *Inequality Watch*, January 12, 2012, http://inequalitywatch.eu/spip.php?article93.
16. Nigel Meager, "The Role of Training and Skills Development in Active Labour Market Policies," working paper, Institute for Employment Studies, April 2008, http://www.employment-studies.co.uk/pdflibrary/wp15.pdf; Bill Briggs, "10 Leading U.S. Private Land Owners," *NBC News*, October 6, 2010, http://www.nbcnews.com/id/39522825/ns/business-real_estate/#.U4WNOC82JsG.
17. "Growing Inequal? Income Distribution and Poverty in OECD Countries," OECD Multilingual Summaries, 2008, p. 2; Andrew Grice, "New Law to Enforce Social Mobility," *Independent*, January 14, 2009; Mia Shanley, "Swedish Equality Fades Away as Rich Get Richer," Reuters, Mar 21, 2012; Joel Kotkin, "The Broken Ladder: The Threat to Upward Mobility in the Global City," Legatum Institute, May 2010, http://www.newgeography.com/files/The-Broken-Ladder-Joel-Kotkin.pdf.

18. Gary Duncan, "Brown's Legacy Is a Nation More Divided than Ever," *Times* (UK), June 8, 2009; Ilona Billington and Nicholas Winning, "U.K. Politicians Vie to Address Fall in Living Standards," *Wall Street Journal*, November 17, 2013.

19. Katya Vasileva, "6.5% of the EU Population Are Foreigners and 9.4% Are Born Abroad," Eurostat, July 7, 2011, http://epp.eurostat.ec.europa.eu/cache/ITY_OFFPUB/KS-SF-11-034/EN/KS-SF-11-034-EN.PDF; World Population Review, "Sweden Population 2014," http://worldpopulationreview.com/countries/sweden-population; U.S. Census Bureau, "Overview of Race and Hispanic Origin: 2010," brief, March 2011, http://www.census.gov/prod/cen2010/briefs/c2010br-02.pdf.

20. Lee Habeeb and Mike Leven, "Where Have You Gone, George Bailey?" *National Review*, May 13, 2004; Donny Shaw, "Refresher Course: TARP," *OpenCongress*, October 27, 2010, http://www.opencongress.org/articles/view/2090-Refresher-Course-TARP.

21. "List of Republicans Who Voted for TARP," *RINO List*, http://www.rinolist.org/2010/08/list-of-republicans-who-voted-for-tarp; Kiplinger Washington Letter, *The New American Boom: Exciting Changes in American Life and Business between Now and the Year 2000* (Washington, DC: Kiplinger Washington Editors, 1986), p. 3.

22. Joel Kotkin, *The Next Hundred Million: America in 2050* (New York: Penguin, 2009), pp. 8–12; Friedman, *The Moral Consequences of Economic Growth*, p. 199.

23. Catherine Rampell, "The Return of China," *Economix* (blog), *New York Times*, March 26, 2010, http://economix.blogs.nytimes.com/2010/03/26/the-return-of-china; UNIDO, "World Manufacturing Production: Statistics for Quarter I, 2013," quarterly report, http://www.unido.org//fileadmin/user_media/Publications/Research_and_statistics/Branch_publications/Research_and_Policy/Files/Reports/World_Manufacturing_Production_Reports/STA_Report_on_Quarterly_production_2013Q1.pdf; John Boudreau, "Japan's Once-Mighty Tech Industry Has Flagged," *Phys.org*, October 19, 2012, http://phys.org/news/2012-10-japan-once-mighty-tech-industry-flagged.html.

24. Liam Pleven and Russell Gold, "U.S. Nears Milestone: Net Fuel Exporter," *Wall Street Journal*, November 30, 2011; Daniel Yergin, "America's New Energy Security," *Wall Street Journal*, December 12, 2011; Vinod Dar, "World's Largest Producer of Natural Gas? Now It's the U.S.," *SeekingAlpha.com*, January 13, 2010; and Robert Bryce, "America Needs the Shale Revolution," *Wall Street Journal*, June 13, 2011.

25. Molly Ryan, "Siemens CEO Emphasizes 'Tectonic Shift' in U.S. Energy, Manufacturing Opportunities," March 5, 2014, *Houston Business Journal*; Harold Meyerson, "The U.S.: Where Europe Comes to Slum," *Los Angeles Times*, May 15, 2011; Justin Lahart and Liam Denning, "Pumping Up the U.S. Economy," *Wall Street Journal*, January 30, 2014; Paolo Scaroni, "Europe Is Being Hobbled by Its Expensive Energy," *Financial Times*, October 31, 2013; Jeffrey Sparshott and Lynn Cook, "Energy a Bright Spot for Trade," *Wall Street Journal*, February 7, 2014.

26. Shepard Daniel with Anuradha Mittal, "The Great Land Grab: Rush for World's Farmland Threatens Food Security for the Poor," report, Oakland Institute, 2009, p. 6, http://www.oaklandinstitute.org/sites/oaklandinstitute.org/files/LandGrab_final_web.pdf; and Seth Lubove, "Betting the Farm-and Winning," *Washington Post*, August 21, 2011.

27. "2005 Nen Wa Nihon No Tagore," *Shokun*, February 2007.

28. Harry Bruinius, "Income Inequality: Does Wider Gap between Rich and Poor Threaten Capitalism?" *Christian Science Monitor*, January 5, 2014; William A. Galston, "Welcome to the Well-Educated-Barista Economy," *Wall Street Journal*, April 29, 2014.

29. Friedrich Engels, *The Condition of the Working Class in England*, trans. W. O. Henderson and W. H. Chaloner (Stanford, CA: Stanford UP, 1958), p. 25; Gertrude Himmelfarb, *The Demoralization of Society: From Victorian Virtues to Modern Values* (New York: Alfred Knopf, 1995), p. 39; William McNeill, *The Rise of the West: A History of the Human Community* (Chicago: Univ. of Chicago Press, 1963), p. 275; Thomas S. Ashton, "Workers Living Standards: A Modern Revision," in Philip A. M. Taylor, *The Industrial Revolution in Britain: Triumph or Disaster?* (Boston: D. C. Heath and Company, 1958), p. 481; Andrew Lees, *Cities Perceived: Urban Society in European and American Thought: 1820–1840* (New York: Columbia UP, 1985), pp. 40–41.

30. Friedman, *The Moral Consequences of Economic Growth*, pp. 232, 349; Marx, *Capital*, p. 112.

31. Engels, *The Condition of the Working Class in England*, p. 335.

32. R. K. Webb, *Modern England: From the Eighteenth Century to the Present* (New York: Dodd, Mead and Company, 1971), pp. 117–18, 235; Ford Maddox Ford, *The Soul of London* (London: Everyman, 1905), p. 69.

33. Hartmut Kaelble, *Historical Research on Social Mobility*, trans. Ingrid Noakes (New York: Columbia UP, 1981), pp. 42–43, 62–65, 96–97; Reuven Brenner, *Rivalry: In Business, Science, among Nations* (Cambridge: Cambridge UP, 1987), p. 43.

34. Beard and Beard, *The Rise of American Civilization*, pp. 423–28; Hays, *The Response to Industrialism*, pp. 84–85; Matthew Josephson, *The Money Lords: The Great Finance Capitalists, 1925–1950* (New York: New American Library, 1972), p. 260.

35. Albert U. Romasco, *The Poverty of Abundance: Hoover, the Nation, the Depression* (New York: Oxford UP, 1965), pp. 3, 230; McNeill, *The Rise of the West*, p. 797.

36. Annie Lowrey, "The Rich Get Richer Through the Recovery," *Economix* (blog), *New York Times*, September 10, 2013, http://economix.blogs.nytimes.com/2013/09/10/the-rich-get-richer-through-the-recovery.

37. Nye, *America as Second Creation*, pp. 294–95.

38. James Ridgeway, *The Politics of Ecology* (New York: Dutton, 1970), p. 203; Friedman, *The Moral Consequences of Economic Growth*, p. 83.

39. Donella H. Meadows, Dennis L. Meadows, Jørgen Randers, and William W. Behrens, *The Limits to Growth* (New York: Potomac Associates, 1972).

40. Lasch, *The Only and True Heaven*, p. 528; Toffler, *Future Shock*, p. 474.

41. Bjørn Lomborg, "The Limits of Panic," *Slate*, June 26, 2013, http://www.slate.com/articles/business/project_syndicate/2013/06/climate_panic_ecological_collapse_is_not_upon_us_and_we_haven_t_run_out.html.

42. Monbiot, "This Is Bigger than Climate Change"; Joel Kotkin, "Capping Emissions, Trading on the Future," *New Geography*, December 8, 2009, http://www.newgeography.com/content/001253-capping-emissions-trading-on-the-future.

43. PBL Netherlands Environmental Assessment Agency and the European Commission Joint Research Centre, "Trends in Global CO_2 Emissions: 2013 Report," October 2013, http://www.pbl.nl/sites/default/files/cms/publicaties/pbl-2013-trends-in-global-co2-emissions-2013-report-1148.pdf.

44. Austin Williams, *The Enemies of Progress: The Dangers of Sustainability* (London: Societas, 2008), pp. 4–8, 13.
45. Christopher Booker, "Climate Change: The True Price of the Warmists' Folly Is Becoming Clear," *Daily Telegraph*, January 9, 2010; Iain Murray, "Alarmism Has Consequences," *OpenMarket.org*, March 2, 2009, http://www.openmarket.org/2009/03/02/alarmism-has-consequences.
46. "Energy Cronies, the Sequel," *Wall Street Journal*, October 25, 2013; Allysia Finley, "How Government Is Making Solar Billionaires," *Wall Street Journal*, October 21, 2013.
47. Paul Rogers, "Silicon Valley May Follow in Richmond, Berkeley Climate Change Efforts," *Contra Costa Times*, August 26, 2013; Vivian Krause, "Rockefellers behind 'Scruffy Little Outfit,'" *Financial Post*, February 14, 2013.
48. Finley, "How Government Is Making Solar Billionaires"; "Energy Cronies, the Sequel"; Bill McKibben, "Cut the Power of Fossil Fuel," *Los Angeles Times*, November 9, 2012.
49. Bill Schneider, "Elites Focus on Inequality; Real People Just Want Growth," Reuters, May 5, 2014; Rebecca Riffkin, "Climate Change Not a Top Worry in U.S.," Gallup, March 12, 2014, http://www.gallup.com/poll/167843/climate-change-not-top-worry.aspx; Gallup Brain, "Gallup Poll Social Series: Mood of the Nation," January 5–8, 2014, http://brain.gallup.com/documents/questionnaire.aspx?STUDY=P1401001; Global Strategy Group, "Focus on Growth to Frame Priorities," report, GSG Compass, April 2014, http://globalstrategygroup.com/wp-content/uploads/2014/04/Focus-on-Growth-to-Frame-Priorities.pdf.
50. Isaiah Berlin, *Karl Marx: His Life and Environment* (Oxford: Oxford UP, 1978), p. 128.
51. W. Arthur Lewis, *The Theory of Economic Growth* (Homewood, IL: R. D. Irwin, 1955), p. 420.
52. Friedman, *The Moral Consequences of Economic Growth*, pp. 325, 383; "The East is Grey," *Economist*, August 10, 2013.
53. Daron Acemoglu, "The Growth Imperative," *American*, February 24, 2009, http://www.american.com/archive/2009/february-2009/the-growth-imperative; Thomas Philippon, "Why Has the U.S. Financial Sector Grown So Much? The Role of Corporate Finance," working paper, NBER Working Paper Series, September 2007, http://www.nber.org/papers/w13405.pdf; William Lazonick, "The Financialization of the U.S. Corporation: What Has Been Lost, and How It Can Be Regained," *Seattle University Law Review*, vol. 26 (2013): 857–909; Suzanne Berger, "How Finance Gutted Manufacturing," *Boston Review*, April 1, 2014.
54. ProPublica, "Bailout Recipients," May 19, 2014, http://projects.propublica.org/bailout/list.
55. Floyd Norris, "Merely Rich and Superrich: The Tax Gap Is Narrowing," *New York Times*, April 17, 2014.
56. John D. McKinnon, "Top Earners Feel the Bite of Tax Increases," *Wall Street Journal*, April 13, 2014; Eric Alterman, "Think Again: The Super-Rich and Their Monster," *Huffington Post*, November 7, 2013, http://www.huffingtonpost.com/eric-alterman/-issues—media-think-agai_b_4232770.html.
57. "Six Years of Low Interest Rates in Search of Some Growth," *Economist*, April 4, 2013; George Anders, "Inside Sequoia Capital: Silicon Valley's Innovation Factory,"

Forbes, March 26, 2014, http://www.forbes.com/sites/georgeanders/2014/03/26/ inside-sequoia-capital-silicon-valleys-innovation-factory; Raymond Hernandez and Stephen Labaton, "In Opposing Tax Plan, Schumer Breaks With Party," *New York Times*, July 30, 2007.

58. Bret Swanson, "Zero GDP Reading Exposes the Real Deficit—Economic Growth," *Maximum Entropy*, February 1, 2013, http://www.bretswanson.com/index. php/2013/02/zero-gdp-reading-exposes-the-real-deficit-%E2%80%93-econom-ic-growth.

59. Walter Russell Mead et al., "The Blue Model Needs Wall Street to Survive," *American Interest*, October 25, 2013, http://www.the-american-interest.com/ blog/2013/10/25/the-blue-model-needs-wall-street-to-survive.

60. American Society of Civil Engineers, "2013 Report Card for America's Infrastruc-ture," http://www.infrastructurereportcard.org.

61. Carl DeMaio, "Revoking the Federal Free Pass on Pensions," *Wall Street Journal*, February 6, 2013; U.S. Department of the Treasury, "A New Economic Analysis of Infrastructure Investment," report, March 23, 2012, http://www.treasury.gov/ resource-center/economic-policy/Documents/20120323InfrastructureReport.pdf.

62. McGraw-Hill Research Foundation, "The Return on Investment (ROI) from Adult Education and Training," May 9, 2011, http://mcgraw-hillresearchfoundation. org/2011/05/09/roi-adult-ed-and-training.

63. Jon Stiles, Michael Hout, and Henry Brady, "California's Economic Payoff: Invest-ing in College Access & Completion," report, April 2012, http://alumni.berkeley. edu/sites/default/files/Californias_Economic_Payoff_Executive_Summary.pdf.

64. Mary Meeker, "USA Inc.: A Basic Summary of America's Financial Statements," report, Kleiner Perkins Caufield Byers, February 2011, http://images.businessweek. com/mz/11/10/1110_mz_49meekerusainc.pdf.

65. Mike Shedlock, "Ominous Looking Picture in Healthcare and Education Jobs," Mish's Global Economic Trend Analysis, February 7, 2014, http://globaleconomic-analysis.blogspot.com/2014/02/ominous-trends-in-healthcare-and.html.

66. Jonathan Rauch, "The No Good, Very Bad Outlook for the Working-Class Ameri-can Man," *National Journal*, December 5, 2012; "States Running Out Of Blue-Collar Jobs," *24/7 Wall Street*, July 11, 2011, http://247wallst.com/investing/2011/07/11/ states-running-out-of-blue-collar-jobs.

67. Joel Kotkin, "Blue-Collar Hot Spots: The Cities Creating the Most High-Pay-ing Working-Class Jobs," *Forbes*, January 30, 2014, http://www.forbes.com/sites/ joelkotkin/2014/01/30/blue-collar-hot-spots-the-cities-creating-the-most-high-paying-working-class-jobs.

68. Reuters, "U.S. Manufacturers Say There Aren't Enough Skilled Workers To Fill Job Openings," October 12, 2011.

69. Harold L. Sirkin, Michael Zinser, and Justin Rose, "The U.S. Skills Gap: Could It Threaten a Manufacturing Renaissance?" *BCG Perspectives* (Boston Consulting Group), August 28, 2013, https://www.bcgperspectives.com/content/articles/lean_ manufacturing_us_skills_gap_could_threaten_manufacturing_renaissance.

70. Stephany Romanow, "WPC '14: ExxonMobil Leader Sees Growing Short-age of Skilled Workers," *Hydrocarbon Processing*, March 26, 2014, http://www. hydrocarbonprocessing.com/Article/3323897/WPC-14-ExxonMobil-leader-

sees-growing-shortage-of-skilled-workers.htm; Stephen D. Pryor, president, ExxonMobil Chemical Co., Houston, letter to the editor, "Friday Letters: The New, Local Energy Shortage: Skilled Workers," *Houston Chronicle*, May 1, 2014; Wayne Grayson, "Energy Boom Contributes to Houston's Shortage of Skilled Construction Workers," *Equipment World*, May 20, 2013, http://www.equipmentworld.com/energy-boom-contributes-to-houstons-shortage-of-skilled-construction-workers.

71. David Leonhardt and Kevin Quealy, "The American Middle Class Is No Longer the World's Richest," *New York Times*, April 23, 2014.
72. Richard Morrill, "Industry, Inequality and the Middle Classes," *New Geography*, October 27, 2008, http://www.newgeography.com/content/00366-industry-inequality-and-middle-classes.
73. Alastair Donald, "A Green Unpleasant Land," in Dave Clements et al., *The Future of Community*, pp. 24, 32.
74. Centers for Disease Control and Prevention, "County Level Estimates: Diabetes and Obesity, 2007: Factsheets," http://www.cdc.gov/diabetes/pubs/factsheets/countylvlestimates.htm.
75. Karen A. Danielsen and Robert E. Lang, "The Case for Higher-Density Housing: A Key to Smart Growth?" in *Smart Growth: Economy, Community, and Environment* (Washington, DC: Urban Land Institute, 1998.), pp. 20–27.
76. Richard Florida, "Obama, Build a Lasting Urban Legacy," *New York Daily News*, February 3, 2013; Wendell Cox, "Still Moving to the Suburbs and Exurbs: The 2011 Census Estimates," *New Geography*, April 9, 2012, http://www.newgeography.com/content/002766-still-moving-suburbs-and-exurbs-the-2011-census-estimates.
77. Calculated from U.S. Census Bureau data, 2010 excepted (no data reported for 2010); Wendell Cox, "Time Magazine Gets it Wrong on the Suburbs," *New Geography*, April 25, 2014, http://www.newgeography.com/content/004283-time-magazine-gets-it-wrong-suburbs. Note: Between 2000 and 2013, among the 52 major metropolitan areas with more than 1 million population, a net 3.4 million moved away from areas with high housing costs. More surprising still, a net 1.8 million domestic migrants moved to smaller areas (outside the major metropolitan areas). Overall, according to the Census, the vast majority of growth has been not in high but in lower density. And after a slowdown in the recession, migration also began to increase in the suburbs by 2013, a process likely to accelerate as millennials reach child-bearing age.
78. Lanier, *Who Owns the Future?*, p. 14; Tom Hamburger and Matea Gold, "Google, Once Disdainful of Lobbying, Now a Master of Washington Influence," *Washington Post*, April 12, 2014; Castells, *The Information Age*, p. 300.
79. Jigar Shah, "Social Media Won't Drive a New Economy," *Stanford Social Innovation Review* (blog), August 30, 2012, http://www.ssireview.org/blog/entry/social_media_wont_drive_a_new_economy.
80. Lanier, *Who Owns the Future?*, 8-13.
81. Polanyi, *The Great Transformation*, p. 249.
82. Lanier, *Who Owns the Future?*, pp. 8–13; David Graeber, "Of Flying Cars and the Declining Rate of Profit," *Baffler*, no. 19 (March 2012): 66–84; Nick Wingfield, "Worries That Microsoft Is Growing Too Tricky to Manage," *New York Times*, September 9, 2013.

83. Murray, *Coming Apart*, p. 48.

84. "Has the Ideas Machine Broken Down?" *Economist*, January 12, 2013; Alexandra Petri, "Dear Google, about These Recent Changes to Gmail," *ComPost* (blog), *Washington Post*, July 18, 2013, http://www.washingtonpost.com/blogs/compost/wp/2013/07/18/dear-google-about-these-recent-changes-to-gmail; Nick Mokey, "What Happened to You, Google?" *Digital Trends*, September 20, 2013, http://www.digitaltrends.com/opinion/what-happened-to-you-google; Drummond Reed, "What Was Google Thinking??? (A Rant about the Gmail Editing Toolbar)," *Equals Drummond*, July 21, 2013, http://equalsdrummond.name/2013/07/21/what-was-google-thinking; Zach Walton, "What Was Worse In 2013: Yahoo Mail Or YouTube Comments?" *WebProNews*, December 29, 2013, http://www.webpronews.com/what-was-worse-in-2013-yahoo-mail-or-youtube-comments-2013-12; Steve Wildstrom, "Windows 8 is Worse Than Vista (for Microsoft)," *TechPinions*, January 22, 2014, http://techpinions.com/windows-8-is-worse-than-vista-for-microsoft/26704.

85. Lasch, *The Only and True Heaven*, p. 26; Joshua Wright, "Data Spotlight: Independent Contractors On the Rise," Economic Modeling Specialists Intl., April 29, 2011, http://www.economicmodeling.com/2011/04/29/independent-contractors-other-noncovered-workers-on-the-rise.

86. U.S. Census Bureau, "Nonemployer Statistics," http://www.census.gov/econ/nonemployer/index.html; Erik Pages, "Living and Working in the 1099 Economy," *New Geography*, July 2, 2011, http://www.newgeography.com/content/002314-living-and-working-1099-economy; Wendell Cox, "Toward a Self Employed Nation?" *New Geography*, June 6, 2013, http://www.newgeography.com/content/003761-toward-a-self-employed-nation; Joshua Wright, "Data Spotlight: Independent Contractors on the Rise," Economic Modeling Specialists Intl., April 29, 2011, http://www.economicmodeling.com/2011/04/29/independent-contractors-other-noncovered-workers-on-the-rise.

87. William Fulton, "Economic Development in the 1099 Economy," *Governing*, May 2011.

88. Wendell Cox, "Decade of the Telecommute," *New Geography*, October 5, 2010, http://www.newgeography.com/content/001798-decade-telecommute; Joel Kotkin, "Marissa Mayer's Misstep and the Unstoppable Rise of Telecommuting," *New Geography*, March 26, 2013, http://www.newgeography.com/content/003597-marissa-mayers-misstep-and-the-unstoppable-rise-of-telecommuting.

89. Toffler, *The Third Wave*, pp. 10, 353; Nicole Belson Goluboff, "Washington Opens the Virtual Office Door," *New Geography*, December 28, 2010, http://www.newgeography.com/content/001923-washington-opens-the-virtual-office-door.

90. Joel Kotkin, "American Cities May Have Hit 'Peak Office,'" *New Geography*, November 5, 2013, http://www.newgeography.com/content/004033-american-cities-may-have-hit-peak-office; Eliot Brown, "Developers Bet Big on Seattle," *Wall Street Journal*, September 10, 2013; Bill McBride, "Office Space: Negative Absorption and New Construction," *Calculated Risk*, July 19, 2009, http://www.calculatedriskblog.com/2009/07/office-space-negative-absorption-and.html.

91. Lasch, *The Only and True Heaven*, p. 519; Neil Irwin, "Why the Housing Market Is Still Stalling the Economy," *New York Times*, April 27, 2014.

92. Vladimir Lenin, quoted in Braudel, *The Perspective of the World*, p. 631.

93. Tocqueville, *Democracy in America*, p. 628.

94. Johan Huizinga, *The Waning of the Middle Ages: A Study of the Forms of Life* (New York: St. Martin's, 1949), pp. 58–59.

95. John Celock, "North Carolina House Speaker Kills Bill to Create State Religion," *Huffington Post*, April 4, 2013, http://www.huffingtonpost.com/2013/04/04/state-religion-bill-north-carolina_n_3016154.html.

96. Klinenberg, *Going Solo*, pp. 4–10.

97. Ernest Callenbach, *Ecotopia: The Notebooks and Reports of William Weston* (Berkeley, CA: Banyan Tree Books, 1975), p. 64; Joel Kotkin, "The Rise of Post-Familialism: Humanity's Future?" *New Geography*, October 10, 2012, http://www.newgeography.com/content/003133-the-rise-post-familialism-humanitys-future; Jennifer Agiesta, "Most Men Aspire to Be Dads, Poll Finds," *USA Today*, June 16, 2013.

98. Robert Maranto and Michael Crouch, "Ignoring an Inequality Culprit: Single-Parent Families," *Wall Street Journal*, April 20, 2014.

99. Pew Research, "'Nones' on the Rise"; Richard Florida, "America's Most (and Least) Religious Metro Areas," *CityLab*, April 4, 2013, http://www.citylab.com/housing/2013/04/americas-most-and-least-religious-metro-areas/5180; Murray, *Coming Apart*, pp. 202–5.

100. Lloyd Green, "The GOP's Huge, Growing Modernity Gap," *Daily Beast*, June 9, 2013, http://www.thedailybeast.com/articles/2013/06/09/the-gop-s-gaping-growing-modernity-gap.html.

101. Murray, *Coming Apart*, pp. 230–31; Ben Domenech, "The Libertarian Populist Agenda," *RealClearPolitics*, June 5, 2013, http://www.realclearpolitics.com/articles/2013/06/05/the_libertarian_populist_agenda_118694.html; Ben Domenech, "Three Challenges to Libertarian Populism," *RealClearPolitics*, June 6, 2013, http://www.realclearpolitics.com/articles/2013/06/06/three_challenges_to_libertarian_populism_118709.html.

102. Connie Robertson, ed., *The Wordsworth Dictionary of Quotations* (London: Wordsworth Editions, 1998), p. 55.

103. Chris Cillizza, "How Democrats Are Trying to Turn the Koch Brothers into Political Bogeymen," *Washington Post*, February 20, 2014; Nolan Finley, "Billionaire Dems Boost Peters," *Detroit News*, March 16, 2014; Frank Rich, "The Billionaires Bankrolling the Tea Party," *New York Times*, August 28, 2010.

104. Lee Drutman, "The Political One Percent of the One Percent," Sunlight Foundation, December 13, 2011, http://sunlightfoundation.com/blog/2011/12/13/the-political-one-percent-of-the-one-percent; Jeffrey Dorfman, "The Democratic Party Is Now the Party of Big Business," *RealClearMarkets*, December 2, 2013, http://www.realclearmarkets.com/articles/2013/12/02/the_democratic_party_is_now_the_party_of_big_business_100768.html.

105. Stein Ringen, "Is American Democracy Headed to Extinction?" *Washington Post*, March 28, 2014; Beard and Beard, *The Rise of American Civilization*, pp. 424, 437.

106. Frank Newport, "Majority in U.S. Want Wealth More Evenly Distributed," Gallup Politics, April 17, 2013, http://www.gallup.com/poll/161927/majority-wealth-evenly-distributed.aspx.

107. Pew Research Center for the People & the Press, "Little Change in Public's Response to 'Capitalism,' 'Socialism,'" report, December 28, 2011, http://www.people-press.org/2011/12/28/little-change-in-publics-response-to-capitalism-socialism.

108. Piketty, *Capital in the Twenty-First Century*, pp. 428–29; Pew Research, "Millennials in Adulthood"; Joshua Miller, "'Millennials' Cynical about Politics," *Boston Globe*, April 29, 2014; Joseph Curl, "White House Panics as Millennials Wise Up, Bail on President Obama," *Washington Times*, January 26, 2014; John Della Volpe, "IOP Releases New Fall Poll, 5 Key Findings And Trends in Millennial Viewpoints," Harvard University Institute of Politics, December 4, 2013, http://iop.harvard.edu/blog/iop-releases-new-fall-poll-5-key-findings-and-trends-millennial-viewpoints.

109. Joel Kotkin, "Political, Economic Power Grow More Concentrated," *New Geography*, January 6, 2014, http://www.newgeography.com/content/004124-political-economic-power-grow-more-concentrated; Ashley Pratte, "New YAF Poll: 53% of Millennials Outraged by NSA Data Collection," *The New Guard* (blog), Young America's Foundation, March 15, 2014, http://www.yaf.org/53PercentofMillennialsOutragedbyNSADataCollection.aspx.

110. Pew Research Center for the People & the Press, "Trust in Government Nears Record Low, But Most Federal Agencies Are Viewed Favorably," report, October 18, 2013, http://www.people-press.org/files/legacy-pdf/10-18-13%20Trust%20in%20Govt%20Update.pdf; Pew Research Center for the People & the Press, "Most See Inequality Growing, but Partisans Differ over Solutions," January 23, 2014, http://www.people-press.org/2014/01/23/most-see-inequality-growing-but-partisans-differ-over-solutions.

111. Peter Osborne, "Europe Is Slowly Strangling the Life out of National Democracy," *Telegraph* (UK), January 1, 2014.

112. Linda Feldmann, "Is Barack Obama an Imperial President?" *Christian Science Monitor*, January 26, 2014; Jacob S. Hacker and Oona A. Hathaway, "Beware an Unchecked President," *Los Angeles Times*, December 8, 2013.

113. Benjamin Landy, "Graph: Can Congress Be Trusted With Tax Reform?" *The Century Foundation*, April 11, 2013, http://www.tcf.org/blog/detail/graph-can-congress-be-trusted-with-tax-reform.

114. Wendell Cox, "Local Government in Ohio: More Accessible and More Efficient," *New Geography*, October 25, 2012, http://www.newgeography.com/content/003180-local-government-ohio-more-accessible-and-more-efficient.

115. Gretchen Morgenson, "From Outside or Inside, the Deck Looks Stacked," *New York Times*, April 27, 2014.

116. Benjamin M. Blau, "Central Bank Intervention and the Role of Political Connections," working paper, Mercatus Center, George Mason University, October 2013, http://mercatus.org/sites/default/files/Blau_CentralBankIntervention_v1.pdf; Samuel Gregg, "Welcome to the New Corporatism," *American Spectator*, November 1, 2013.

117. Heidi Przybyla and Phil Mattingly, "Tea Party Congressmen Accept Cash from Bailed-Out Bankers," *Bloomberg*, April 30, 2012, http://www.bloomberg.com/news/2012-04-30/tea-party-congressmen-accept-cash-from-bailed-out-bankers.html; Kate Ackley, "Financial Industry Warily Looks to Tea Party Conservatives for Tax Support," *Roll Call*, March 11, 2014, http://www.rollcall.com/news/financial_industry_warily_looks_to_tea_party_conservatives_for_tax_support-231443-1.html.

118. Rasmussen Reports, "31% Believe U.S. Has Crony Capitalist System," April 9, 2014, http://www.rasmussenreports.com/public_content/politics/general_politics/

april_2014/31_believe_u_s_has_crony_capitalist_system;   Rasmussen   Reports, "63% Say Government Contracts Go to Those with Most Political Connections," January   29,   2014,   http://www.rasmussenreports.com/public_content/politics/ general_politics/january_2014/63_say_government_contracts_go_to_those_with_ most_political_connections.

Also from Telos Press Publishing

The Forest Passage
Ernst Jünger

The Adventurous Heart: Figures and Capriccios
Ernst Jünger

The Democratic Contradictions of Multiculturalism
Jens-Martin Eriksen and Frederik Stjernfelt

A Journal of No Illusions:
Telos, *Paul Piccone, and the Americanization of Critical Theory*
Timothy W. Luke and Ben Agger, eds.

Hamlet or Hecuba:
The Intrusion of the Time into the Play
Carl Schmitt

On Pain
Ernst Jünger

Class Cleansing: The Massacre at Katyn
Victor Zaslavsky

Jihad and Jew-Hatred:
Islamism, Nazism, and the Roots of 9/11
Matthias Küntzel

Confronting the Crisis: Writings of Paul Piccone
Paul Piccone

Theory of the Partisan
Carl Schmitt

The Nomos *of the Earth*
in the International Law of the Jus Publicum Europaeum
Carl Schmitt